Look you here,
Here is himself, marred, as you see, with traitors.

—Act III. Scene 2.

The Academy Classics

SHAKESPEARE

JULIUS CÆSAR

EDITED WITH A LIFE OF SHAKESPEARE, AN ACCOUNT OF
THE THEATRE IN HIS TIME, AND NUMEROUS
AIDS TO THE STUDY OF THE PLAY

BY

SAMUEL THURBER, Jr.

NEWTON HIGH SCHOOL, NEWTONVILLE
MASSACHUSETTS

ALLYN AND BACON

Boston   New York   Chicago

OAR

Norwood Press
J. S. Cushing Co. — Berwick & Smith Co.
Norwood, Mass., U.S.A.

FOREWORD

In revising my father's edition of "Julius Cæsar," I have been influenced by changed conditions of English teaching in high schools since the time when his work was done. The greater number of pupils, the consequent inadequacy of reference material, the more general and less specialized literary preparation, and the broader aims and ideals of the rising generation, — all these conditions demand a different type of annotation from that of twenty-five years ago.

My own recent problems in teaching "Julius Cæsar" with college preparatory, commercial, and technical classes have led me to include in the present edition the following six features not found in my father's work: a fuller and more informational array of notes; a study of the structural elements of the play; a discussion of the sources of the tragedy, with numerous quotations from North's "Plutarch"; a list of familiar quotations from "Julius Cæsar"; an account of Shakespeare, the man, — his life, work, reputation, and the theatre for which he wrote; and finally a list of practical, usable topics for oral and written composition. These six new features will be found in the appendix following the text of the play.

It is hoped that this additional material will not only increase the interest of the student, but that it will also lighten the labor of the teacher.

Samuel Thurber, Jr.

CONTENTS

LIST OF ILLUSTRATIONS

v

List of Illustrations.

SHAKESPEARE

WHAT needs my Shakespeare for his honored bones
The labor of an age in piléd stones?
Or that his hallowed reliques should be hid
Under a star-ypointing pyramid?
Dear son of memory, great heir of fame,
What need'st thou such weak witness of thy name?
Thou in our wonder and astonishment
Hast built thyself a live-long monument.
For whilst to the shame of slow-endeavoring art
Thy easy numbers flow, and that each heart
Hath from the leaves of thy unvalued book
Those Delphic lines with deep impression took,
Then thou, our fancy of itself bereaving,
Dost make us marble with too much conceiving;
And, so sepúlchred, in such pomp dost lie
That kings for such a tomb would wish to die.

JOHN MILTON.

JULIUS CÆSAR.

DRAMATIS PERSONÆ.

JULIUS CÆSAR,

OCTAVIUS CÆSAR,
MARCUS ANTONIUS,
M. ÆMILIUS LEPIDUS,
} triumvirs after the death of Julius Cæsar.

CICERO,
PUBLIUS,
POPILIUS LENA,
} senators.

MARCUS BRUTUS,
CASSIUS,
CASCA,
TREBONIUS,
LIGARIUS,
DECIUS BRUTUS,
METELLUS CIMBER,
CINNA,
} conspirators against Julius Cæsar.

FLAVIUS AND MARULLUS, tribunes.

ARTEMIDORUS of Cnidos, a teacher of Rhetoric.

A Soothsayer.

CINNA, a Poet.   Another Poet.

LUCILIUS,
TITINIUS,
MESSALA,
YOUNG CATO,
VOLUMNIUS,
} friends to Brutus and Cassius.

VARRO,
CLITUS,
CLAUDIUS,
STRATO,
LUCIUS,
DARDANIUS,
} servants to Brutus.

PINDARUS, servant to Cassius.

CALPURNIA, wife to Cæsar.

PORTIA, wife to Brutus.

Senators, Citizens, Guards, Attendants, etc.

SCENE: *Rome; the neighborhood of Sardis; the neighborhood of Philippi.*

ACT I.

Scene I. *Rome. A Street.*

Enter Flavius, Marullus, *and certain* Commoners.

Flav. Hence! home, you idle creatures, get you home:
Is this a holiday? what! know you not,
Being mechanical, you ought not walk
Upon a laboring day without the sign
Of your profession? Speak, what trade art thou?   5

Speak, what trade art thou?
— Act I.   Scene I.

First Com. Why, sir, a carpenter.
Mar. Where is thy leather apron and thy rule?
What dost thou with thy best apparel on?
You, sir, what trade are you?

I

Sec. Com.　Truly, sir, in respect of a fine workman, I am but, as you would say, a cobbler.

Mar.　But what trade art thou? answer me directly.

Sec. Com.　A trade, sir, that, I hope, I may use with a safe conscience ; which is, indeed, sir, a mender of bad soles.

Mar.　What trade, thou knave? thou naughty knave,
　　　　 what trade?

Sec. Com.　Nay, I beseech you, sir, be not out with me : yet, if you be out, sir, I can mend you.

Mar.　What meanest thou by that? mend me, thou saucy fellow !

Sec. Com.　Why, sir, cobble you.　　　　　　　　　20

Flav.　Thou art a cobbler, art thou?

Sec. Com.　Truly, sir, all that I live by is with the awl : I meddle with no tradesman's matters, nor women's matters, but with awl. I am, indeed, sir, a surgeon to old shoes ; when they are in great danger, I recover them. As proper men as ever trod upon neat's-leather have gone upon my handiwork.

Flav.　But wherefore art not in thy shop to-day?
Why dost thou lead these men about the streets?

Sec. Com.　Truly, sir, to wear out their shoes, to get myself into more work. But indeed, sir, we make holiday to see Cæsar and to rejoice in his triumph.

Mar.　Wherefore rejoice? What conquest brings he
　　　　 home?
What tributaries follow him to Rome,
To grace in captive bonds his chariot-wheels?　　　35
You blocks, you stones, you worse than senseless things !
O you hard hearts, you cruel men of Rome,
Knew you not Pompey? Many a time and oft
Have you climbed up to walls and battlements,

To towers and windows, yea, to chimney-tops,   40
Your infants in your arms, and there have sat
The live-long day, with patient expectation,
To see great Pompey pass the streets of Rome :
And when you saw his chariot but appear,
Have you not made an universal shout,   45
That Tiber trembled underneath her banks,
To hear the replication of your sounds
Made in her concave shores ?
And do you now put on your best attire ?
And do you now cull out a holiday ?   50
And do you now strew flowers in his way
That comes in triumph over Pompey's blood ?
Be gone !
Run to your houses, fall upon your knees,
Pray to the gods to intermit the plague   55
That needs must light on this ingratitude.
    Flav.   Go, go, good countrymen, and, for this fault,
Assemble all the poor men of your sort ;
Draw them to Tiber banks, and weep your tears
Into the channel, till the lowest stream   60
Do kiss the most exalted shores of all.
                         [*Exeunt all the Commoners.*
See, whether their basest metal be not moved ;
They vanish tongue-tied in their guiltiness.
Go you down that way towards the Capitol ;
This way will I : disrobe the images,   65
If you do find them decked with ceremonies.
    Mar.   May we do so ?
You know it is the feast of Lupercal.
    Flav.   It is no matter ; let no images
Be hung with Cæsar's trophies.   I'll about,   70

3

And drive away the vulgar from the streets:
So do you too, where you perceive them thick.
These growing feathers plucked from Cæsar's wing
Will make him fly an ordinary pitch,
Who else would soar above the view of men   75
And keep us all in servile fearfulness.   [*Exeunt.*

SCENE II.   *A public place.*

Flourish.   Enter CÆSAR ; ANTONY, *for the course;* CAL-
    PURNIA, PORTIA, DECIUS, CICERO, BRUTUS, CASSIUS,
    and CASCA ; *a great crowd following, among them a*
    Soothsayer.

Cæs.   Calpurnia !

Casca.   Peace, ho !   Cæsar speaks.

Cæs.   Calpurnia !

Cal.   Here ! my lord.

Cæs.   Stand you directly in Antonius' way,
When he doth run his course.   Antonius !

Ant.   Cæsar, my lord ?

Cæs.   Forget not, in your speed, Antonius,
To touch Calpurnia ; for our elders say,
The barren, touchéd in this holy chase,
Shake off their sterile curse.

Ant.   I shall remember :
When Cæsar says " do this," it is performed.   10

Cæs.   Set on ; and leave no ceremony out.   [*Flourish.*

Sooth.   Cæsar !

Cæs.   Ha ! who calls ?

Casca.   Bid every noise be still : peace yet again !

Cæs.   Who is it in the press that calls on me ?   15

4

I hear a tongue, shriller than all the music,
Cry " Cæsar ! "   Speak ; Cæsar is turned to hear.

  Sooth.   Beware the ides of March.

  Cæs.   What man is that ?

  Bru.   A soothsayer bids you beware the ides of March.

  Cæs.   Set him before me ; let me see his face.   20

  Cas.   Fellow, come from the throng ; look upon Cæsar.

  Cæs.   What say'st thou to me now ? speak once again.

  Sooth.   Beware the ides of March.

  Cæs.   He is a dreamer ; let us leave him : pass.

              [*Sennet.   Exeunt all but Brutus and Cassius.*

  Cas.   Will you go see the order of the course ?   25

  Bru.   Not I.

  Cas.   I pray you, do.

  Bru.   I am not gamesome : I do lack some part
Of that quick spirit that is in Antony.
Let me not hinder, Cassius, your desires ;   30
I'll leave you.

  Cas.   Brutus, I do observe you now of late :
I have not from your eyes that gentleness
And show of love as I was wont to have :
You bear too stubborn and too strange a hand   35
Over your friend that loves you.

  Bru.   Cassius,
Be not deceived : if I have veiled my look,
I turn the trouble of my countenance
Merely upon myself.   Vexed I am
Of late with passions of some difference,   40
Conceptions only proper to myself,
Which give some soil perhaps to my behaviors ;
But let not therefore my good friends be grieved —
Among which number, Cassius, be you one —

Nor construe any further my neglect,   45
Than that poor Brutus, with himself at war,
Forgets the shows of love to other men.
   Cas.   Then, Brutus, I have much mistook your passion ;
By means whereof this breast of mine hath buried
Thoughts of great value, worthy cogitations.   50
Tell me, good Brutus, can you see your face ?
   Bru.   No, Cassius ; for the eye sees not itself,
But by reflection, by some other things.
   Cas.   'T is just :
And it is very much lamented, Brutus,   55
That you have no such mirrors as will turn
Your hidden worthiness into your eye,
That you might see your shadow.   I have heard,
Where many of the best respect in Rome,
Except immortal Cæsar, speaking of Brutus   60
And groaning underneath this age's yoke,
Have wished that noble Brutus had his eyes.
   Bru.   Into what dangers would you lead me, Cassius,
That you would have me seek into myself
For that which is not in me ?   65
   Cas.   Therefore, good Brutus, be prepared to hear :
And since you know you cannot see yourself
So well as by reflection, I, your glass,
Will modestly discover to yourself
That of yourself which you yet know not of.   70
And be not jealous on me, gentle Brutus :
Were I a common laugher, or did use
To stale with ordinary oaths my love
To every new protester ; if you know
That I do fawn on men and hug them hard,   75
And after scandal them ; or if you know

That I profess myself in banqueting
To all the rout, then hold me dangerous.

> [*Flourish and shout.*

   Bru.   What means this shouting?   I do fear, the people
Choose Cæsar for their king.

   Cas.   Ay, do you fear it?   80
Then must I think you would not have it so.

   Bru.   I would not, Cassius; yet I love him well.
But wherefore do you hold me here so long?
What is it that you would impart to me?
If it be ought toward the general good,   85
Set honor in one eye and death i' the other,
And I will look on both indifferently:
For let the gods so speed me as I love
The name of honor more than I fear death.

   Cas.   I know that virtue to be in you, Brutus,   90
As well as I do know your outward favor.
Well, honor is the subject of my story.
I cannot tell what you and other men
Think of this life; but, for my single self,
I had as lief not be as live to be   95
In awe of such a thing as I myself.
I was born free as Cæsar; so were you:
We both have fed as well, and we can both
Endure the winter's cold as well as he:
For once, upon a raw and gusty day,   100
The troubled Tiber chafing with her shores,
Cæsar said to me, " Darest thou, Cassius, now
Leap in with me into this angry flood,
And swim to yonder point? "   Upon the word,
Accoutred as I was, I plungéd in   105
And bade him follow; so indeed he did.

The torrent roared, and we did buffet it
With lusty sinews, throwing it aside
And stemming it with hearts of controversy;
But ere we could arrive the point proposed,   110
Cæsar cried, "Help me, Cassius, or I sink!"
I, as Æneas, our great ancestor,
Did from the flames of Troy upon his shoulder
The old Anchises bear, so from the waves of Tiber
Did I the tired Cæsar: and this man   115
Is now become a god, and Cassius is
A wretched creature and must bend his body,
If Cæsar carelessly but nod on him.
He had a fever when he was in Spain,
And when the fit was on him, I did mark   120
How he did shake: 'tis true, this god did shake:
His coward lips did from their color fly,
And that same eye whose bend doth awe the world
Did lose his lustre: I did hear him groan:
Ay, and that tongue of his that bade the Romans   125
Mark him and write his speeches in their books,
Alas, it cried, "Give me some drink, Titinius,"
As a sick girl.   Ye gods! it doth amaze me
A man of such a feeble temper should
So get the start of the majestic world   130
And bear the palm alone.   [*Shout.   Flourish.*
     Bru.   Another general shout!
I do believe that these applauses are
For some new honors that are heaped on Cæsar.
     Cas.   Why, man, he doth bestride the narrow world   135
Like a Colossus, and we petty men
Walk under his huge legs and peep about
To find ourselves dishonorable graves.

Men at some time are masters of their fates:
The fault, dear Brutus, is not in our stars,   140
But in ourselves, that we are underlings.
Brutus and Cæsar: what should be in that "Cæsar"?
Why should that name be sounded more than yours?
Write them together, yours is as fair a name;
Sound them, it doth become the mouth as well;   145
Weigh them, it is as heavy; conjure with 'em,
Brutus will start a spirit soon as Cæsar.
Now, in the names of all the gods at once,
Upon what meat doth this our Cæsar feed,
That he is grown so great?   Age, thou art shamed!   150
Rome, thou hast lost the breed of noble bloods!
When went there by an age, since the great flood,
But it was famed with more than with one man?
When could they say till now, that talked of Rome,
That her wide walls encompassed but one man?   155
Now is it Rome indeed and room enough,
When there is in it but one only man.
O, you and I have heard our fathers say,
There was a Brutus once that would have brooked
The eternal devil to keep his state in Rome   160
As easily as a king.
   Bru.   That you do love me, I am nothing jealous;
What you would work me to, I have some aim:
How I have thought of this and of these times,
I shall recount hereafter; for this present,   165
I would not, so with love I might entreat you,
Be any further moved.   What you have said
I will consider; what you have to say
I will with patience hear, and find a time
Both meet to hear and answer such high things.   170

Till then, my noble friend, chew upon this:
Brutus had rather be a villager
Than to repute himself a son of Rome
Under these hard conditions as this time
Is like to lay upon us.   175
    Cas.   I am glad that my weak words
Have struck but thus much show of fire from Brutus.
    Bru.   The games are done and Cæsar is returning.
    Cas.   As they pass by, pluck Casca by the sleeve;
And he will, after his sour fashion, tell you   180
What hath proceeded worthy note to-day.

         Re-enter Cæsar *and his Train.*

    Bru.   I will do so.   But, look you, Cassius,
The angry spot doth glow on Cæsar's brow,
And all the rest look like a chidden train:
Calpurnia's cheek is pale; and Cicero   185
Looks with such ferret and such fiery eyes
As we have seen him in the Capitol,
Being crossed in conference by some senators.
    Cas.   Casca will tell us what the matter is.
    Cæs.   Antonius!   190
    Ant.   Cæsar?
    Cæs.   Let me have men about me that are fat,
Sleek-headed men and such as sleep o' nights:
Yond Cassius has a lean and hungry look;
He thinks too much: such men are dangerous.   195
    Ant.   Fear him not, Cæsar; he's not dangerous;
He is a noble Roman and well given.
    Cæs.   Would he were fatter!   But I fear him not:
Yet if my name were liable to fear,
I do not know the man I should avoid   200

So soon as that spare Cassius.　He reads much;
He is a great observer, and he looks
Quite through the deeds of men; he loves no plays,
As thou dost, Antony; he hears no music;
Seldom he smiles, and smiles in such a sort　　　　205
As if he mocked himself and scorned his spirit
That could be moved to smile at any thing.
Such men as he be never at heart's ease
Whiles they behold a greater than themselves,
And therefore are they very dangerous.　　　　　210
I rather tell thee what is to be feared
Than what I fear; for always I am Cæsar.
Come on my right hand, for this ear is deaf,
And tell me truly what thou think'st of him.
　　　[*Sennet.　Exeunt Cæsar and all his Train but Casca.*
　Casca.　You pulled me by the cloak; would you speak
with me?
　Bru.　Ay, Casca; tell us what hath chanced to-day,
That Cæsar looks so sad.
　Casca.　Why, you were with him, were you not?　　218
　Bru.　I should not then ask Casca what had chanced.
　Casca.　Why, there was a crown offered him: and be-
ing offered him, he put it by with the back of his hand,
thus; and then the people fell a-shouting.
　Bru.　What was the second noise for?
　Casca.　Why, for that too.
　Cas.　They shouted thrice; what was the last cry for?
　Casca.　Why, for that too.
　Bru.　Was the crown offered him thrice?
　Casca.　Ay, marry, was't, and he put it by thrice, every
time gentler than other; and at every putting-by mine
honest neighbors shouted.　　　　　　　　　　230

11

Cas.   Who offered him the crown?

Casca.   Why, Antony.

Bru.   Tell us the manner of it, gentle Casca.

Casca.   I can as well be hanged as tell the manner of it: it was mere foolery; I did not mark it.   I saw Mark Antony offer him a crown; — yet 'twas not a crown neither, 'twas one of these coronets; — and, as I told you, he put it by once: but, for all that, to my thinking, he would fain have had it.   Then he offered it to him again; then he put it by again; but, to my thinking, he was very loath to lay his fingers off it.   And then he offered it the third time; he put it the third time by: and still as he refused it, the rabblement shouted and clapped their chopt hands and threw up their sweaty nightcaps, and uttered such a deal of stinking breath because Cæsar refused the crown, that it had almost choked Cæsar; for he swounded and fell down at it: and for mine own part, I durst not laugh, for fear of opening my lips and receiving the bad air.   249

Cas.   But, soft, I pray you: what, did Cæsar swound?

Casca.   He fell down in the market-place, and foamed at mouth, and was speechless.

Bru.   'Tis very like: he hath the falling-sickness.

Cas.   No, Cæsar hath it not; but you, and I, And honest Casca, we have the falling-sickness.   255

Casca.   I know not what you mean by that; but, I am sure Cæsar fell down.   If the tag-rag people did not clap him and hiss him, according as he pleased and displeased them, as they used to do the players in the theatre, I am no true man.   260

Bru.   What said he when he came unto himself?

Casca.   Marry, before he fell down, when he perceived

I 2

the common herd was glad he refused the crown, he plucked me ope his doublet and offered them his throat to cut. An I had been a man of any occupation, if I would not have taken him at a word, I would I might go to hell among the rogues. And so he fell. When he came to himself again, he said, If he had done or said any thing amiss, he desired their worships to think it was his infirmity. Three or four wenches, where I stood, cried, " Alas, good soul!" and forgave him with all their hearts: but there's no heed to be taken of them; if Cæsar had stabbed their mothers, they would have done no less.   273

Bru. And after that, he came, thus sad, away?

Casca. Ay.

Cas. Did Cicero say any thing?

Casca. Ay, he spoke Greek.

Cas. To what effect?   278

Casca. Nay, an I tell you that, I'll ne'er look you i' the face again: but those that understood him smiled at one another and shook their heads; but, for mine own part, it was Greek to me. I could tell you more news too: Marullus and Flavius, for pulling scarfs off Cæsar's images, are put to silence. Fare you well. There was more foolery yet, if I could remember it.   285

Cas. Will you sup with me to-night, Casca?

Casca. No, I am promised forth.

Cas. Will you dine with me to-morrow?

Casca. Ay, if I be alive, and your mind hold, and your dinner worth the eating.   290

Cas. Good: I will expect you.

Casca. Do so. Farewell, both.   *[Exit.*

Bru. What a blunt fellow is this grown to be! He was quick mettle when he went to school.

   Cas.   So is he now in execution   295
Of any bold or noble enterprise,
However he puts on this tardy form.
This rudeness is a sauce to his good wit,
Which gives men stomach to digest his words
With better appetite.   300
   Bru.   And so it is.   For this time I will leave you:
To-morrow, if you please to speak with me,
I will come home to you ; or, if you will,
Come home to me, and I will wait for you.
   Cas.   I will do so : till then, think of the world.   305
                                                [Exit Brutus.

Well, Brutus, thou art noble ; yet, I see,
Thy honorable metal may be wrought
From that it is disposed : therefore it is meet
That noble minds keep ever with their likes ;
For who so firm that cannot be seduced ?   310
Cæsar doth bear me hard ; but he loves Brutus :
If I were Brutus now and he were Cassius,
He should not humor me.   I will this night,
In several hands, in at his windows throw,
As if they came from several citizens,   315
Writings all tending to the great opinion
That Rome holds of his name ; wherein obscurely
Cæsar's ambition shall be glanced at :
And after this let Cæsar seat him sure ;   319
For we will shake him, or worse days endure.   *[Exit.*

Scene III.   *The same.   A street.*

Thunder and lightning.   Enter, from opposite sides, Casca,
with his sword drawn, and Cicero.

   Cic.   Good even, Casca: brought you Cæsar home?
Why are you breathless? and why stare you so?
   Casca.   Are not you moved, when all the sway of earth
Shakes like a thing unfirm?   O Cicero,
I have seen tempests, when the scolding winds   5
Have rived the knotty oaks, and I have seen
The ambitious ocean swell and rage and foam,
To be exalted with the threatening clouds:
But never till to-night, never till now,
Did I go through a tempest dropping fire.   10
Either there is a civil strife in heaven,
Or else the world, too saucy with the gods,
Incenses them to send destruction.
   Cic.   Why, saw you anything more wonderful?
   Casca.   A common slave — you know him well by sight —
Held up his left hand, which did flame and burn
Like twenty torches joined, and yet his hand,
Not sensible of fire, remained unscorched.
Besides — I ha' not since put up my sword —
Against the Capitol I met a lion,   20
Who glared upon me, and went surly by,
Without annoying me: and there were drawn
Upon a heap a hundred ghastly women,
Transformed with their fear, who swore they saw
Men all in fire walk up and down the streets.   25
And yesterday the bird of night did sit
Even at noon-day upon the market place,

Hooting and shrieking. When those prodigies
Do so conjointly meet, let not men say,
" These are their reasons ; they are natural ; "   30

Against the Capitol I met a lion,
Who glared upon me, and went surly by.
             — Act I.   Scene 3.

For, I believe, they are portentous things
Unto the climate that they point upon.
   Cic.   Indeed, it is a strange-disposéd time :
But men may construe things after their fashion,
Clean from the purpose of the things themselves.   35
Comes Cæsar to the Capitol to-morrow ?
   Casca.   He doth ; for he did bid Antonius
Send word to you he would be there to-morrow.

Cic.   Good night, then, Casca : this disturbéd sky
Is not to walk in.
   Casca.   Farewell, Cicero.   *[Exit Cicero.* 40

              Enter Cassius.

   Cas.   Who's there ?
   Casca.   A Roman.
   Cas.   Casca, by your voice.
   Casca.   Your ear is good.   Cassius, what night is this !
   Cas.   A very pleasing night to honest men.
   Casca.   Who ever knew the heavens menace so ?
   Cas.   Those that have known the earth so full of faults.
For my part, I have walked about the streets,
Submitting me unto the perilous night,
And thus unbracéd, Casca, as you see,
Have bared my bosom to the thunder-stone ;
And when the cross blue lightning seemed to open   50
The breast of heaven, I did present myself
Even in the aim and very flash of it.   [heavens ?
   Casca.   But wherefore did you so much tempt the
It is the part of men to fear and tremble,
When the most mighty gods by tokens send   55
Such dreadful heralds to astonish us.
   Cas.   You are dull, Casca, and those sparks of life
That should be in a Roman you do want,
Or else you use not.   You look pale and gaze
And put on fear and cast yourself in wonder,   60
To see the strange impatience of the heavens :
But if you would consider the true cause
Why all these fires, why all these gliding ghosts,
Why birds and beasts from quality and kind,
Why old men fool and children calculate,   65

Why all these things change from their ordinance
Their natures and preforméd faculties,
To monstrous quality, why, you shall find
That heaven hath infused them with these spirits,
To make them instruments of fear and warning   70
Unto some monstrous state.
Now could I, Casca, name to thee a man
Most like this dreadful night,
That thunders, lightens, opens graves, and roars
As doth the lion in the Capitol;   75
A man no mightier than thyself or me
In personal action, yet prodigious grown
And fearful, as these strange eruptions are.

    Casca.   'Tis Cæsar that you mean; is it not, Cassius?

    Cas.   Let it be who it is: for Romans now   80
Have thews and limbs like to their ancestors;
But, woe the while! our fathers' minds are dead,
And we are governed with our mothers' spirits;
Our yoke and sufferance show us womanish.

    Casca.   Indeed, they say the senators to-morrow   85
Mean to establish Cæsar as a king;
And he shall wear his crown by sea and land,
In every place save here in Italy.

    Cas.   I know where I will wear this dagger then;
Cassius from bondage will deliver Cassius: 90
Therein, ye gods, you make the weak most strong;
Therein, ye gods, you tyrants do defeat:
No stony tower, nor walls of beaten brass,
Nor airless dungeon, nor strong links of iron,
Can be retentive to the strength of spirit;   95
But life, being weary of these worldly bars,
Never lacks power to dismiss itself.

If I know this, know all the world besides,
That part of tyranny that I do bear
I can shake off at pleasure.　　　　　　*[Thunder still.*
　　Casca.　　　　　　　　So can I:　　　　　100
So every bondman in his own hand bears
The power to cancel his captivity.
　　Cas.　And why should Cæsar be a tyrant then?
Poor man! I know he would not be a wolf,
But that he sees the Romans are but sheep:　　105
He were no lion, were not Romans hinds.
Those that with haste will make a mighty fire
Begin it with weak straws: what trash is Rome,
What rubbish and what offal, when it serves
For the base matter to illuminate　　　　　110
So vile a thing as Cæsar! But, O grief,
Where hast thou led me? I perhaps speak this
Before a willing bondman; then I know
My answer must be made. But I am armed,
And dangers are to me indifferent.　　　　115
　　Casca.　You speak to Casca, and to such a man
That is no fleering tell-tale. Hold, my hand:
Be factious for redress of all these griefs,
And I will set this foot of mine as far
As who goes farthest.
　　Cas.　　　　　　There's a bargain made.　　120
Now know you, Casca, I have moved already
Some certain of the noblest-minded Romans
To undergo with me an enterprise
Of honorable-dangerous consequence;
And I do know, by this they stay for me　　125
In Pompey's porch: for now, this fearful night,
There is no stir or walking in the streets;

And the complexion of the element
In favor's like the work we have in hand,
Most bloody, fiery, and most terrible.   130

Enter CINNA.

   Casca.   Stand close awhile, for here comes one in haste.
   Cas.   'Tis Cinna; I do know him by his gait;
He is a friend.   Cinna, where haste you so?
   Cin.   To find out you.   Who's that?   Metellus Cimber?
   Cas.   No, it is Casca; one incorporate   135
To our attempts.   Am I not stayed for, Cinna?
   Cin.   I am glad on't.   What a fearful night is this!
There's two or three of us have seen strange sights.
   Cas.   Am I not stayed for? tell me.
   Cin.   Yes, you are.
O Cassius, if you could   140
But win the noble Brutus to our party—
   Cas.   Be you content: good Cinna, take this paper,
And look you lay it in the prætor's chair,
Where Brutus may but find it; and throw this
In at his window; set this up with wax   145
Upon old Brutus' statue; all this done,
Repair to Pompey's porch, where you shall find us.
Is Decius Brutus and Trebonius there?
   Cin.   All but Metellus Cimber; and he's gone
To seek you at your house.   Well, I will hie,   150
And so bestow these papers as you bade me.
   Cas.   That done, repair to Pompey's theatre.   [*Exit*
Come, Casca, you and I will yet ere day   *Cinna.*
See Brutus at his house: three parts of him
Is ours already, and the man entire   155
Upon the next encounter yields him ours.

Casca.   O, he sits high in all the people's hearts :
And that which would appear offence in us
His countenance, like richest alchemy,
Will change to virtue and to worthiness.   160

Cas.   Him and his worth and our great need of him
You have right well conceited.   Let us go,
For it is after midnight ; and ere day
We will awake him and be sure of him.   [*Exeunt.*

ACT II.

Scene I.   *Rome.   Brutus' orchard.*

Enter Brutus.

Bru.   What, Lucius, ho !
I cannot, by the progress of the stars,
Give guess how near to day.   Lucius, I say !
I would it were my fault to sleep so soundly.
When, Lucius, when ? awake, I say ! what, Lucius !   5

Enter Lucius.

Luc.   Called you, my lord ?
Bru.   Get me a taper in my study, Lucius :
When it is lighted, come and call me here.
Luc.   I will, my lord.   [*Exit.*
Bru.   It must be by his death : and for my part,   10
I know no personal cause to spurn at him,
But for the general.   He would be crowned :
How that might change his nature, there's the question
It is the bright day that brings forth the adder ;
And that craves wary walking.   Crown him ? — that ; —   15
And then, I grant, we put a sting in him,

That at his will he may do danger with.
The abuse of greatness is, when it disjoins
Remorse from power : and, to speak truth of Cæsar,
I have not known when his affections swayed   20
More than his reason.   But 'tis a common proof,
That lowliness is young ambition's ladder,
Whereto the climber-upward turns his face ;
But when he once attains the utmost round,
He then unto the ladder turns his back,   25
Looks in the clouds, scorning the base degrees
By which he did ascend : so Cæsar may ;
Then, lest he may, prevent.   And, since the quarrel
Will bear no color for the thing he is,
Fashion it thus ; that what he is, augmented,   30
Would run to these and these extremities :
And therefore think him as a serpent's egg
Which, hatched, would, as his kind, grow mischievous,
And kill him in the shell.

Re-enter LUCIUS.

   Luc.   The taper burneth in your closet, sir.   35
Searching the window for a flint, I found
This paper thus sealed up, and I am sure
It did not lie there when I went to bed.
                                   [*Gives him the letter.*
   Bru.   Get you to bed again ; it is not day.
Is not to-morrow, boy, the ides of March ?   40
   Luc.   I know not, sir.
   Bru.   Look in the calendar, and bring me word.
   Luc.   I will, sir.   [*Exit.*
   Bru.   The exhalations whizzing in the air
Give so much light that I may read by them.   45

22

[Opens the letter and reads.
" Brutus, thou sleep'st : awake, and see thyself.
Shall Rome, etc.   Speak, strike, redress !
Brutus, thou sleep'st : awake ! "
Such instigations have been often dropped
Where I have took them up.   50
" Shall Rome, etc."   Thus must I piece it out :
Shall Rome stand under one man's awe ?   What, Rome ?
My ancestors did from the streets of Rome
The Tarquin drive, when he was called a king.
" Speak, strike, redress ! "   Am I entreated   55
To speak and strike ?   O Rome, I make thee promise ;
If the redress will follow, thou receivest
Thy full petition at the hand of Brutus !

Re-enter Lucius.

Luc.   Sir, March is wasted fifteen days.
                                        [Knocking within.
Bru.   'Tis good.   Go to the gate ; somebody knocks. 60
                                        [Exit Lucius.
Since Cassius first did whet me against Cæsar,
I have not slept.
Between the acting of a dreadful thing
And the first motion, all the interim is
Like a phantasma, or a hideous dream :   65
The genius and the mortal instruments
Are then in council ; and the state of man,
Like to a little kingdom, suffers then
The nature of an insurrection.

Re-enter Lucius.

Luc.   Sir, 'tis your brother Cassius at the door,   70
Who doth desire to see you.

23

Bru.   Is he alone?

Luc. No, sir, there are moe with him.

Bru.   Do you know them?

Luc. No, sir; their hats are plucked about their ears,
And half their faces buried in their cloaks,
That by no means I may discover them   75
By any mark of favor.

Bru.   Let 'em enter.   [*Exit Lucius.*
They are the faction.   O conspiracy,
Shamest thou to show thy dangerous brow by night,
When evils are most free?   O, then, by day
Where wilt thou find a cavern dark enough   80
To mask thy monstrous visage?   Seek none, conspiracy;
Hide it in smiles and affability:
For if thou path, thy native semblance on,
Not Erebus itself were dim enough
To hide thee from prevention.   85

Enter the Conspirators, CASSIUS, CASCA, DECIUS, CINNA,
     METELLUS CIMBER, *and* TREBONIUS.

Cas.   I think we are too bold upon your rest:
Good morrow, Brutus; do we trouble you?

Bru.   I have been up this hour, awake all night.
Know I these men that come along with you?

Cas.   Yes, every man of them: and no man here   90
But honors you; and every one doth wish
You had but that opinion of yourself
Which every noble Roman bears of you.
This is Trebonius.

Bru.   He is welcome hither.

Cas.   This, Decius Brutus.

Bru.   He is welcome too.   95

24

Cas. This, Casca; this, Cinna; and this, Metellus
    Cimber.

Bru. They are all welcome.
What watchful cares do interpose themselves
Betwixt your eyes and night?

Cas. Shall I entreat a word?   100

                 [*Brutus and Cassius whisper.*

Dec. Here lies the east: doth not the day break here?

Casca. No.

Cin. O, pardon, sir, it doth; and yon gray lines
That fret the clouds are messengers of day.

Casca. You shall confess that you are both deceived.
Here, as I point my sword, the sun arises,
Which is a great way growing on the south,
Weighing the youthful season of the year.
Some two months hence up higher toward the north
He first presents his fire; and the high east   110
Stands, as the Capitol, directly here.

Bru. Give me your hands all over, one by one.

Cas. And let us swear our resolution.

Bru. No, not an oath: if not the face of men,
The sufferance of our souls, the time's abuse,—   115
If these be motives weak, break off betimes,
And every man hence to his idle bed;
So let high-sighted tyranny range on,
Till each man drop by lottery. But if these,
As I am sure they do, bear fire enough   120
To kindle cowards and to steel with valor
The melting spirits of women, then, countrymen,
What need we any spur but our own cause,
To prick us to redress? what other bond
Than secret Romans, that have spoke the word,   125

And will not palter? and what other oath
Than honesty to honesty engaged,
That this shall be, or we will fall for it?
Swear priests and cowards and men cautelous,
Old feeble carrions and such suffering souls   130
That welcome wrongs; unto bad causes swear
Such creatures as men doubt; but do not stain
The even virtue of our enterprise,
Nor the insuppressive mettle of our spirits,
To think that or our cause or our performance   135
Did need an oath; when every drop of blood
That every Roman bears, and nobly bears,
Is guilty of a several bastardy,
If he do break the smallest particle
Of any promise that hath passed from him.   140
    Cas.   But what of Cicero? shall we sound him?
I think he will stand very strong with us.
    Casca.   Let us not leave him out.
    Cin.   No, by no means.
    Met.   O, let us have him, for his silver hairs
Will purchase us a good opinion,   145
And buy men's voices to commend our deeds:
It shall be said, his judgment ruled our hands;
Our youths and wildness shall no whit appear,
But all be buried in his gravity.
    Bru.   O, name him not: let us not break with him,
For he will never follow anything   151
That other men begin.
    Cas.   Then leave him out.
    Casca.   Indeed he is not fit.
    Dec.   Shall no man else be touched but only Cæsar?
    Cas.   Decius, well urged: I think it is not meet,   155

Mark Antony, so well beloved of Cæsar,
Should outlive Cæsar: we shall find of him
A shrewd contriver; and, you know, his means,
If he improve them, may well stretch so far
As to annoy us all: which to prevent,   160
Let Antony and Cæsar fall together.
   Bru. Our course will seem too bloody, Caius Cassius,
To cut the head off and then hack the limbs,
Like wrath in death and envy afterwards;
For Antony is but a limb of Cæsar;   165
Let us be sacrificers, but not butchers, Caius.
We all stand up against the spirit of Cæsar:
And in the spirit of men there is no blood,
O, that we then could come by Cæsar's spirit,
And not dismember Cæsar! But, alas,   170
Cæsar must bleed for it! And, gentle friends,
Let's kill him boldly, but not wrathfully;
Let's carve him as a dish fit for the gods,
Not hew him as a carcass fit for hounds:
And let our hearts, as subtle masters do,   175
Stir up their servants to an act of rage,
And after seem to chide 'em. This shall make
Our purpose necessary and not envious:
Which so appearing to the common eyes,
We shall be called purgers, not murderers.   180
And for Mark Antony, think not of him;
For he can do no more than Cæsar's arm
When Cæsar's head is off.
   Cas.   Yet I fear him;
For in the ingrafted love he bears to Cæsar —
   Bru. Alas, good Cassius, do not think of him   185
If he love Cæsar, all that he can do

Is to himself, take thought and die for Cæsar:
And that were much he should; for he is given
To sports, to wildness, and much company.

  Treb. There is no fear in him; let him not die; 190
For he will live, and laugh at this hereafter. [*Clock strikes.*

  Bru. Peace! count the clock.

  Cas.   The clock hath stricken three.

  Treb. 'Tis time to part.

  Cas.   But it is doubtful yet,
Whether Cæsar will come forth to-day, or no;
For he is superstitious grown of late,   195
Quite from the main opinion he held once
Of fantasy, of dreams, and ceremonies:
It may be, these apparent prodigies,
The unaccustomed terror of this night,
And the persuasion of his augurers,   200
May hold him from the Capitol to-day.

  Dec. Never fear that; if he be so resolved,
I can o'ersway him; for he loves to hear
That unicorns may be betrayed with trees,
And bears with glasses, elephants with holes,   205
Lions with toils, and men with flatterers;
But when I tell him he hates flatterers,
He says he does, being then most flattered.
Let me work;
For I can give his humor the true bent,   210
And I will bring him to the Capitol.

  Cas. Nay, we will all of us be there to fetch him.

  Bru. By the eighth hour: is that the uttermost?

  Cin. Be that the uttermost, and fail not then.

  Met. Caius Ligarius doth bear Cæsar hard,   215
Who rated him for speaking well of Pompey:

I wonder none of you have thought of him.

   Bru. Now, good Metellus, go along by him:
He loves me well, and I have given him reasons;
Send him but hither, and I'll fashion him.   [Brutus.

   Cas. The morning comes upon's: we'll leave you,
And, friends, disperse yourselves; but all remember
What you have said, and show yourselves true Romans.

   Bru. Good gentlemen, look fresh and merrily;
Let not our looks put on our purposes,   225
But bear it as our Roman actors do,
With untired spirits and formal constancy:
And so good morrow to you every one.

                [*Exeunt all but Brutus.*

Boy! Lucius! Fast asleep? It is no matter;
Enjoy the honey-heavy dew of slumber: 230
Thou hast no figures nor no fantasies,
Which busy care draws in the brains of men;
Therefore thou sleep'st so sound.

           Enter PORTIA.

   Por.   Brutus, my lord!

   Bru. Portia, what mean you? wherefore rise you now?
It is not for your health thus to commit   235
Your weak condition to the raw cold morning.

   Por. Nor for yours neither. You've ungently, Brutus,
Stole from my bed: and yesternight at supper,
You suddenly arose, and walked about,
Musing and sighing, with your arms across;   240
And when I asked you what the matter was,
You stared upon me with ungentle looks;
I urged you further; then you scratched your head,
And too impatiently stamped with your foot;

Yet I insisted, yet you answered not,   245
But, with an angry wafture of your hand,
Gave sign for me to leave you: so I did,
Fearing to strengthen that impatience
Which seemed too much enkindled, and withal
Hoping it was but an effect of humor,   250
Which sometime hath his hour with every man.
It will not let you eat, nor talk, nor sleep,
And could it work so much upon your shape
As it hath much prevailed on your condition,
I should not know you, Brutus.   Dear my lord,   255
Make me acquainted with your cause of grief.
   Bru.   I am not well in health, and that is all.
   Por.   Brutus is wise, and, were he not in health,
He would embrace the means to come by it.
   Bru.   Why, so I do.   Good Portia, go to bed.   260
   Por.   Is Brutus sick? and is it physical
To walk unbracéd and suck up the humors
Of the dank morning?   What, is Brutus sick,
And will he steal out of his wholesome bed,
To dare the wild contagion of the night   265
And tempt the rheumy and unpurgéd air
To add unto his sickness?   No, my Brutus;
You have some sick offence within your mind,
Which, by the right and virtue of my place,
I ought to know of: and, upon my knees,   270
I charm you, by my once commended beauty,
By all your vows of love and that great vow
Which did incorporate and make us one,
That you unfold to me, yourself, your half,
Why you are heavy, and what men to-night   275
Have had resort to you: for here have been

Some six or seven, who did hide their faces
Even from darkness.

   Bru.   Kneel not, gentle Portia.

   Por.   I should not need, if you were gentle Brutus.
Within the bond of marriage, tell me, Brutus,   280
Is it excepted I should know no secrets
That appertain to you?   Am I yourself
But, as it were, in sort or limitation,
To keep with you at meals, comfort your bed,
And talk to you sometimes?   Dwell I but in the suburbs
Of your good pleasure?   If it be no more,   286
Portia is Brutus' harlot, not his wife.

   Bru.   You are my true and honorable wife,
As dear to me as are the ruddy drops
That visit my sad heart.   290

   Por.   If this were true, then should I know this secret.
I grant I am a woman; but withal
A woman that Lord Brutus took to wife:
I grant I am a woman; but withal
A woman well-reputed, Cato's daughter.   295
Think you I am no stronger than my sex,
Being so fathered and so husbanded?
Tell me your counsels, I will not disclose 'em:
I have made strong proof of my constancy,
Giving myself a voluntary wound   300
Here in the thigh: can I bear that with patience,
And not my husband's secrets?

   Bru.   O ye gods,
Render me worthy of this noble wife!   [*Knocking within.*
Hark, hark! one knocks: Portia, go in awhile;
And by and by thy bosom shall partake   305
The secrets of my heart:

All my engagements I will construe to thee,
All the charactery of my sad brows: [knocks?
Leave me with haste. [*Exit Portia.*] Lucius, who's that

Re-enter LUCIUS *with* LIGARIUS.

Luc. Here is a sick man that would speak with you.

Bru. Caius Ligarius, that Metellus spake of.   311
Boy, stand aside. Caius Ligarius! how?

Lig. Vouchsafe good morrow from a feeble tongue.

Bru. O, what a time have you chose out, brave Caius,
To wear a kerchief! Would you were not sick!   315

Lig. I am not sick, if Brutus have in hand
Any exploit worthy the name of honor.

Bru. Such an exploit have I in hand, Ligarius,
Had you a healthful ear to hear of it.

Lig. By all the gods that Romans bow before,   320
I here discard my sickness! Soul of Rome!
Brave son, derived from honorable loins!
Thou, like an exorcist, has conjured up
My mortified spirit. Now bid me run,
And I will strive with things impossible;   325
Yea, get the better of them. What's to do?

Bru. A piece of work that would make sick men whole.

Lig. But are not some whole that we must make sick?

Bru. That must we also. What it is, my Caius,
I shall unfold to thee, as we are going   330
To whom it must be done.

Lig.   Set on your foot,
And with a heart new-fired I follow you,
To do I know not what: but it sufficeth
That Brutus leads me on.

Bru.   Follow me, then.   [*Exeunt.*

SCENE II. *Cæsar's House.*

Thunder and lightning. Enter CÆSAR, *in his night-gown.*

Cæs.   Nor heaven nor earth have been at peace to-night :
Thrice hath Calpurnia in her sleep cried out,
"Help, ho! they murder Cæsar!" Who's within ?

Enter a Servant.

Serv.   My lord ?
Cæs.   Go bid the priests do present sacrifice,   5
And bring me their opinions of success.
Serv.   I will, my lord.   [*Exit.*

Enter CALPURNIA.

Cal.   What mean you, Cæsar ? think you to walk forth ?
You shall not stir out of your house to-day.
Cæs.   Cæsar shall forth : the things that threatened me
Ne'er looked but on my back ; when they shall see   11
The face of Cæsar, they are vanished.
Cal.   Cæsar, I never stood on ceremonies,
Yet now they fright me.   There is one within,
Besides the things that we have heard and seen,   15
Recounts most horrid sights seen by the watch.
A lioness hath whelpéd in the streets ;
And graves have yawned, and yielded up their dead ;
Fierce fiery warriors fought upon the clouds,
In ranks and squadrons and right form of war,   20
Which drizzled blood upon the Capitol ;
The noise of battle hurtled in the air,
Horses did neigh, and dying men did groan,
And ghosts did shriek and squeal about the streets.

O Cæsar ! these things are beyond all use,   25
And I do fear them.

    Cæs.   What can be avoided
Whose end is purposed by the mighty gods?

O Caesar ! these things are beyond all use,
And I do fear them.

                     — Act II.   Scene 2.

Yet Cæsar shall go forth ; for these predictions
Are to the world in general as to Cæsar.

    Cal.   When beggars die, there are no comets seen ;   30
The heavens themselves blaze forth the death of princes.

    Cæs.   Cowards die many times before their deaths ;
The valiant never taste of death but once.

Of all the wonders that I yet have heard,
It seems to me most strange that men should fear;   35
Seeing that death, a necessary end,
Will come when it will come.

Re-enter Servant.

                          What say the augurers?
    Serv.   They would not have you to stir forth to-day.
Plucking the entrails of an offering forth,
They could not find a heart within the beast.   40
    Cæs.   The gods do this in shame of cowardice:
Cæsar should be a beast without a heart,
If he should stay at home to-day for fear.
No, Cæsar shall not: danger knows full well
That Cæsar is more dangerous than he: 45
We are two lions littered in one day,
And I the elder and more terrible:
And Cæsar shall go forth.
    Cal.   Alas, my lord,
Your wisdom is consumed in confidence.
Do not go forth to-day: call it my fear   50
That keeps you in the house, and not your own.
We'll send Mark Antony to the senate-house;
And he shall say you are not well to-day:
Let me, upon my knee, prevail in this.
    Cæs.   Mark Antony shall say I am not well   55
And, for thy humor, I will stay at home.

Enter DECIUS.

Here's Decius Brutus, he shall tell them so.
    Dec.   Cæsar, all hail! good morrow, worthy Cæsar:
I come to fetch you to the senate-house.

35

Cæs.   And you are come in very happy time,   60
To bear my greeting to the senators
And tell them that I will not come to-day:
Cannot, is false, and that I dare not, falser:
I will not come to-day: tell them so, Decius.
   Cal.   Say he is sick.
   Cæs.   Shall Cæsar send a lie?   65
Have I in conquest stretched mine arm so far,
To be afeard to tell graybeards the truth?
Decius, go tell them Cæsar will not come.
   Dec.   Most mighty Cæsar, let me know some cause,
Lest I be laughed at when I tell them so.   70
   Cæs.   The cause is in my will: I will not come ;
That is enough to satisfy the senate.
But for your private satisfaction,
Because I love you, I will let you know:
Calpurnia here, my wife, stays me at home: 75
She dreamt to-night she saw my statuë,
Which, like a fountain with an hundred spouts,
Did run pure blood ; and many lusty Romans
Came smiling, and did bathe their hands in it:
And these does she apply for warnings, and portents,   80
And evils imminent ; and on her knee
Hath begged that I will stay at home to-day.
   Dec.   This dream is all amiss interpreted ;
It was a vision fair and fortunate:
Your statue spouting blood in many pipes,   85
In which so many smiling Romans bathed,
Signifies that from you great Rome shall suck
Reviving blood, and that great men shall press
For tinctures, stains, relics and cognizance.
This by Calpurnia's dream is signified.   90

Cæs.   And this way have·you well expounded it.

Dec.   I have, when you have heard what I can say:
And know it now: the senate have concluded
To give this day a crown to mighty Cæsar.
If you shall send them word you will not come,   95
Their minds may change.   Besides, it were a mock
Apt to be rendered, for some one to say,
" Break up the senate till another time,
When Cæsar's wife shall meet with better dreams."
If Cæsar hide himself, shall they not whisper,   100
"Lo, Cæsar is afraid ! "
Pardon me, Cæsar; for my dear dear love
To your proceeding bids me tell you this,
And reason to my love is liable.

Cæs.   How foolish do your fears seem now, Calpurnia !
I am ashaméd I did yield to them.
Give me my robe, for I will go.

Enter PUBLIUS, BRUTUS, LIGARIUS, METELLUS, CASCA,
TREBONIUS, *and* CINNA.

And look where Publius is come to fetch me.

Pub.   Good morrow, Cæsar.

Cæs.   Welcome, Publius.
What, Brutus, are you stirred so early too?   110
Good morrow, Casca.   Caius Ligarius,
Cæsar was ne'er so much your enemy
As that same ague which hath made you lean.
What is 't o'clock?

Bru.   Cæsar, 'tis strucken eight.

Cæs.   I thank you for your pains and courtesy.   115

Enter ANTONY.

See!   Antony, that revels long o' nights,
Is notwithstanding up.   Good morrow, Antony.

   Ant.   So to most noble Cæsar.

   Cæs.   Bid them prepare within:
I am to blame to be thus waited for.
Now, Cinna: now, Metellus: what, Trebonius!   120
I have an hour's talk in store for you;
Remember that you call on me to-day:
Be near me, that I may remember you.

   Treb.   Cæsar, I will: [*Aside*] and so near will I be,
That your best friends shall wish I had been further.   125

   Cæs.   Good friends, go in, and taste some wine with
     me;
And we, like friends, will straightway go together.

   Bru.   [*Aside*] That every like is not the same, O Cæsar,
The heart of Brutus yearns to think upon!   [*Exeunt.*

SCENE III.   *A street near the Capitol.*

Enter ARTEMIDORUS, *reading a paper.*

   Art.   "Cæsar, beware of Brutus; take heed of Cassius; come not near Casca; have an eye to Cinna; trust
not Trebonius; mark well Metellus Cimber: Decius
Brutus loves thee not: thou hast wronged Caius Ligarius.
There is but one mind in all these men, and it is bent
against Cæsar.   If thou beest not immortal, look about
you: security gives way to conspiracy.   The mighty gods
defend thee!   Thy lover ARTEMIDORUS."
Here will I stand till Cæsar pass along,
And as a suitor will I give him this.   10

38

My heart laments that virtue cannot live
Out of the teeth of emulation.
If thou read this, O Cæsar, thou mayst live ;
If not, the Fates with traitors do contrive.   [*Exit.*

SCENE IV. *Another part of the same street, before the*
house of Brutus.

Enter PORTIA *and* LUCIUS.

Por.   I prithee, boy, run to the senate-house ;
Stay not to answer me, but get thee gone :
Why dost thou stay ?

O constancy, be strong upon my side.
— Act II.   Scene 4.

Luc.   To know my errand, madam.
Por.   I would have had thee there, and here again,

Ere I can tell thee what thou shouldst do there.   5
O constancy, be strong upon my side,
Set a huge mountain 'tween my heart and tongue!
I have a man's mind, but a woman's might.
How hard it is for women to keep counsel!
Art thou here yet?

    Luc.   Madam, what should I do?   10
Run to the Capitol, and nothing else?
And so return to you, and nothing else?

    Por.   Yes, bring me word, boy, if thy lord look well,
For he went sickly forth: and take good note
What Cæsar doth, what suitors press to him.   15
Hark, boy! what noise is that?

    Luc.   I hear none, madam.

    Por.   Prithee, listen well;
I heard a bustling rumor, like a fray,
And the wind brings it from the Capitol.

    Luc.   Sooth, madam, I hear nothing.

Enter the Soothsayer.

    Por.   Come hither, fellow: 20
Which way hast thou been?

    Sooth.   At mine own house, good lady.

    Por.   What is 't o'clock?

    Sooth.   About the ninth hour, lady.

    Por.   Is Cæsar yet gone to the Capitol?

    Sooth.   Madam, not yet: I go to take my stand,
To see him pass on to the Capitol.   25

    Por.   Thou hast some suit to Cæsar, hast thou not?

    Sooth.   That I have, lady: if it will please Cæsar
To be so good to Cæsar as to hear me,
I shall beseech him to befriend himself.

40

Por. Why, know'st thou any harm's intended towards
   him?   30
   Sooth. None that I know will be, much that I fear may
   chance.
Good morrow to you.   Here the street is narrow:
The throng that follow Cæsar at the heels,
Of senators, of prætors, common suitors,
Will crowd a feeble man almost to death: 35
I'll get me to a place more void, and there
Speak to great Cæsar as he comes along.   [*Exit.*
   Por. I must go in.   Ay me, how weak a thing
The heart of woman is !   O Brutus,
The heavens speed thee in thine enterprise !   40
Sure, the boy heard me : Brutus hath a suit
That Cæsar will not grant.   O, I grow faint.
Run, Lucius, and commend me to my lord ;
Say I am merry : come to me again,
And bring me word what he doth say to thee.   45
                    [*Exeunt severally.*

ACT III.   — *question*

SCENE I. *Rome.   Before the Capitol; the Senate sitting
above.*

A crowd of people; among them ARTEMIDORUS *and the*
Soothsayer. *Flourish.   Enter* CÆSAR, BRUTUS, CAS-
SIUS, CASCA, DECIUS, METELLUS, TREBONIUS, CINNA,
ANTONY, LEPIDUS, POPILIUS, PUBLIUS, *and others.*

   Cæs. [*To the Soothsayer*] The ides of March are come.
   Sooth. Ay, Cæsar ; but not gone.
   Art. Hail, Cæsar ! read this schedule.

Dec.   Trebonius doth desire you to o'er-read,
At your best leisure, this his humble suit.   5

Art.   O Cæsar, read mine first; for mine's a suit
That touches Cæsar nearer: read it, great Cæsar.

Cæs.   What touches us ourself shall be last served.

Art.   Delay not, Cæsar; read it instantly.

Cæs.   What, is the fellow mad?

Pub.   Sirrah, give place.   10

Cas.   What, urge you your petitions in the street?
Come to the Capitol.

    CÆSAR *goes up to the Senate-House, the rest following.*

Pop.   I wish your enterprise to-day may thrive.

Cas.   What enterprise, Popilius?

Pop.   Fare you well.

                    [*Advances to Cæsar.*

Bru.   What said Popilius Lena?   15

Cas.   He wished to-day our enterprise might thrive.
I fear our purpose is discovered.

Bru.   Look, how he makes to Cæsar: mark him.

Cas.   Casca,
Be sudden, for we fear prevention.
Brutus, what shall be done?   If this be known,   20
Cassius or Cæsar never shall turn back,
For I will slay myself.

Bru.   Cassius, be constant:
Popilius Lena speaks not of our purposes;
For, look, he smiles, and Cæsar doth not change.

Cas.   Trebonius knows his time; for, look you, Brutus,
He draws Mark Antony out of the way.   26

           [*Exeunt Antony and Trebonius.*

Dec.   Where is Metellus Cimber?   Let him go,

And presently prefer his suit to Cæsar.

Bru. He is addressed: press near and second him.

Cin. Casca, you are the first that rears your hand.   30

Cæs. Are we all ready? What is now amiss
That Cæsar and his senate must redress?

Met. Most high, most mighty, and most puissant Cæsar,
Metellus Cimber throws before thy seat
An humble heart: —   [*Kneeling.*

Cæs.   I must prevent thee, Cimber.   35
These couchings and these lowly courtesies
Might thaw the blood of ordinary men,
And turn pre-ordinance and first decree
Into the law of children. Be not fond,
To think that Cæsar bears such rebel blood   40
That will be thawed from the true quality
With that which melteth fools; I mean, sweet words,
Low-crookéd court'sies and base spaniel-fawning.
Thy brother by decree is banishéd:
If thou dost bend and pray and fawn for him,   45
I spurn thee like a cur out of my way.
Know, Cæsar doth not wrong, nor without cause
Will he be satisfied.

Met. Is there no voice more worthy than my own,
To sound more sweetly in great Cæsar's ear   50
For the repealing of my banished brother?

Bru. I kiss thy hand, but not in flattery, Cæsar;
Desiring thee that Publius Cimber may
Have an immediate freedom of repeal.

Cæs. What, Brutus!

43

Cas.   Pardon, Cæsar; Cæsar, pardon;   55
As low as to thy foot doth Cassius fall,
To beg enfranchisement for Publius Cimber.

Cæs.   I could be well moved, if I were as you;
If I could pray to move, prayers would move me;
But I am constant as the northern star,   60
Of whose true-fixed and resting quality
There is no fellow in the firmament.
The skies are painted with unnumbered sparks,
They are all fire and every one doth shine;
But there's but one in all doth hold his place: 65
So in the world; 'tis furnished well with men,
And men are flesh and blood, and apprehensive;
Yet in the number I do know but one
That unassailable holds on his rank,
Unshaked of motion: and that I am he,   70
Let me a little show it, even in this;
That I was constant Cimber should be banished,
And constant do remain to keep him so.

Cin.   O Cæsar, —

Cæs.   Hence! wilt thou lift up Olympus?

Dec.   Great Cæsar, —

Cæs.   Doth not Brutus bootless kneel?   75

Casca.   Speak, hands, for me!

[*Casca first, then the other conspirators and Marcus
    Brutus stab Cæsar.*

Cæs.   Et tu, Brute! Then fall, Cæsar!   [*Dies.*

Cin.   Liberty! Freedom! Tyranny is dead!
Run hence, proclaim, cry it about the streets.

Cas.   Some to the common pulpits, and cry out
" Liberty, freedom, and enfranchisement! "

Bru.   People and senators, be not affrighted;
Fly not; stand still: ambition's debt is paid.

Casca.   Go to the pulpit, Brutus.

Dec.   And Cassius too.   85

Bru.   Where's Publius?

Cin.   Here, quite confounded with this mutiny.

Met.   Stand fast together, lest some friend of Cæsar's
Should chance —

Bru.   Talk not of standing.   Publius, good cheer;   90
There is no harm intended to your person,
Nor to no Roman else: so tell them, Publius.

Cas.   And leave us, Publius: lest that the people,
Rushing on us, should do your age some mischief.

Bru.   Do so: and let no man abide this deed,   95
But we the doers.

Re-enter TREBONIUS.

Cas.   Where is Antony?

Tre.   Fled to his house amazed:
Men, wives, and children stare, cry out, and run
As it were doomsday.

Bru.   Fates, we will know your pleasures:
That we shall die, we know; 'tis but the time   100
And drawing days out, that men stand upon.

Cas.   Why, he that cuts off twenty years of life
Cuts off so many years of fearing death.

Bru.   Grant that, and then is death a benefit:
So are we Cæsar's friends, that have abridged   105
His time of fearing death.   Stoop, Romans, stoop,
And let us bathe our hands in Cæsar's blood
Up to the elbows, and besmear our swords:
Then walk we forth, even to the market-place,

45

And, waving our red weapons o'er our heads,   110
Let's all cry " Peace, freedom, and liberty ! "

Cas.   Stoop then, and wash.   How many ages hence
Shall this our lofty scene be acted over
In states unborn and accents yet unknown !

Bru.   How many times shall Cæsar bleed in sport,   115
That now on Pompey's basis lies along
No worthier than the dust !

Cas.   So oft as that shall be,
So often shall the knot of us be called
The men that gave their country liberty.

Dec.   What, shall we forth ?

Cas.   Ay, every man away :   120
Brutus shall lead ; and we will grace his heels
With the most boldest and best hearts of Rome.

Enter a Servant.

Bru.   Soft ! who comes here ?   A friend of Antony's.

Serv.   Thus, Brutus, did my master bid me kneel ;
Thus did Mark Antony bid me fall down ;   125
And, being prostrate, thus he bade me say :
Brutus is noble, wise, valiant and honest ;
Cæsar was mighty, bold, royal and loving :
Say I love Brutus, and I honor him ;
Say I feared Cæsar, honored him, and loved him.   130
If Brutus will vouchsafe that Antony
May safely come to him, and be resolved
How Cæsar hath deserved to lie in death,
Mark Antony shall not love Cæsar dead
So well as Brutus living ; but will follow   135
The fortunes and affairs of noble Brutus
Thorough the hazards of this untrod state

46

And, waving our red weapons o'er our heads,
Let's all cry "Peace, freedom, and liberty!"

— Act III. Scene 1.

With all true faith.   So says my master Antony.

Bru.   Thy master is a wise and valiant Roman;
I never thought him worse.   140
Tell him, so please him come unto this place,
He shall be satisfied, and, by my honor,
Depart untouched.

Serv.   I'll fetch him presently.   [*Exit.*

Bru.   I know that we shall have him well to friend.

Cas.   I wish we may: but yet have I a mind   145
That fears him much; and my misgiving still
Falls shrewdly to the purpose.

Bru.   But here comes Antony.

Re-enter ANTONY.

                              Welcome, Mark Antony.

Ant.   O mighty Cæsar! dost thou lie so low?
Are all thy conquests, glories, triumphs, spoils,   150
Shrunk to this little measure?   Fare thee well.
I know not, gentlemen, what you intend,
Who else must be let blood, who else is rank:
If I myself, there is no hour so fit
As Cæsar's death's hour, nor no instrument   155
Of half that worth as those your swords, made rich
With the most noble blood of all this world.
I do beseech ye, if you bear me hard,
Now whilst your purpled hands do reek and smoke,
Fulfil your pleasure.   Live a thousand years,   160
I shall not find myself so apt to die:
No place will please me so, no mean of death,
As here by Cæsar, and by you cut off,
The choice and master spirits of this age.

Bru.   O Antony, beg not your death of us.   165

Though now we must appear bloody and cruel,
As, by our hands and this our present act,
You see we do, yet see you but our hands
And this the bleeding business they have done:

Welcome, Mark Antony.
— Act III.   Scene i.

Our hearts you see not; they are pitiful;   170
And pity to the general wrong of Rome —
As fire drives out fire, so pity pity —
Hath done this deed on Cæsar.   For your part,
To you our swords have leaden points, Mark Antony:
Our arms in strength of malice, and our hearts   175
Of brothers' temper, do receive you in
With all kind love, good thoughts, and reverence.

Cas.   Your voice shall be as strong as any man's
In the disposing of new dignities.

Bru.   Only be patient till we have appeased   180
The multitude, beside themselves with fear,
And then we will deliver you the cause,
Why I, that did love Cæsar when I struck him,
Have thus proceeded.

Ant.   I doubt not of your wisdom.
Let each man render me his bloody hand: 185
First, Marcus Brutus, will I shake with you;
Next, Caius Cassius, do I take your hand;
Now, Decius Brutus, yours; now yours, Metellus;
Yours, Cinna; and, my valiant Casca, yours;
Though last, not least in love, yours, good Trebonius.   190
Gentlemen all,— alas, what shall I say?
My credit now stands on such slippery ground,
That one of two bad ways you must conceit me,
Either a coward or a flatterer.
That I did love thee, Cæsar, O, 'tis true: 195
If then thy spirit look upon us now,
Shall it not grieve thee dearer than thy death,
To see thy Antony making his peace,
Shaking the bloody fingers of thy foes,
Most noble! in the presence of thy corse?   200
Had I as many eyes as thou hast wounds,
Weeping as fast as they stream forth thy blood,
It would become me better than to close
In terms of friendship with thine enemies.
Pardon me, Julius! Here wast thou bayed, brave hart;   205
Here didst thou fall, and here thy hunters stand,
Signed in thy spoil, and crimsoned in thy lethe.
O world, thou wast the forest to this hart;

And this, indeed, O world, the heart of thee.
How like a deer strucken by many princes,   210
Dost thou here lie !
   Cas.   Mark Antony, —
   Ant.   Pardon me, Caius Cassius ;
The enemies of Cæsar shall say this ;
Then, in a friend, it is cold modesty.
   Cas.   I blame you not for praising Cæsar so ;   215
But what compact mean you to have with us ?
Will you be pricked in number of our friends,
Or shall we on, and not depend on you ?
   Ant.   Therefore I took your hands, but was, indeed,
Swayed from the point, by looking down on Cæsar.   220
Friends am I with you all and love you all,
Upon this hope, that you shall give me reasons
Why and wherein Cæsar was dangerous.
   Bru.   Or else were this a savage spectacle :
Our reasons are so full of good regard   225
That were you, Antony, the son of Cæsar,
You should be satisfied.
   Ant.   That's all I seek :
And am moreover suitor that I may
Produce his body to the market-place ;
And in the pulpit, as becomes a friend,   230
Speak in the order of his funeral.
   Bru.   You shall, Mark Antony.
   Cas.   Brutus, a word with you.
[*Aside to Brutus.*] You know not what you do : do not
    consent
That Antony speak in his funeral :
Know you how much the people may be moved   235
By that which he will utter ?

Bru.   By your pardon ;
I will myself into the pulpit first,
And show the reason of our Cæsar's death :
What Antony shall speak, I will protest
He speaks by leave and by permission,   240
And that we are contented Cæsar shall
Have all true rites and lawful ceremonies.
It shall advantage more than do us wrong.
    Cas.   I know not what may fall ; I like it not.
    Bru.   Mark Antony, here, take you Cæsar's body.   245
You shall not in your funeral speech blame us,
But speak all good you can devise of Cæsar,
And say you do't by our permission ;
Else shall you not have any hand at all
About his funeral : and you shall speak   250
In the same pulpit whereto I am going,
After my speech is ended.
    Ant.   Be it so ;
I do desire no more.
    Bru.   Prepare the body then, and follow us.
                              [*Exeunt all but Antony.*
    Ant.   O, pardon me, thou bleeding piece of earth,   255
That I am meek and gentle with these butchers !
Thou art the ruins of the noblest man
That ever lived in the tide of times.
Woe to the hand that shed this costly blood !
Over thy wounds now do I prophesy,—   260
Which, like dumb mouths, do ope their ruby lips,
To beg the voice and utterance of my tongue,—
A curse shall light upon the limbs of men ;
Domestic fury and fierce civil strife
Shall cumber all the parts of Italy ;   265

Blood and destruction shall be so in use,
And dreadful objects so familiar,
That mothers shall but smile when they behold
Their infants quartered with the hands of war;
All pity choked with custom of fell deeds: 270
And Cæsar's spirit, ranging for revenge,
With Ate by his side come hot from hell,
Shall in these confines with a monarch's voice
Cry "Havoc," and let slip the dogs of war;
That this foul deed shall smell above the earth   275
With carrion men, groaning for burial.

Enter a Servant.

You serve Octavius Cæsar, do you not?
    Serv.   I do, Mark Antony.
    Ant.   Cæsar did write for him to come to Rome.
    Serv.   He did receive his letters, and is coming;   280
And bid me say to you by word of mouth —
O Cæsar! —   [*Seeing the body.*
    Ant.   Thy heart is big; get thee apart and weep.
Passion, I see, is catching; for mine eyes,
Seeing those beads of sorrow stand in thine,   285
Began to water.   Is thy master coming?
    Serv.   He lies to-night within seven leagues of Rome.
    Ant.   Post back with speed, and tell him what hath
        chanced:
Here is a mourning Rome, a dangerous Rome,
No Rome of safety for Octavius yet;   290
Hie hence, and tell him so.   Yet, stay awhile:
Thou shalt not back till I have borne this corse
Into the market-place: there shall I try,
In my oration, how the people take

53

The cruel issue of these bloody men;   295
According to the which, thou shalt discourse
To young Octavius of the state of things.
Lend me your hand.   [*Exeunt with Cæsar's body.*

SCENE II.   *The Forum.*

Enter BRUTUS *and* CASSIUS, *and a throng of* Citizens.

Citizens.   We will be satisfied; let us be satisfied.
Bru.   Then follow me, and give me audience, friends.
Cassius, go you into the other street,
And part the numbers.
Those that will hear me speak, let 'em stay here ·   5
Those that will follow Cassius, go with him;
And public reasons shall be rendered
Of Cæsar's death.
First Cit.   I will hear Brutus speak.
Sec. Cit.   I will hear Cassius; and compare their reasons,
When severally we hear them rendered.   10
   [*Exit Cassius, with some of the Citizens. Brutus goes
      into the pulpit.*
Third Cit.   The noble Brutus is ascended: silence!
Bru.   Be patient till the last.
Romans, countrymen, and lovers! hear me for my cause,
and be silent that you may hear: believe me for mine
honor, and have respect to mine honor, that you may be-
lieve: censure me in your wisdom, and awake your senses,
that you may the better judge. If there be any in this
assembly, any dear friend of Cæsar's, to him I say, that
Brutus' love to Cæsar was no less than his. If then that
friend demand why Brutus rose against Cæsar, this is my

answer: — Not that I loved Cæsar less, but that I loved
Rome more. Had you rather Cæsar were living and die
all slaves, than that Cæsar were dead, to live all free
men? As Cæsar loved me, I weep for him; as he was
fortunate, I rejoice at it; as he was valiant, I honor him:
but as he was ambitious, I slew him. There is tears for
his love; joy for his fortune; honor for his valor; and
death for his ambition. Who is here so base that would
be a bondman? If any, speak; for him have I offended.
Who is here so rude that would not be a Roman? If any,
speak; for him have I offended. Who is here so vile
that will not love his country? If any, speak; for him
have I offended. I pause for a reply.   33

All. None, Brutus, none.

Bru. Then none have I offended. I have done no
more to Cæsar than you shall do to Brutus. The question of his death is enrolled in the Capitol; his glory not
extenuated, wherein he was worthy, nor his offences enforced, for which he suffered death.

Enter ANTONY *and others, with* CÆSAR'S *body.*

Here comes his body, mourned by Mark Antony: who,
though he had no hand in his death, shall receive the
benefit of his dying, a place in the commonwealth; as
which of you shall not? With this I depart, — that, as
I slew my best lover for the good of Rome, I have the
same dagger for myself, when it shall please my country
to need my death.   46

All. Live, Brutus! live, live!

First Cit. Bring him with triumph home unto his house.

Sec. Cit. Give him a statue with his ancestors.

Third Cit. Let him be Cæsar.

Fourth Cit.   Cæsar's better parts 50
Shall be crowned in Brutus.

First Cit. We'll bring him to his house with shouts
and clamors.

Here comes his body, mourned by Mark Antony.
— Act III. Scene 2.

Bru. My countrymen, —

Sec. Cit.   Peace, silence ! Brutus speaks.

First Cit. Peace, ho !

Bru. Good countrymen, let me depart alone,   55
And, for my sake, stay here with Antony :
Do grace to Cæsar's corpse, and grace his speech
Tending to Cæsar's glories ; which Mark Antony,

By our permission, is allowed to make.
I do entreat you, not a man depart,   60
Save I alone, till Antony have spoke.   [*Exit.*

    First Cit.   Stay, ho! and let us hear Mark Antony.

    Third Cit.   Let him go up into the public chair;
We'll hear him.   Noble Antony, go up.

    Ant.   For Brutus' sake, I am beholding to you.   65
                        [*Goes into the pulpit.*

    Fourth Cit.   What does he say of Brutus?

    Third Cit.   He says, for Brutus' sake,
He finds himself beholding to us all.

    Fourth Cit.   'Twere best he speak no harm of Brutus
    here.

    First Cit.   This Cæsar was a tyrant.

    Third Cit.   Nay, that's certain:
We are blest that Rome is rid of him.   70

    Sec. Cit.   Peace! let us hear what Antony can say.

    Ant.   You gentle Romans, —

    Citizens.   Peace, ho! let us hear him.

    Ant.   Friends, Romans, countrymen, lend me your ears;
I come to bury Cæsar, not to praise him.
The evil that men do lives after them;   75
The good is oft interréd with their bones;
So let it be with Cæsar.   The noble Brutus
Hath told you Cæsar was ambitious:
If it were so, it was a grievous fault,
And grievously hath Cæsar answered it.   80
Here, under leave of Brutus and the rest, —
For Brutus is an honorable man;
So are they all, all honorable men, —
Come I to speak in Cæsar's funeral.
He was my friend, faithful and just to me: 85

But Brutus says he was ambitious;
And Brutus is an honorable man.
He hath brought many captives home to Rome,
Whose ransoms did the general coffers fill:
Did this in Cæsar seem ambitious?   90
When that the poor have cried, Cæsar hath wept:
Ambition should be made of sterner stuff:
Yet Brutus says he was ambitious;
And Brutus is an honorable man.
You all did see that on the Lupercal   95
I thrice presented him a kingly crown,
Which he did thrice refuse: was this ambition?
Yet Brutus says he was ambitious;
And, sure, he is an honorable man.
I speak not to disprove what Brutus spoke,   100
But here I am to speak what I do know.
You all did love him once, not without cause:
What cause withholds you then to mourn for him?
O judgment! thou art fled to brutish beasts,
And men have lost their reason.   Bear with me;   105
My heart is in the coffin there with Cæsar,
And I must pause till it come back to me.

    First Cit.   Methinks there is much reason in his say-
    ings.

    Sec. Cit.   If thou consider rightly of the matter,
Cæsar has had great wrong.

    Third Cit.   Has he, masters?   110
I fear there will a worse come in his place.

    Fourth Cit.   Marked ye his words? He would not
    take the crown;
Therefore 'tis certain he was not ambitious.

    First Cit.   If it be found so, some will dear abide it.

Sec. Cit. Poor soul! his eyes are red as fire with
   weeping.   115
Third Cit. There's not a nobler man in Rome than
   Antony.
Fourth Cit.   Now mark him, he begins again to speak.
   Ant.   But yesterday the word of Caesar might
Have stood against the world; now lies he there,
And none so poor to do him reverence.   120
O masters, if I were disposed to stir
Your hearts and minds to mutiny and rage,
I should do Brutus wrong, and Cassius wrong,
Who, you all know, are honorable men:
I will not do them wrong; I rather choose   125
To wrong the dead, to wrong myself and you,
Than I will wrong such honorable men.
But here's a parchment with the seal of Cæsar;
I found it in his closet   'tis his will:
Let but the commons hear this testament —   130
Which, pardon me, I do not mean to read —
And they would go and kiss dead Cæsar's wounds
And dip their napkins in his sacred blood,
Yea, beg a hair of him for memory,
And, dying, mention it within their wills,   135
Bequeathing it as a rich legacy
Unto their issue.
   Fourth Cit.   We'll hear the will: read it, Mark Antony.
   All.   The will! the will! we will hear Cæsar's will.
   Ant.   Have patience, gentle friends, I must not read it;
It is not meet you know how Cæsar loved you.   141
You are not wood, you are not stones, but men;
And, being men, hearing the will of Cæsar,
It will inflame you, it will make you mad:

'Tis good you know not that you are his heirs;   145
For, if you should, O, what would come of it!

Fourth Cit.   Read the will; we'll hear it, Antony;
You shall read us the will, Cæsar's will.

Ant.   Will you be patient? will you stay awhile?
I have o'ershot myself to tell you of it: 150
I fear I wrong the honorable men
Whose daggers have stabbed Cæsar; I do fear it.

Fourth Cit.   They were traitors: honorable men!

All.   The will! the testament!

Sec. Cit.   They were villains, murderers: the will! read
the will.   156

Ant.   You will compel me, then, to read the will?
Then make a ring about the corpse of Cæsar,
And let me show you him that made the will.
Shall I descend? and will you give me leave?   160

All.   Come down.

Sec. Cit.   Descend.   [*He comes down from the pulpit.*

Third Cit.   You shall have leave.

Fourth Cit.   A ring; stand round.

First Cit.   Stand from the hearse, stand from the
body.

Sec. Cit.   Room for Antony, most noble Antony.   166

Ant.   Nay, press not so upon me; stand far off.

Several Cit.   Stand back.   Room!   Bear back.

Ant.   If you have tears, prepare to shed them now.
You all do know this mantle: I remember   170
The first time ever Cæsar put it on;
'Twas on a summer's evening, in his tent,
That day he overcame the Nervii:
Look, in this place ran Cassius' dagger through:
See what a rent the envious Casca made: 175

60

Through this the well-belovéd Brutus stabbed ;
And as he plucked his curséd steel away,
Mark how the blood of Cæsar followed it,
As rushing out of doors, to be resolved
If Brutus so unkindly knocked, or no ;   180
For Brutus, as you know, was Cæsar's angel :
Judge, O you gods, how dearly Cæsar loved him !
This was the most unkindest cut of all ;
For when the noble Cæsar saw him stab,
Ingratitude, more strong than traitors' arms,   185
Quite vanquished him : then burst his mighty heart ;
And, in his mantle muffling up his face,
Even at the base of Pompey's statuë,
Which all the while ran blood, great Cæsar fell.
O, what a fall was there, my countrymen !   190
Then I, and you, and all of us fell down,
Whilst bloody treason flourished over us.
O, now you weep, and I perceive you feel
The dint of pity : these are gracious drops.
Kind souls, what, weep you when you but behold   195
Our Cæsar's vesture wounded ?   Look you here,
Here is himself, marred, as you see, with traitors.

   First Cit.   O piteous spectacle !
   Sec. Cit.   O noble Cæsar !
   Third Cit.   O woful day !   200
   Fourth Cit.   O traitors, villains !
   First Cit.   O most bloody sight !
   Sec. Cit.   We will be revenged.
   All.   Revenge !   About !   Seek !   Burn !   Fire !   Kill !
Slay !   Let not a traitor live !   205
   Ant.   Stay, countrymen.
   First Cit.   Peace there ! hear the noble Antony.

Sec. Cit. We'll hear him, we'll follow him, we'll die
    with him.

Ant. Good friends, sweet friends, let me not stir you up
To such a sudden flood of mutiny   211
They that have done this deed are honorable :
What private griefs they have, alas, I know not,
That made them do it : they are wise and honorable,
And will, no doubt, with reasons answer you.   215
I come not, friends, to steal away your hearts :
I am no orator, as Brutus is ;
But, as you know me all, a plain blunt man,
That love my friend ; and that they know full well
That gave me public leave to speak of him :   220
For I have neither wit, nor words, nor worth,
Action, nor utterance, nor the power of speech,
To stir men's blood : I only speak right on ;
I tell you that which you yourselves do know ;
Show you sweet Cæsar's wounds, poor, poor dumb mouths,
And bid them speak for me : but were I Brutus,   226
And Brutus Antony, there were an Antony
Would ruffle up your spirits and put a tongue
In every wound of Cæsar that should move
The stones of Rome to rise and mutiny.   230

All. We'll mutiny.

First Cit. We'll burn the house of Brutus.

Third Cit. Away then ! come, seek the conspirators.

Ant. Yet hear me, countrymen ; yet hear me speak.

All. Peace, ho ! Hear Antony. Most noble Antony !

Ant. Why, friends, you go to do you know not what :
Wherein hath Cæsar thus deserved your loves ?   237
Alas, you know not : I must tell you then :
You have forgot the will I told you of.

All.   Most true : the will ! Let's stay and hear the
                will.   240
Ant.   Here is the will, and under Cæsar's seal.
To every Roman citizen he gives,
To every several man, seventy-five drachmas.
Sec. Cit.   Most noble Cæsar ! We'll revenge his death.
Third Cit.   O royal Cæsar !   245
Ant.   Hear me with patience.
All.   Peace, ho !
Ant.   Moreover, he hath left you all his walks,
His private arbors and new-planted orchards;
On this side Tiber ; he hath left them you,   250
And to your heirs for ever ; common pleasures,
To walk abroad and recreate yourselves.
Here was a Cæsar ! when comes such another ?
First Cit.   Never, never. Come, away, away !
We'll burn his body in the holy place,   255
And with the brands fire the traitors' houses.
Take up the body.
Sec. Cit.   Go fetch fire.
Third Cit.   Pluck down benches.
Fourth Cit.   Pluck down forms, windows, anything.
                [*Exeunt Citizens with the body.*
Ant.   Now let it work. Mischief, thou art afoot,   261
Take thou what course thou wilt !

Enter a Servant.

                                How now, fellow !
Serv.   Sir, Octavius is already come to Rome.
Ant.   Where is he ?
Serv.   He and Lepidus are at Cæsar's house.   265
Ant.   And thither will I straight to visit him :

He comes upon a wish.   Fortune is merry,
And in this mood will give us any thing.
    Serv.   I heard him say, Brutus and Cassius
Are rid like madmen through the gates of Rome.   270
    Ant.   Belike they had some notice of the people,
How I had moved them.   Bring me to Octavius.

                                        [*Exeunt.*

SCENE III.   *A street.*

Enter CINNA *the poet.*

    Cin.   I dreamt to-night that I did feast with Cæsar,
And things unlucky charge my fantasy :
I have no will to wander forth of doors,
Yet something leads me forth.

Enter Citizens.

    First Cit.   What is your name ?   5
    Sec. Cit.   Whither are you going ?
    Third Cit.   Where do you dwell ?
    Fourth Cit.   Are you a married man or a bachelor ?
    Sec. Cit.   Answer every man directly.
    First Cit.   Ay, and briefly.   10
    Fourth Cit.   Ay, and wisely.
    Third Cit.   Ay, and truly, you were best.
    Cin.   What is my name ?   Whither am I going ?
Where do I dwell ? am I a married man or a bachelor ?
Then, to answer every man directly and briefly, wisely
and truly : wisely I say, I am a bachelor.   16
    Sec. Cit.   That's as much as to say, they are fools that
marry : you'll bear me a bang for that, I fear.   Proceed ;
directly.
    Cin.   Directly, I am going to Cæsar's funeral.   20

64

First Cit.   As a friend or an enemy?

Cin.   As a friend.

Sec. Cit.   That matter is answered directly.

Fourth Cit.   For your dwelling, briefly.

Cin.   Briefly, I dwell by the Capitol.   25

Third Cit.   Your name, sir, truly.

Cin.   Truly, my name is Cinna.

First Cit.   Tear him to pieces; he's a conspirator.

Cin.   I am Cinna the poet, I am Cinna the poet.

Fourth Cit.   Tear him for his bad verses, tear him for his bad verses.   31

Cin.   I am not Cinna the conspirator.

Fourth Cit.   It is no matter, his name's Cinna; pluck but his name out of his heart, and turn him going.

Third Cit.   Tear him, tear him! Come, brands, ho! fire-brands: to Brutus', to Cassius'; burn all: some to Decius' house, and some to Casca's; some to Ligarius': away, go!   [*Exeunt.*

ACT IV.

SCENE I.   *A house in Rome.*

ANTONY, OCTAVIUS, *and* LEPIDUS, *seated at a table.*

Ant.   These many, then, shall die; their names are
     pricked.

Oct.   Your brother too must die; consent you, Lepi-
     dus?

Lep.   I do consent —

Oct.   Prick him down, Antony.

Lep.   Upon condition Publius shall not live,
Who is your sister's son, Mark Antony.   5

Ant. He shall not live; look, with a spot I damn him.
But Lepidus, go you to Cæsar's house;
Fetch the will hither, and we shall determine
How to cut off some charge in legacies.

He shall not live; look, with a spot I damn him.

— Act IV. Scene 1.

   Lep. What, shall I find you here?   10
   Oct. Or here, or at the Capitol.   [*Exit Lepidus.*
   Ant. This is a slight unmeritable man,
Meet to be sent on errands: is it fit,
The three-fold world divided, he should stand
One of the three to share it?
   Oct.   So you thought him,   15
And took his voice who should be pricked to die,
In our black sentence and proscription.
   Ant. Octavius, I have seen more days than you:
And though we lay these honors on this man,
To ease ourselves of divers slanderous loads,   20

He shall but bear them as the ass bears gold,
To groan and sweat under the business,
Either led or driven, as we point the way;
And having brought our treasure where we will,
Then take we down his load and turn him off,   25
Like to the empty ass, to shake his ears,
And graze in commons.
   Oct.   You may do your will;
But he's a tried and valiant soldier.
   Ant.   So is my horse, Octavius; and for that
I do appoint him store of provender: 30
It is a creature that I teach to fight,
To wind, to stop, to run directly on,
His corporal motion governed by my spirit.
And, in some taste, is Lepidus but so;
He must be taught, and trained, and bid go forth;   35
A barren-spirited fellow; one that feeds
On abjects, orts, and imitations,
Which, out of use and staled by other men,
Begin his fashion: do not talk of him,
But as a property.   And now, Octavius,   40
Listen great things: Brutus and Cassius
Are levying powers: we must straight make head:
Therefore let our alliance be combined,
Our best friends made, our means stretched;
And let us presently go sit in council,   45
How covert matters may be best disclosed,
And open perils surest answeréd.
   Oct.   Let us do so: for we are at the stake,
And bayed about with many enemies;
And some that smile have in their hearts, I fear,   50
Millions of mischiefs.   *[Exeunt*

Scene II.   *Camp near Sardis.   Before Brutus' tent.*

Drum.   Enter Brutus, Lucilius, Lucius, *and* Soldiers :
      Titinius *and* Pindarus *meeting them.*

Bru.   Stand, ho !
Lucil.   Give the word, ho ! and stand.
Bru.   What now, Lucilius ! is Cassius near ?
  Lucil.   He is at hand ; and Pindarus is come
To do you salutation from his master.   5
  Bru.   He greets me well.   Your master, Pindarus,
In his own change, or by ill officers,
Hath given me some worthy cause to wish
Things done, undone ; but if he be at hand,
I shall be satisfied.
  Pin.   I do not doubt   10
But that my noble master will appear
Such as he is, full of regard and honor.
  Bru.   He is not doubted.   A word, Lucilius,
How he received you : let me be resolved.
  Lucil.   With courtesy and with respect enough ;   15
But not with such familiar instances,
Nor with such free and friendly conference,
As he hath used of old.
  Bru.   Thou hast described
A hot friend cooling : ever note, Lucilius,
When love begins to sicken and decay,   20
It useth an enforcéd ceremony.
There are no tricks in plain and simple faith ;
But hollow men, like horses hot at hand,
Make gallant show and promise of their mettle ;
But when they should endure the bloody spur,   25

68

They fall their crests, and, like deceitful jades,
Sink in the trial.   Comes his army on?
   Lucil.   They mean this night in Sardis to be quartered;
The greater part, the horse in general,
Are come with Cassius.   [*Low march within.*
   Bru.   Hark! he is arrived.   30
March gently on to meet him.

       Enter CASSIUS *and his powers.*

   Cas.   Stand, ho!
   Bru.   Stand, ho!   Speak the word along.
   First Sol.   Stand!
   Sec. Sol.   Stand!   35
   Third Sol.   Stand!
   Cas.   Most noble brother, you have done me wrong.
   Bru.   Judge me, you gods! wrong I mine enemies?
And, if not so, how should I wrong a brother?
   Cas.   Brutus, this sober form of yours hides wrongs;   40
And when you do them —
   Bru.   Cassius, be content;
Speak your griefs softly: I do know you well.
Before the eyes of both our armies here,
Which should perceive nothing but love from us,
Let us not wrangle: bid them move away;   45
Then in my tent, Cassius, enlarge your griefs,
And I will give you audience.
   Cas.   Pindarus,
Bid our commanders lead the charges off
A little from this ground.
   Bru.   Lucilius, do you the like; and let no man   50
Come to our tent till we have done our conference.
Let Lucius and Titinius guard our door.   [*Exeunt.*

SCENE III. *Brutus' tent.*

Enter BRUTUS *and* CASSIUS.

Cas.   That you have wronged me doth appear in this:
You have condemned and noted Lucius Pella
For taking bribes here of the Sardians;
Wherein my letters, praying on his side,
Because I knew the man, were slighted off.   5
   Bru.   You wronged yourself to write in such a case.
   Cas.   In such a time as this it is not meet
That every nice offence should bear his comment.
   Bru.   Let me tell you, Cassius, you yourself
Are much condemned to have an itching palm,   10
To sell and mart your offices for gold
To undeservers.
   Cas.   I an itching palm!
You know that you are Brutus that speaks this,
Or, by the gods, this speech were else your last.
   Bru.   The name of Cassius honors this corruption,   15
And chastisement doth therefore hide his head.
   Cas.   Chastisement!
   Bru.   Remember March, the ides of March remember ·
Did not great Julius bleed for justice' sake?
What villain touched his body, that did stab,   20
And not for justice?   What, shall one of us,
That struck the foremost man of all this world
But for supporting robbers, shall we now
Contaminate our fingers with base bribes,
And sell the mighty space of our large honors   25
For so much trash as may be grasped thus?
I had rather be a dog, and bay the moon,
Than such a Roman.

Cas.   Brutus, bait not me ;
I'll not endure it : you forget yourself,
To hedge me in ; I am a soldier, I,   30
Older in practice, abler than yourself
To make conditions.
    Bru.   Go to ; you are not, Cassius.
    Cas.   I am.
    Bru.   I say you are not.
    Cas.   Urge me no more, I shall forget myself ;   35
Have mind upon your health, tempt me no farther.
    Bru.   Away, slight man !
    Cas.   Is't possible ?
    Bru.   Hear me, for I will speak.
Must I give way and room to your rash choler ?
Shall I be frighted when a madman stares ?   40
    Cas.   O ye gods, ye gods ! must I endure all this ?
    Bru.   All this ! ay, more : fret till your proud heart
      break ;
Go show your slaves how choleric you are,
And make your bondmen tremble.   Must I budge,
Must I observe you ? must I stand and crouch   45
Under your testy humor ?   By the gods,
You shall digest the venom of your spleen,
Though it do split you ; for, from this day forth,
I'll use you for my mirth, yea, for my laughter,
When you are waspish.
    Cas.   Is it come to this ?   50
    Bru.   You say you are a better soldier :
Let it appear so ; make your vaunting true,
And it shall please me well : for mine own part,
I shall be glad to learn of noble men.
    Cas.   You wrong me every way ; you wrong me, Brutus ;

I said, an elder soldier, not a better: 56
Did I say, better?

Bru. If you did, I care not.

Cas. When Cæsar lived, he durst not thus have moved me.

Bru. Peace, peace! you durst not so have tempted him.

Cas. I durst not! 60

Bru. No.

Cas. What, durst not tempt him!

Bru. For your life you durst not.

Cas. Do not presume too much upon my love;
I may do that I shall be sorry for.

Bru. You have done that you should be sorry for. 65
There is no terror, Cassius, in your threats;
For I am armed so strong in honesty
That they pass by me as the idle wind,
Which I respect not. I did send to you
For certain sums of gold, which you denied me: 70
For I can raise no money by vile means:
By heaven, I had rather coin my heart,
And drop my blood for drachmas, than to wring
From the hard hands of peasants their vile trash
By any indirection: I did send 75
To you for gold to pay my legions,
Which you denied me: was that done like Cassius?
Should I have answered Caius Cassius so?
When Marcus Brutus grows so covetous,
To lock such rascal counters from his friends, 80
Be ready, gods, with all your thunderbolts;
Dash him to pieces!

Cas.   I denied you not.

Bru. You did.

Cas.   I did not: he was but a fool
That brought my answer back. Brutus hath rived my
    heart:
A friend should bear his friend's infirmities,   85
But Brutus makes mine greater than they are.

Bru. I do not, till you practise them on me.

Cas. You love me not.

Bru.   I do not like your faults.

Cas. A friendly eye could never see such faults.

Bru. A flatterer's would not, though they do appear   90
As huge as high Olympus.

Cas. Come, Antony, and young Octavius, come;
Revenge yourselves alone on Cassius,
For Cassius is aweary of the world;
Hated by one he loves; braved by his brother;   95
Checked like a bondman; all his faults observed,
Set in a note-book, learned, and conned by rote,
To cast into my teeth.   O, I could weep
My spirit from mine eyes!   There is my dagger,
And here my naked breast; within, a heart   100
Dearer than Plutus' mine, richer than gold:
If that thou be'st a Roman, take it forth;
I, that denied thee gold, will give my heart:
Strike, as thou didst at Cæsar; for I know,
When thou didst hate him worst, thou lovedst him
    better   105
Than ever thou lovedst Cassius.

Bru.   Sheathe your dagger:
Be angry when you will, it shall have scope;
Do what you will, dishonor shall be humor.

O Cassius, you are yokéd with a lamb
That carries anger as the flint bears fire,   110
Who, much enforcéd, shows a hasty spark
And straight is cold again.

   Cas.   Hath Cassius lived
To be but mirth and laughter to his Brutus,
When grief and blood ill-tempered vexeth him?

   Bru.   When I spoke that, I was ill-tempered too.   115

   Cas.   Do you confess so much? Give me your hand.

   Bru.   And my heart too.

   Cas.   O Brutus!

   Bru.   What's the matter?

   Cas.   Have not you love enough to bear with me,
When that rash humor which my mother gave me
Makes me forgetful?

   Bru.   Yes, Cassius, and from henceforth, 120
When you are over-earnest with your Brutus,
He'll think your mother chides, and leave you so.

   Poet.   [*Within.*]   Let me go in to see the generals;
There is some grudge between 'em: 'tis not meet
They be alone.

   Lucil.   [*Within.*]   You shall not come to them.   125

   Poet.   [*Within.*]   Nothing but death shall stay me.

Enter Poet, *followed by* LUCILIUS, TITINIUS, *and* LUCIUS.

   Cas.   How now! what's the matter?

   Poet.   For shame, you generals! what do you mean?
Love, and be friends, as two such men should be;
For I have seen more years, I'm sure, than ye.   130

   Cas.   Ha, ha! how vilely doth this cynic rhyme!

   Bru.   Get you hence, sirrah; saucy fellow, hence!

   Cas.   Bear with him, Brutus; 'tis his fashion.

Bru. I'll know his humor, when he knows his time:
What should the wars do with these jigging fools?   135
Companion, hence!

Cas.   Away, away, be gone!   [*Exit Poet.*

Bru. Lucilius and Titinius, bid the commanders
Prepare to lodge their companies to-night.

Cas. And come yourselves, and bring Messala with you
Immediately to us.   [*Exeunt Lucilius and Titinius.*

Bru.   Lucius, a bowl of wine!   *Exit Lucius.*

Cas. I did not think you could have been so angry.   141

Bru. O Cassius, I am sick of many griefs.

Cas. Of your philosophy you make no use,
If you give place to accidental evils.

Bru. No man bears sorrow better: Portia is dead.   145

Cas. Ha! Portia!

Bru. She is dead.

Cas. How scaped I killing when I crossed you so?
O insupportable and touching loss!
Upon what sickness?

Bru.   Impatient of my absence,   150
And grief that young Octavius with Mark Antony
Have made themselves so strong: for with her death
That tidings came: with this she fell distract,
And, her attendants absent, swallowed fire.

Cas. And died so?

Bru.   Even so.

Cas.   O ye immortal gods!   155

Re-enter LUCIUS, *with wine and taper.*

Bru. Speak no more of her. Give me a bowl of wine.
In this I bury all unkindness, Cassius.   [*Drinks.*

Cas. My heart is thirsty for that noble pledge.

75

Fill, Lucius, till the wine o'erswell the cup ;   159
I cannot drink too much of Brutus' love.   [*Drinks.*

    Bru.   Come in, Titinius !   [*Exit Lucius.*

     Re-enter TITINIUS, *with* MESSALA.

                 Welcome, good Messala.
Now sit we close about this taper here,
And call in question our necessities.

    Cas.   Portia, art thou gone ?

    Bru.   No more, I pray you.
Messala, I have here receivéd letters,   165
That young Octavius and Mark Antony
Come down upon us with a mighty power,
Bending their expedition toward Philippi.

    Mes.   Myself have letters of the selfsame tenor.

    Bru.   With what addition ?   170

    Mes.   That by proscription and bills of outlawry,
Octavius, Antony, and Lepidus,
Have put to death an hundred senators.

    Bru.   Therein our letters do not well agree ;
Mine speak of seventy senators that died   175
By their proscriptions, Cicero being one.

    Cas.   Cicero one !

    Mes.   Cicero is dead,
And by that order of proscription.
Had you your letters from your wife, my lord ?

    Bru.   No, Messala.   180

    Mes.   Nor nothing in your letters writ of her ?

    Bru.   Nothing, Messala.

    Mes.   That, methinks, is strange.

    Bru.   Why ask you ? hear you aught of her in yours ?

    Mes.   No, my lord.

Bru.   Now, as you are a Roman, tell me true.   185
  Mes.   Then like a Roman bear the truth I tell:
For certain she is dead, and by strange manner.
  Bru.   Why, farewell, Portia.   We must die, Messala:
With meditating that she must die once
I have the patience to endure it now.   190
  Mes.   Even so great men great losses should endure.
  Cas.   I have as much of this in art as you,
But yet my nature could not bear it so.
  Bru.   Well, to our work alive.   What do you think
Of marching to Philippi presently?   195
  Cas.   I do not think it good.
  Bru.   Your reason?
  Cas.   This it is:
'Tis better that the enemy seek us:
So shall he waste his means, weary his soldiers,
Doing himself offence; whilst we, lying still,
Are full of rest, defence, and nimbleness.   200
  Bru.   Good reasons must of force give place to
      better.
The people 'twixt Philippi and this ground
Do stand but in a forced affection,
For they have grudged us contribution:
The enemy, marching along by them,   205
By them shall make a fuller number up,
Come on refreshed, new-added, and encouraged;
From which advantage shall we cut him off,
If at Philippi we do face him there,
These people at our back.
  Cas.   Hear me, good brother.   210
  Bru.   Under your pardon.   You must note beside,
That we have tried the utmost of our friends,

Our legions are brim-full, our cause is ripe :
The enemy increaseth every day ;
We, at the height, are ready to decline.   215
There is a tide in the affairs of men,
Which, taken at the flood, leads on to fortune ;
Omitted, all the voyage of their life
Is bound in shallows and in miseries.
On such a full sea are we now afloat ;   220
And we must take the current when it serves,
Or lose our ventures.
   Cas.   Then, with your will, go on ;
We'll along ourselves, and meet them at Philippi.
   Bru.   The deep of night is crept upon our talk,
And nature must obey necessity ;   225
Which we will niggard with a little rest.
There is no more to say ?
   Cas.   No more.   Good night :
Early to-morrow will we rise and hence.
   Bru.   Lucius ! [*Enter Lucius.*] My gown. [*Exit Lucius.*]
     Farewell, good Messala :
Good night, Titinius : noble, noble Cassius,   230
Good night, and good repose.
   Cas.   O my dear brother !
This was an ill beginning of the night :
Never come such division 'tween our souls !
Let it not, Brutus.
   Bru.   Everything is well.
   Cas.   Good night, my lord.
   Bru.   Good night, good brother.   235
   Tit. Mes.   Good night, lord Brutus.
   Bru.   Farewell, every one.
                 [*Exeunt all but Brutus.*

78

Re-enter LUCIUS, *with the gown.*

Give me the gown.   Where is thy instrument?
Luc.   Here in the tent.
Bru.   What, thou speak'st drowsily?
Poor knave, I blame thee not; thou art o'erwatched.
Call Claudius and some other of my men;   240
I'll have them sleep on cushions in my tent.
   Luc.   Varro and Claudius!

Enter VARRO *and* CLAUDIUS.

   Var.   Calls my lord?
   Bru.   I pray you, sirs, lie in my tent and sleep;
It may be I shall raise you by and by   245
On business to my brother Cassius.
   Var.   So please you, we will stand and watch your
    pleasure.
   Bru.   I will not have it so: lie down, good sirs;
It may be I shall otherwise bethink me.
Look, Lucius, here's the book I sought for so;   250
I put it in the pocket of my gown.
              [Varro and Claudius lie down.
   Luc.   I was sure your lordship did not give it me.
   Bru.   Bear with me, good boy, I am much forgetful.
Canst thou hold up thy heavy eyes awhile,
And touch thy instrument a strain or two?   255
   Luc.   Ay, my lord, an't please you.
   Bru.   It does, my boy:
I trouble thee too much, but thou art willing.
   Luc.   It is my duty, sir.
   Bru.   I should not urge thy duty past thy might;
I know young bloods look for a time of rest.   260

Luc.   I have slept, my lord, already.
Bru.   It was well done; and thou shalt sleep again;
I will not hold thee long; if I do live,
I will be good to thee.   [*Music, and a song.*
This is a sleepy tune.   O murderous slumber,   265
Lay'st thou thy leaden mace upon my boy,
That plays thee music?   Gentle knave, good night;
I will not do thee so much wrong to wake thee:
If thou dost nod, thou break'st thy instrument;
I'll take it from thee; and, good boy, good night.   270
Let me see, let me see; is not the leaf turned down
Where I left reading?   Here it is, I think.

Enter the Ghost of CÆSAR.

How ill this taper burns!   Ha! who comes here?
I think it is the weakness of mine eyes
That shapes this monstrous apparition.   275
It comes upon me.   Art thou any thing?
Art thou some god, some angel, or some devil,
That makest my blood cold and my hair to stare?
Speak to me what thou art.
    Ghost.   Thy evil spirit, Brutus.
    Bru.   Why comest thou?   280
    Ghost.   To tell thee thou shalt see me at Philippi.
    Bru.   Well; then I shall see thee again?
    Ghost.   Ay, at Philippi.
    Bru.   Why, I will see thee at Philippi, then.
                                        [*Exit Ghost.*
Now I have taken heart thou vanishest: 285
Ill spirit, I would hold more talk with thee.
Boy, Lucius!   Varro!   Claudius!   Sirs, awake!
Claudius!

Luc.   The strings, my lord, are false.

Bru.   He thinks he still is at his instrument.   290

Lucius, awake!

Luc.   My lord?

Bru.   Didst thou dream, Lucius, that thou so criedst out?

Thou shalt see me at Philippi.
— Act IV.   Scene 3.

Luc.   My lord, I do not know that I did cry.   294

Bru.   Yes, that thou didst: didst thou see any thing?

Luc.   Nothing, my lord.

Bru.   Sleep again, Lucius.   Sirrah, Claudius!

[*To Varro*] Fellow thou, awake!

Var.   My lord?
Clau.   My lord?   300
Bru.   Why did you so cry out, sirs, in your sleep?
Var. Clau.   Did we, my lord?
Bru.   Ay: saw you any thing?
Var.   No, my lord, I saw nothing.
Clau.   Nor I, my lord.
Bru.   Go and commend me to my brother Cassius;
Bid him set on his powers betimes before,   305
And we will follow.
Var. Clau.   It shall be done, my lord.   [*Exeunt.*

ACT V.

Scene I.   *The plains of Philippi.*

Enter Octavius, Antony, *and their* Army.

Oct.   Now, Antony, our hopes are answeréd:
You said the enemy would not come down,
But keep the hills and upper regions;
It proves not so: their battles are at hand;
They mean to warn us at Philippi here,   5
Answering before we do demand of them.
Ant.   Tut, I am in their bosoms, and I know
Wherefore they do it: they could be content
To visit other places; and come down
With fearful bravery, thinking by this face   10
To fasten in our thoughts that they have courage;
But 'tis not so.

Enter a Messenger.

Mess.   Prepare you, generals:
The enemy comes on in gallant show;

Their bloody sign of battle is hung out,
And something to be done immediately. 15
Ant. Octavius, lead your battle softly on,
Upon the left hand of the even field.
Oct. Upon the right hand I; keep thou the left.

Now, Antony, our hopes are answeréd.
— Act V. Scene 1.

Ant. Why do you cross me in this exigent? 19
Oct. I do not cross you; but I will do so. [*March.*

Drum. *Enter* BRUTUS, CASSIUS, *and their* Army; LU-
CILIUS, TITINIUS, MESSALA, *and others.*

Bru. They stand, and would have parley.
Cas. Stand fast, Titinius: we must out and talk.
Oct. Mark Antony, shall we give sign of battle?
Ant. No, Cæsar, we will answer on their charge.
Make forth, the generals would have some words. 25
Oct. Stir not until the signal.
Bru. Words before blows: is it so, countrymen?

Oct.   Not that we love words better, as you do.

Bru.   Good words are better than bad strokes, Octavius.

Ant.   In your bad strokes, Brutus, you give good
words :

Witness the hole you made in Cæsar's heart,   31
Crying "Long live! hail, Cæsar!"

Cas.   Antony,
The posture of your blows are yet unknown ;
But for your words, they rob the Hybla bees,
And leave them honeyless.

Ant.   Not stingless too.   35

Bru.   O, yes, and soundless too ;
For you have stolen their buzzing, Antony,
And very wisely threat before you sting.

Ant.   Villains, you did not so, when your vile daggers
Hacked one another in the sides of Cæsar :   40
You showed your teeth like apes, and fawned like hounds,
And bowed like bondmen, kissing Cæsar's feet ;
Whilst damnéd Casca, like a cur, behind
Struck Cæsar on the neck. O you flatterers!

Cas.   Flatterers! Now, Brutus, thank yourself :   45
This tongue had not offended so to-day,
If Cassius might have ruled.

Oct.   Come, come, the cause : if arguing make us sweat,
The proof of it will turn to redder drops.
Look ;   50
I draw a sword against conspirators ;
When think you that the sword goes up again ?
Never, till Cæsar's three and thirty wounds
Be well avenged, or till another Cæsar
Have added slaughter to the sword of traitors.   55

Bru.   Cæsar, thou canst not die by traitors' hands,
Unless thou bring'st them with thee.
   Oct.   So I hope ;
I was not born to die on Brutus' sword.
   Bru.   O, if thou wert the noblest of thy strain,
Young man, thou couldst not die more honorable.   60
   Cas.   A peevish schoolboy, worthless of such honor,
Joined with a masker and a reveller !
   Ant.   Old Cassius still !
   Oct.   Come, Antony, away.
Defiance, traitors, hurl we in your teeth :
If you dare fight to-day, come to the field ;   65
If not, when you have stomachs.
         [Exeunt Octavius, Antony, and their army.
   Cas.   Why, now, blow wind, swell billow, and swim bark !
The storm is up, and all is on the hazard.
   Bru.   Ho, Lucilius ! hark, a word with you.
   Lucil.   *[Standing forth.]*   My lord !
         [Brutus and Lucilius converse apart.
   Cas.   Messala.
   Mes.   *[Standing forth.]*   What says my general ?
   Cas.   Messala,
This is my birthday ; as this very day   70
Was Cassius born.   Give me thy hand, Messala :
Be thou my witness that against my will,
As Pompey was, am I compelled to set
Upon one battle all our liberties.   75
You know that I held Epicurus strong
And his opinion : now I change my mind,
And partly credit things that do presage.
Coming from Sardis, on our former ensign
Two mighty eagles fell, and there they perched,   80

Gorging and feeding from our soldiers' hands;
Who to Philippi here consorted us:
This morning are they fled away and gone;
And in their steads do ravens, crows and kites
Fly o'er our heads and downward look on us,   85
As we were sickly prey: their shadows seem
A canopy most fatal, under which
Our army lies, ready to give up the ghost.
 Mes. Believe not so.
 Cas.   I but believe it partly;
For I am fresh of spirit and resolved   90
To meet all perils very constantly.
 Bru. Even so, Lucilius.
 Cas.   Now, most noble Brutus,
The gods to-day stand friendly, that we may,
Lovers in peace, lead on our days to age!
But since the affairs of men rest still incertain,   95
Let's reason with the worst that may befall.
If we do lose this battle, then is this
The very last time we shall speak together:
What are you then determinèd to do?
 Bru. Even by the rule of that philosophy   100
By which I did blame Cato for the death
Which he did give himself: I know not how,
But I do find it cowardly and vile,
For fear of what might fall, so to prevent
The time of life: arming myself with patience   105
To stay the providence of some high powers
That govern us below.
 Cas.   Then, if we lose this battle,
You are contented to be led in triumph
Thorough the streets of Rome?

Bru. No, Cassius, no : think not, thou noble Roman,
That ever Brutus will go bound to Rome ;   111
He bears too great a mind.   But this same day
Must end that work the ides of March begun ;
And whether we shall meet again I know not.
Therefore our everlasting farewell take :   115
For ever, and for ever, farewell Cassius !
If we do meet again, why, we shall smile ;
If not, why then this parting was well made.
   Cas.   For ever, and for ever, farewell, Brutus !
If we do meet again, we'll smile indeed ;   120
If not, 'tis true this parting was well made.
   Bru.   Why, then, lead on.   O, that a man might know
The end of this day's business ere it come !
But it sufficeth that the day will end,
And then the end is known.   Come, ho ! away ! [*Exeunt.*

SCENE II.   *The same.   The field of battle.*

Alarum.   Enter BRUTUS *and* MESSALA.

   Bru.   Ride, ride, Messala, ride, and give these bills
Unto the legions on the other side.   [*Loud alarum.*
Let them set on at once ; for I perceive
But cold demeanor in Octavius' wing,
And sudden push gives them the overthrow.   5
Ride, ride, Messala : let them all come down.   [*Exeunt.*

SCENE III.   *Another part of the field.*

Alarums.   Enter CASSIUS *and* TITINIUS.

   Cas.   O, look, Titinius, look, the villains fly !
Myself have to my own turned enemy :

This ensign here of mine was turning back;
I slew the coward, and did take it from him.

Titin. O Cassius, Brutus gave the word too early; 5
Who, having some advantage on Octavius,
Took it too eagerly: his soldiers fell to spoil,
Whilst we by Antony are all enclosed.

Enter PINDARUS.

Pin. Fly further off, my lord, fly further off;
Mark Antony is in your tents, my lord: 10
Fly, therefore, noble Cassius, fly far off.

Cas. This hill is far enough. Look, look, Titinius;
Are those my tents where I perceive the fire?

Titin. They are, my lord.

Cas.   Titinius, if thou lovest me,
Mount thou my horse and hide thy spurs in him, 15
Till he have brought thee up to yonder troops
And here again; that I may rest assured
Whether yond troops are friend or enemy.

Titin. I will be here again, even with a thought. [*Exit.*

Cas. Go, Pindarus, get higher on that hill; 20
My sight was ever thick; regard Titinius,
And tell me what thou not'st about the field.
                              [*Pindarus ascends the hill.*
This day I breathèd first: time is come round,
And where I did begin, there shall I end;
My life is run his compass. Sirrah, what news? 25

Pin. [*Above.*] O my lord!

Cas. What news?

Pin. [*Above.*] Titinius is enclosèd round about
With horsemen, that make to him on the spur;
Yet he spurs on. Now they are almost on him. 30

88

Now, Titinius!   Now some light.   O, he lights too.
He's ta'en.   [*Shout.*]   And, hark! they shout for joy.
  Cas.   Come down, behold no more.

*Titinius is enclosèd round about
With horsemen, that make to him on the spur.*
                        — Act V.   Scene 3.

O, coward that I am, to live so long,
To see my best friend ta'en before my face !   35
                        [*Pindarus descends.*

Come hither, sirrah :
In Parthia did I take thee prisoner ;
And then I swore thee, saving of thy life,
That whatsoever I did bid thee do,
Thou shouldst attempt it.   Come now, keep thine oath ;
Now be a freeman : and with this good sword,   41

That ran through Cæsar's bowels, search this bosom.
Stand not to answer : here, take thou the hilts ;
And, when my face is covered, as 'tis now,
Guide thou the sword. [*Pindarus stabs him.*] Cæsar,
    thou art revenged,
                                      45
Even with the sword that killed thee.   [*Dies.*

   Pin. So, I am free ; yet would not so have been,
Durst I have done my will. O Cassius !
Far from this country Pindarus shall run,
Where never Roman shall take note of him.   [*Exit.*

       Re-enter Titinius *with* Messala.

   Mes. It is but change, Titinius ; for Octavius   5ᴀ
Is overthrown by noble Brutus' power,
As Cassius' legions are by Antony.
   Titin. These tidings will well comfort Cassius.
   Mes. Where did you leave him ?
   Titin.   All disconsolate,   55
With Pindarus his bondman, on this hill.
   Mes. Is not that he that lies upon the ground ?
   Titin. He lies not like the living. O my heart !
   Mes. Is not that he ?
   Titin.   No, this was he, Messala,
But Cassius is no more. O setting sun,   60
As in thy red rays thou dost sink to-night,
So in his red blood Cassius' day is set ;
The sun of Rome is set ! Our day is gone ;
Clouds, dews, and dangers come ; our deeds are done !
Mistrust of my success hath done this deed.   65
   Mes. Mistrust of good success hath done this deed.
O hateful error, melancholy's child,
Why dost thou show to the apt thoughts of men

The things that are not?   O error, soon conceived,
Thou never comest unto a happy birth,   70
But kill'st the mother that engendered thee.

   Titin.   What, Pindarus! where art thou, Pindarus?

   Mes.   Seek him, Titinius, whilst I go to meet
The noble Brutus, thrusting this report
Into his ears: I may say, thrusting it;   75
For piercing steel and darts envenoméd
Shall be as welcome to the ears of Brutus
As tidings of this sight.

   Titin.   Hie you, Messala,
And I will seek for Pindarus the while.   [*Exit Messala.*
Why didst thou send me forth, brave Cassius?   80
Did I not meet thy friends? and did not they
Put on my brows this wreath of victory,
And bid me give it thee? Didst thou not hear their
    shouts ?
Alas, thou hast miscónstrued every thing!
But, hold thee, take this garland on thy brow;   85
Thy Brutus bid me give it thee, and I
Will do his bidding.   Brutus, come apace,
And see how I regarded Caius Cassius.
By your leave, gods: this is a Roman's part:
Come, Cassius' sword, and find Titinius' heart.

                       [*Kills himself.*

Alarum.   Re-enter MESSALA, *with* BRUTUS, *young* CATO,
    STRATO, VOLUMNIUS, *and* LUCILIUS.

   Bru.   Where, where, Messala, doth his body lie?   91

   Mes.   Lo, yonder, and Titinius mourning it.

   Bru.   Titinius' face is upward.

   Cato.   He is slain.

Bru.   O Julius Cæsar, thou art mighty yet!
Thy spirit walks abroad, and turns our swords   95
In our own proper entrails.   [*Low alarums.*
Cato.   Brave Titinius!
Look, whether he have not crowned dead Cassius!
Bru.   Are yet two Romans living such as these?
The last of all the Romans, fare thee well!
It is impossible that ever Rome
Should breed thy fellow.   Friends, I owe more tears   100
To this dead man than you shall see me pay.
I shall find time, Cassius, I shall find time.
Come, therefore, and to Thasos send his body:
His funerals shall not be in our camp,
Lest it discomfort us.   Lucilius, come;   105
And come, young Cato; let us to the field.
Labeo and Flavius, set our battles on:
'Tis three o'clock; and, Romans, yet ere night
We shall try fortune in a second fight.   [*Exeunt.* 110

SCENE IV.   *Another part of the field.*

Alarum.   Enter, fighting, Soldiers *of both armies; then*
BRUTUS, *young* CATO, LUCILIUS, *and others.*

Bru.   Yet, countrymen, O, yet hold up your heads!
Cato.   What bastard doth not?   Who will go with me?
I will proclaim my name about the field;
I am the son of Marcus Cato, ho!
A foe to tyrants, and my country's friend;   5
I am the son of Marcus Cato, ho!
Bru.   And I am Brutus, Marcus Brutus, I;
Brutus, my country's friend; know me for Brutus! [*Exit.*

Lucil.   O young and noble Cato, art thou down?
Why, now thou diest as bravely as Titinius;   10
And mayst be honored, being Cato's son.
  First Sold.   Yield, or thou diest.
  Lucil.   Only I yield to die;
There is so much that thou wilt kill me straight;
                                        [*Offering money.*
Kill Brutus, and be honored in his death.
  First Sold.   We must not.   A noble prisoner!   15
  Sec. Sold.   Room, ho!   Tell Antony, Brutus is ta'en.
  First Sold.   I'll tell the news.   Here comes the general.

Enter ANTONY.

Brutus is ta'en, Brutus is ta'en, my lord.
  Ant.   Where is he?
  Lucil.   Safe, Antony; Brutus is safe enough: 20
I dare assure thee that no enemy
Shall ever take alive the noble Brutus:
The gods defend him from so great a shame!
When you do find him, or alive or dead,
He will be found like Brutus, like himself.   25
  Ant.   This is not Brutus, friend; but, I assure you,
A prize no less in worth: keep this man safe;
Give him all kindness; I had rather have
Such men my friends than enemies.   Go on,
And see whether Brutus be alive or dead;   30
And bring us word unto Octavius' tent
How every thing is chanced.   [*Exeunt.*

SCENE V. *Another part of the field.*

Enter BRUTUS, DARDANIUS, CLITUS, STRATO, *and*
VOLUMNIUS.

Bru.   Come, poor remains of friends, rest on this rock
Cli.   Statilius show'd the torch-light, but, my lord,
He came not back : he is or ta'en or slain.
Bru.   Sit thee down, Clitus : slaying is the word ;
It is a deed in fashion. Hark thee, Clitus. [*Whispering.* 5
Cli.   What, I, my lord ?   No, not for all the world.
Bru.   Peace, then ! no words.
Cli.   I'll rather kill myself.
Bru.   Hark thee, Dardanius.   [*Whispering.*
Dar.   Shall I do such a deed ?
Cli.   O Dardanius !
Dar.   O Clitus !   10
Cli.   What ill request did Brutus make to thee ?
Dar.   To kill him, Clitus.   Look, he meditates.
Cli.   Now is that noble vessel full of grief,
That it runs over even at his eyes.
Bru.   Come hither, good Volumnius ; list a word.   15
Vol.   What says my lord ?
Bru.   Why, this, Volumnius :
The ghost of Cæsar hath appeared to me
Two several times by night ; at Sardis once,
And this last night here in Philippi fields ;
I know my hour is come.
Vol.   Not so, my lord.   20
Bru.   Nay, I am sure it is, Volumnius.
Thou seest the world, Volumnius, how it goes ;
Our enemies have beat us to the pit ;   [*Low alarums.*
It is more worthy to leap in ourselves,

Than tarry till they push us.   Good Volumnius,   25
Thou know'st that we two went to school together :
Even for that our love of old, I prithee,
Hold thou my sword-hilts, whilst I run on it.

    Vol.   That's not an office for a friend, my lord.

                           [Alarum still.

    Cli.   Fly, fly, my lord ; there is no tarrying here.   30

    Bru.   Farewell to you ; and you ; and you, Volumnius.
Strato, thou hast been all this while asleep ;
Farewell to thee too, Strato.   Countrymen,
My heart doth joy that yet in all my life
I found no man but he was true to me.   35
I shall have glory by this losing day,
More than Octavius and Mark Antony
By this vile conquest shall attain unto.
So, fare you well at once ; for Brutus' tongue
Hath almost ended his life's history :   40
Night hangs upon mine eyes ; my bones would rest,
That have but labored to attain this hour.

              [Alarum.   Cry within, " Fly, fly, fly ! "

    Cli.   Fly, my lord, fly.

    Bru.   Hence !   I will follow.

        [Exeunt Clitus, Dardanius, and Volumnius.

I prithee, Strato, stay thou by thy lord :
Thou art a fellow of a good respect ;   45
Thy life hath had some smatch of honor in it :
Hold then my sword, and turn away thy face,
While I do run upon it.   Wilt thou, Strato ?

    Stra.   Give me your hand first.   Fare you well, my lord.

    Bru.   Farewell, good Strato.   *[Runs on his sword.*

                      Cæsar, now be still :   50
I killed not thee with half so good a will.   *[Dies.*

Alarum.   Retreat.   Enter OCTAVIUS, ANTONY, MESSALA, LUCILIUS, *and the army.*

Oct.   What man is that?

Mes.   My master's man.   Strato, where is thy master?

Stra.   Free from the bondage you are in, Messala:
The conquerors can but make a fire of him;   55
For Brutus only overcame himself,

This was the noblest Roman of them all.
                    —Act V.   Scene 5.

And no man else hath honor by his death.

Lucil.   So Brutus should be found.   I thank thee, Brutus
That thou hast proved Lucilius' saying true.

Oct.   All that served Brutus, I will entertain them.   60
Fellow, wilt thou bestow thy time with me?
    Stra.   Ay, if Messala will prefer me to you.
    Oct.   Do so, good Messala.
    Mes.   How died my master, Strato?
    Stra.   I held the sword, and he did run on it.   65
    Mes.   Octavius, then take him to follow thee,
That did the latest service to my master.
    Ant.   This was the noblest Roman of them all.
All the conspirators, save only he,
Did that they did in envy of great Cæsar;   70
He only, in a general honest thought
And common good to all, made one of them.
His life was gentle, and the elements
So mixed in him that Nature might stand up
And say to all the world, "This was a man!"   75
    Oct.   According to his virtue let us use him,
With all respect and rites of burial.
Within my tent his bones to-night shall lie,
Most like a soldier, ordered honorably.
So call the field to rest; and let's away,   80
To part the glories of this happy day.   [*Exeunt.*

A LIST OF THE PERSONS OF THE DRAMA, WITH THE SCENES IN WHICH THEY APPEAR

JULIUS CÆSAR . . . . . . I, 2; II, 2; III, 1.

OCTAVIUS CÆSAR, *a triumvir after the death of* Julius Cæsar . IV, 1; V, 1, 5.

MARCUS ANTONIUS, *a triumvir after the death of* Julius Cæsar . I, 2; II, 2; III, 1, 2; IV, 1; V, 1, 4, 5.

M. ÆMILIUS LEPIDUS, *a triumvir after the death of* Cæsar. III, 1; IV, 1.

CICERO, *a senator* . . . . . I, 2, 3.

PUBLIUS, *a senator* . . . . . II, 2; III, 1.

POPILIUS LENA, *a senator* . . III, 1.

MARCUS BRUTUS, *a conspirator* . I, 2; II, 1, 2; III, 1, 2; IV, 2, 3; V, 1, 2, 3, 4, 5.

CASSIUS, *a conspirator* . . . . I, 2, 3; II, 1; III, 1, 2; IV, 2, 3; V, 1, 3.

CASCA, *a conspirator* . . . . I, 2, 3; II, 1, 2; III, 1.

TREBONIUS, *a conspirator* . . . II, 1, 2; III, 1.

LIGARIUS, *a conspirator* . . . II, 1, 2.

DECIUS BRUTUS, *a conspirator* . I, 2; II, 1, 2; III, 1.

METELLUS CIMBER, *a conspirator* II, 1, 2; III, 1.

CINNA, *a conspirator* . . . . I, 3; II, 1, 2; III, 1.

FLAVIUS, *a tribune* . . . . . I, 1.

MARULLUS, *a tribune* . . . . I, 1.

ARTEMIDORUS, *a sophist of* Cnidos . . . . II, 3; III, 1.

A Soothsayer . . . . I, 2; II, 4; III, 1.

CINNA, *a poet* . . . . III, 3.

A Poet . . . . IV, 3.

LUCILIUS, *a friend to* Brutus *and* Cassius . . . . IV, 2, 3; V, 1, 3, 4, 5.

TITINIUS, *a friend to* Brutus *and* Cassius . . . . IV, 2, 3; V, 1, 3.

List of Characters.

MESSALA, *a friend to* Brutus *and*
    Cassius . . . . IV, 3; V, 1, 2, 3, 5.

Young CATO, *a friend to* Brutus
    and Cassius . . . . . . V, 3, 4.

VOLUMNIUS, *a friend to* Brutus
    and Cassius . . . . . . V, 3, 5.

VARRO, *servant to* Brutus . . . IV, 3.

CLITUS, *servant to* Brutus . . . V, 5.

CLAUDIUS, *servant to* Brutus . . IV, 3.

STRATO, *servant to* Brutus . . V, 3, 5.

LUCIUS, *servant to* Brutus . . . II, 1, 4; IV, 2, 3.

DARDANIUS, *servant to* Brutus . V, 5.

PINDARUS, *servant to* Cassius . IV, 2; V, 3.

CALPURNIA, *wife to* Cæsar . . I, 2; II; 2.

PORTIA, *wife to* Brutus . . . I, 2; II, 1, 4.

Senators, Citizens, Guards, Attendants, etc.

SCENE. DURING A GREAT PART OF THE PLAY AT ROME; AFTER
    WARDS AT SARDIS, AND NEAR PHILIPPI.

APPENDIX

THE WRITING AND PUBLICATION OF JULIUS CÆSAR

Shakespeare produced his plays and poems during a period of about twenty years, which is almost equally divided by the close of the 16th century. "Julius Cæsar" must have been written between 1598 and 1603. Most critics agree now in assigning it to the year 1601. It therefore stands almost exactly at the middle of the dramatist's career, and is the first of those great tragedies, "Hamlet," "Othello," "King Lear," "Macbeth," "Antony and Cleopatra," which have given their author world-wide and enduring fame. In 1601 all the popular comedies had been written; with the exception of "Romeo and Juliet" none of the tragedies had appeared. Thus "Julius Cæsar" marks an important turning-point in Shakespeare's life and dramatic work.

The place of "Julius Cæsar" in Shakespeare's works.

From external and internal evidence the play belongs to the same period as "Hamlet." The language of these two great tragedies has several points of marked resemblance. As Brandes and other critics have pointed out, there is also an interesting similarity in the chief characters of the two plays. "Brutus and Hamlet are both thrust into action from a life of contemplation: Brutus is an idealist; Hamlet, a scholar and dreamer. Both are unfit for the work they are called upon to do, and both, in the end, bungle it badly; Hamlet from delay and uncertainty,

The relation of "Julius Cæsar" to "Hamlet."

Appendix.

Brutus from mistaken judgment. The study of the idealist thrown into the world of action must have appealed to Shakespeare's imagination, and those critics do not seem far afield who consider Brutus the sketch from which Hamlet is built up."[1] A passage in "Hamlet" which enumerates the prodigies that preceded Cæsar's death an allusion to Roman suicides, and the statement by Polonius, "I did enact Julius Cæsar: I was killed i' the Capitol; Brutus killed me," — all seem to indicate that "Julius Cæsar" was written, if not in the same year, certainly not long before the greatest of all Shakespeare's tragedies, "Hamlet."

As far as we know, "Julius Cæsar" was never printed in the poet's lifetime. As was the case with nineteen of **The first publication of "Julius Cæsar."** his other plays, it first appeared in print in the Folio of 1623 (see page 133), where it stands among the tragedies before "Macbeth" and following "Coriolanus" and "Timon of Athens." The fact that the play is remarkably short has been accounted for by supposing that the copy which came into the hands of the publishers, Heminge and Condell, had been cut down and adapted for stage purposes There are some reasons, moreover, for thinking that this shortening was done by Shakespeare's friend, Ben Jonson Whether this is so or not, the text is remarkably free from doubtful passages and evident misprints. The fact, also that the poet's diction in 1601 was simpler, his style more flowing, and to modern readers easier than it became in the later tragedies, makes "Julius Cæsar" one of the least difficult plays for young people to read.

[1] George C. D. Odell, Shakespeare's " Julius Cæsar," page xviii.

SOURCES OF JULIUS CÆSAR

Young persons studying a Shakespearian play for the first time are often surprised, and sometimes even distressed, to learn that the stories of the dramatist's works were not original with him. Originality of plot seems to them the chief requisite of greatness ; a worker in second-hand material **Originality of plot unimportant.** falls under their scorn ; they begin to wonder just why this borrower of other men's ideas has been rated so highly and so profoundly admired by their elders. This is not strange. Action, movement, complication of events, — all that goes to make up a plot, — is interesting and therefore important to boys and girls. They are naturally more concerned with what the hero *does*, than how he does it, or how he talks, or what he is like. Moreover, in our novel-reading, inventive age, — in our age of " movies " and of everything new and startling, — it is not surprising that false values are given to things just because they are original. It is difficult even for mature people to see that originality of plot in story or play is really the least important element in the final test of its worth. They must be reminded that any one with a little clever inventiveness can work out a complicated and entirely new series of events. Thousands of short stories and novels appear every year in our magazines with plots that are skilfully woven and often remarkably original. Beyond that they have nothing to recommend them, so that after a moment's curiosity to see " how they come out," they are completely neglected and soon forgotten. The fact that in plot and action they are "something new" and clever gives them no claim whatsoever to the enduring fame of literature.

It is therefore not a sign of weakness or of a shallow mind to find Shakespeare making use of material already **Shakespeare not a writer of original stories.** at his disposal. On the contrary, it is evidence of wisdom and good judgment. He was above bothering his head with new plots to amuse his audiences. All his mind and skill and strength were needed for more essential things. Old plays, Italian novels, Plutarch's Lives, chronicles of English history, furnished him with incidents and characters with which to work. The best elements of these he skilfully chose, made over, and combined; but next to nothing did he himself invent. The force of his wonderful genius was spent in drawing character so clearly and so true to human nature that the men and women of his plays became distinct personalities that have lived now for three hundred years in the hearts of the people. Falstaff, Portia, Shylock, Rosalind, Hamlet, Desdemona, Macbeth, Juliet, Lear, — these are as real as any who have lived in the annals of history. Then again, the language and the poetry of the plays, the sentiments, the wit, and above all the artistic blending of thought and character and action, are his and his alone. The sources of the stories which Shakespeare used no one ever reads. They are commonplace, flat, and unworthy of our interest. Yet these same stories remoulded, polished, and filled with the inspiration of Shakespeare's genius, have become masterpieces of literature.

It is well that Shakespeare was not attracted to the inventing of elaborate and original plots, for he must have been busy enough as it was.   In their demand for novelty in stage attractions audiences then required a new play, on an average, every sixteen or seventeen days.   Intense rivalry existed between the various companies of actors.   In their struggle for popularity, which meant their daily bread, playwrights turned off their work with astonishing rapidity.   Thus in the twenty years of his London activity Shakespeare wrote, in whole or in part, about forty plays. "Driven by the necessity of speed on the one hand, and by anxiety to catch the popular fancy on the other, is it any wonder that he never stopped to devise a plot?   What need was there that he should do so?   The manager of the company had many an old play which, at one time or another, had been submitted to the test of public approval. . . .   To such plays, if selected for revision, a certain amount of popularity was thus assured in advance ; and as for the plot, — the barest skeleton sufficed for Shakespeare.   He knew that he could remodel it into fair proportions and relume it with life.   Of all that goes to make up one of his dramas, the plot in itself, in its mere outlines, is of less importance than any other element in it.   Of course, in the nature of things, it is not to be supposed that after he had selected the old play to be rejuvenated he either adhered to it closely, or refused hints from other sources.   Old ballads, books of travels, histories, the gossip of the day, — all were put under contribution.   As Emerson says : 'Every master has found his materials collected, and his power lay in his sympathy with his people, and in his love for the materials he wrought in.' "[1]

Advantages of using old material for plays.

[1] Dr. H. H. Furness : New Variorum Edition, "Merchant of Venice."

105

Appendix.

In "Julius Cæsar," though Shakespeare is not writing history or chronicle, he is dramatizing a chapter of history. The theme of his tragedy is the fall of Cæsar,—the conspiracy, the assassination, and the fate of the men who brought about his death. The poet, to be sure, treats historical facts with great freedom. Exactness of time and place give way to the necessity of making a good story; for his purpose is not primarily to educate his audience in details of Roman history, but rather to make an interesting, stirring play. Yet the spirit and ideals of the times are well portrayed in the drama; indeed, the person may well count himself fortunate whose introduction to the times of Cæsar is Shakespeare's drama rather than the pages of a textbook of history.

"Julius Cæsar," a historical tragedy.

The history of Julius Cæsar had probably been seen on the stage, in several different forms, before Shakespeare's time. A Latin play on this subject was performed at Oxford in 1582, from which the poet's "Et tu, Brute" may have been taken. References are also found to other plays dealing with the same theme, though it is extremely doubtful whether Shakespeare was at all influenced by them.

Shakespeare's use of Plutarch's Lives.

His chief source of "Julius Cæsar" was Plutarch's lives of Cæsar, Brutus, and Antony, written in Greek in the first century A.D., and translated into French by Jacques Amyot, Bishop of Auxerre, in 1559. Twenty years later, when Shakespeare was seven years old, this French edition was translated into English by Sir Thomas North, and it was this version of Plutarch that the poet read and used when writing his play. Probably in no other of his works did he follow his sources so closely. Many expres-

sions he took word for word from North, and several passages are little more than the language of the biographer
turned into stately blank verse. The structure of the
play, however, is wholly the poet's own. So, too, are
the life, the color, the movement, the imaginative power,
the lines that have become familiar quotations, — everything that makes the tragedy a work of art and a master-
piece of literature. The sources from which he drew his
facts are seldom read. Except to the student of the poet's
methods they are of but little interest to-day; whereas the
play, which Shakespeare's genius made out of them, lives
and gives pleasure to young and old in the twentieth century, as it did in the days of Queen Elizabeth three hundred years ago.

SELECTIONS FROM NORTH'S PLUTARCH

The following two short passages from North's *Plutarch* will suffice to show how closely Shakespeare often followed the words of the biographies which he used when writing his play.

1. *It rejoiceth my heart that not one of my friends hath failed me at my need.* . . . For as for me, I think myself happier than they that have overcome, considering that I leave a perpetual fame of virtue and honesty, the which our enemies *the conquerors* shall never *attain unto* by force or money, etc.

In V, 5, 33–38, we find these words cast into verse and ennobled by Shakespeare.

> Countrymen,
> My heart doth joy that yet in all my life
> I found no man but he was true to me.
> I shall have glory by this losing day
> More than Octavius and Mark Antony
> By this vile conquest shall attain unto.

2. For it was said that Antonius spake it openly divers times that he thought that of all them that had slain Cæsar, there was none but Brutus only that was moved to do it, as thinking the act commendable of itself; but that all the other conspirators did conspire his death for some private malice or envy that they otherwise did bear against him.

In the play we have these four lines : —

> All the conspirators, save only he,
> Did that they did in envy of great Cæsar;
> He only, in a general honest thought
> And common good to all, made one of them.

V, 5, 69–72.

Following are a number of the more interesting passages in North's *Plutarch* which the poet followed closely, or from which he took an idea. It will be a profitable study to compare word for word these selections with the corresponding lines in the play. Nothing can show more clearly the method of the dramatist, or the skill which he used in working over his prose material into poetry of the highest type.

1. Cæsar sat to behold that sport upon the pulpit for orations, in a chain of gold, apparelled in triumphant manner. Antonius, who was Consul at that time, was one of them that ran this holy course. So when he came into the market-place, the people made a lane for him to run at liberty, and he came to Cæsar, and presented him a diadem wreathed about with laurel. Whereupon there rose a certain cry of rejoicing, not very great, done only by a few appointed for the purpose. But when Cæsar refused the diadem, then all the people together made an outcry of joy. Then Antonius offering it him again, there was a second shout of joy, but yet of a few. But when Cæsar refused it again the second time, then all the whole people shouted. Cæsar, having made this proof, found that the people did not like of it, and thereupon rose out of his chair and commanded the crown to be carried unto Jupiter in the Capitol. After that there were set up images of Cæsar in the city, with diadems upon their heads like kings. Those the two tribunes, Flavius and Marullus, went and pulled down, and furthermore, meeting with them that first saluted Cæsar as king, they committed them to prison.

Plutarch, *Julius Cæsar*.   Shakespeare, I, 2.

2. Furthermore, there was a certaine Soothsayer, that had given Cæsar warning long afore, to take heed of the day of the Ides of March (which is the fifteenth of the moneth), for on that day he should be in great danger. That day being come, Cæsar going unto the Senate-house, and speaking merrily to the sooth-sayer, told him, "The Ides of March be come." "So they be," softly answered the soothsayer, "but yet are they not past."

Plutarch, *Julius Cæsar*.   Shakespeare, I, 2, and III, 1.

3. Then going to bed the same night, as his manner was, and lying with his wife Calpurnia, all the windows and doors of his chamber flying open, the noise awoke him, and made him afraid when he saw such light; but more, when he heard his wife Calpurnia, being fast asleep, weep and sigh, and put forth many fumbling lamentable speeches; for she dreamed that Cæsar was slain, and that she had him in her arms. . . . Insomuch that Cæsar, rising in the morning, she prayed him, if it were possible, not to go out of the doors that day, but to adjourn the session of the Senate until another day. And if that he made no reckoning of her dream, yet that he would search further of the soothsayers by their sacrifices, to know what should happen him that day. Thereby it seemed that Cæsar likewise did fear or suspect somewhat, because his wife Calpurnia until that time was never given to any fear and superstition, and that then he saw her so troubled in mind with this dream she had. But much more afterwards, when the soothsayers having sacrificed many beasts one after another, told him that none did like them; then he determined to send Antonius to adjourn the session of the Senate.

Plutarch, *Julius Cæsar.*   Shakespeare, II, 2.

4. But when they had opened Cæsar's testament, and found a liberal legacy of money bequeathed unto every citizen of Rome, and that they saw his body (which was brought into the market-place) all bemangled with gashes of swords, then there was no order to keep the multitude and common people quiet, but they plucked up forms, tables, and stools, and laid them all about the body; and setting them afire, burnt the corse. Then when the fire was well kindled, they took the fire-brands, and went unto their houses that had slain Cæsar, to set them afire. Other also ran up and down the city to see if they could meet with any of them, to cut them in pieces: howbeit they could meet with never a man of them, because they had locked themselves up safely in their houses. There was one of Cæsar's friends called Cinna, that had a marvellous strange and terrible dream the night

before. He dreamed that Cæsar bade him to supper, and that he refused, and would not go; then that Cæsar took him by the hand, and led him against his will. Now Cinna, hearing at that time that they burnt Cæsar's body in the market-place, notwithstanding that he feared his dream, and had an ague on him besides, he went into the market-place to honour his funerals. When he came thither, one of mean sort asked him what his name was? He was straight called by his name. The first man told it to another, and that other unto another, so that it ran straight through them all, that he was one of them that murthered Cæsar (for indeed one of the traitors to Cæsar was also called Cinna as himself), wherefore taking him for Cinna the murtherer, they fell upon him with such fury that they presently despatched him in the market-place.

Plutarch, *Julius Cæsar*.   Shakespeare, III, 2 and 3.

5. Now Cæsar, on the other side, did not trust him overmuch, nor was without tales brought unto him against him, howbeit he feared his great mind, authority, and friends. Yet, on the other side also, he trusted his good nature and fair conditions. For intelligence being brought him one day that Antonius and Dolabella did conspire against him, he answered "That these fat long-haired men made him not afraid, but the lean and whitely-faced fellows," meaning by that Brutus and Cassius.

Plutarch, *Brutus*.   Shakespeare, I, 2.

6. But for Brutus, his friends and countrymen, both by divers procurements and sundry rumours of the city, and by many bills also, did openly call and procure him to do that he did. For under the image of his ancestor Junius Brutus (that drave the kings out of Rome) they wrote, "Oh, that it pleased the gods thou wert now alive, Brutus!" and again, "That thou wert here among us now!" His tribunal or chair where he gave audience during the time he was prætor was full of such bills: "Brutus, thou art asleep, and art not Brutus indeed."

Plutarch, *Brutus*.   Shakespeare, II, 1.

7. Brutus, who went to see him being sick in his bed, and said unto him, "Ligarius, in what time art thou sick?" Ligarius rising up in his bed, and taking him by the right hand, said unto him, "Brutus," said he, "if thou hast any great enterprise in hand worthy of thyself, I am whole."

Plutarch, *Brutus*.   Shakespeare, II, 2.

8. Then perceiving her husband was marvellously out of quiet, and that he could take no rest, even in her greatest pain of all she spake in this sort unto him: "I being, O Brutus," said she, "the daughter of Cato, was married unto thee; not to be thy bed-fellow and companion in bed and at board only, like a harlot, but to be partaker also with thee thy good and evil fortune. Now for thyself, I can find no cause of fault in thee touching our match; but for my part, how may I shew my duty towards thee and how much I would do for thy sake, if I cannot constantly bear a secret mischance or grief with thee, which requireth secrecy and fidelity? I confess that a woman's wit commonly is too weak to keep a secret safely, but yet, Brutus, good education and the company of virtuous men have some power to reform the defect of nature. And for myself, I have this benefit moreover, that I am the daughter of Cato and wife of Brutus. This notwithstanding, I did not trust to any of these things before, until that now I have found by experience that no pain or grief whatsoever can overcome me." With those words she shewed him her wound on her thigh, and told him what she had done to prove herself. Brutus was amazed to hear what she said unto him, and lifting up his hands to heaven, he besought the gods to give him the grace he might bring his enterprise to so good pass, that he might be found a husband worthy of so noble a wife as Porcia; so he then did comfort her the best he could.

Plutarch, *Brutus*.   Shakespeare, II, 1.

9. When this was done, they came to talk of Cæsar's will and testament and of his funerals and tomb. Then Antonius, thinking good his testament should be read openly, and also

that his body should be honourably buried, and not in hugger-mugger, lest the people might thereby take occasion to be worse offended if they did otherwise, Cassius stoutly spake against it. But Brutus went with the motion and agreed unto it, wherein it seemeth he committed a second fault. For the first fault he did was when he would not consent to his fellow-conspirators that Antonius should be slain; and therefore he was justly accused that thereby he had saved and strengthened a strong and grievous enemy of their conspiracy. The second fault was when he agreed that Cæsar's funerals should be as Antonius would have them, the which indeed marred all. For first of all, when Cæsar's testament was openly read among them, whereby it appeared that he bequeathed unto every citizen of Rome 75 drachmas a man, and that he left his gardens and arbours unto the people, which he had on this side of the river Tiber, in the place where now the temple of Fortune is built, the people then loved him, and were marvellous sorry for him. Afterwards, when Cæsar's body was brought into the market-place, Antonius making his funeral oration in praise of the dead, according to the ancient custom of Rome, and perceiving that his words moved the common people to compassion, he framed his eloquence to make their hearts yearn the more, and taking Cæsar's gown all bloody in his hand, he laid it open to the sight of them all, shewing what a number of cuts and holes it had upon it. Therewithal the people fell presently into such a rage and mutiny, that there was no more order kept amongst the common people. For some of them cried out, "Kill the murtherers!" others plucked up forms, tables, and stalls about the market-place, as they had done before at the funerals of Clodius, and having laid them all in a heap together, they set them on fire, and thereupon did put the body of Cæsar, and burnt it in the midst of the most holy places. And furthermore, when the fire was thoroughly kindled, some here, some there, took burning firebrands, and ran with them to the murtherers' houses that killed him, to set them on fire. Howbeit the conspirators, forseeing the danger before, had wisely provided for themselves and fled.

Plutarch, *Brutus*.   Shakespeare, III, 2.

10. About that time Brutus sent to pray Cassius to come to the city of Sardis, and so he did. Brutus, understanding of his coming, went to meet him with all his friends. There both their armies being armed, they called them both *Emperors*. Now as it commonly happened in great affairs between two persons, both of them having many friends and so many captains under them, there ran tales and complaints betwixt them. Therefore, before they fell in hand with any other matter, they went into a little chamber together, and bade every man avoid, and did shut the doors to them. Then they began to pour out their complaints one to the other, and grew hot and loud, earnestly accusing one another, and at length fell both a-weeping. Their friends that were without the chamber, hearing them loud within, and angry between themselves, they were both amazed and afraid also, lest it would grow to further matter, but yet they were commanded that no man should come to them.

Plutarch, *Brutus*.   Shakespeare, IV, 3.

11. This Phaonius at that time, in despite of the doorkeepers, came into the chamber, and with a certain scoffing and mocking gesture, which he counterfeited of purpose, he rehearsed the verses which old Nestor said in Homer:

> My lords, I pray you hearken both to me,
> For I have seen moe years than suchie three.

Cassius fell a-laughing at him; but Brutus thrust him out of the chamber, and called him dog, and counterfeit Cynic. Howbeit his coming in brake their strife at that time, and so they left each other.

Plutarch, *Brutus*.   Shakespeare, IV, 3.

12. So, being ready to go into Europe, one night very late (when all the camp took quiet rest) as he was in his tent with a

little light, thinking of weighty matters, he thought he heard one come in to him, and casting his eye towards the door of his tent, that he saw a wonderful strange and monstrous shape of a body coming towards him, and said never a word. So Brutus boldly asked what he was, a god or a man, and what cause brought him thither? The spirit answered him, "I am thy evil spirit, Brutus, and thou shalt see me by the city of Philippes." Brutus being no otherwise afraid, replied again unto it, "Well, then I shall see thee again."

Plutarch, *Brutus*. Shakespeare, IV, 3.

13. Now the night being far spent, Brutus as he sat bowed towards Clitus, one of his men, and told him somewhat in his ear: the other answered him not, but fell a-weeping. Thereupon he proved Dardanus, and said somewhat also to him; at length he came to Volumnius himself, and speaking to him in Greek, prayed him for the studies' sake which brought them acquainted together, that he would help him to put his hand to his sword, to thrust it in him to kill him. Volumnius denied his request, and so did many others; and amongst the rest, one of them said, there was no tarrying for them there, but that they must needs fly. Then Brutus, rising up, "We must fly indeed," said he, "but it must be with our hands, not with our feet." Having so said, he prayed every man to shift for himself, and then he went a little aside with two or three only, among the which Strato was one with whom he came first acquainted by the study of rhetoric. He came as near to him as he could, and taking his sword by the hilt with both his hands, and falling down upon the point of it, ran himself through. Others say that not he, but Strato (at his request) held the sword in his hand, and turned his head aside, and that Brutus fell down upon it, and so ran himself through, and died presently.

Plutarch, *Brutus*. Shakespeare, V, 5.

FAMILIAR PASSAGES IN JULIUS CÆSAR

When you first take a play of Shakespeare's in hand, you soon begin to have the feeling that you have read this before, though you know you have not. The fact is, Shakespeare expressed the general mind and common feeling of us all in phrases so packed with meaning, so full of insight into human nature, so happy in figure and choice of words, that we have adopted them and added them to our stock of everyday language. Only the Bible has contributed more of these stock phrases to modern English speech. The result is that we are constantly quoting words and even whole lines from Shakespeare's plays without knowing it. Some of these unconscious quotations are "the king's English," "sweets to the sweet," "at a pin's fee," "what's in a name?" "last, but not least," "single blessedness," "the short and long of it," "forever and a day," "in my mind's eye," "the game is up," "what's done is done," "the pink of courtesy," "parting is such sweet sorrow," "I'll not budge an inch," etc.

With the exception of "Hamlet," "Macbeth," and "The Merchant of Venice," none of the plays have contributed a greater number of familiar phrases to our speech to-day than "Julius Cæsar." Here are some of the most interesting. Others may be found in Bartlett's "Familiar Quotations." It will interest you to try to place them by recalling when and where and by whom they were spoken. How many of them had you heard before you studied the play? Learn as many of them as you can.

Familiar Passages

1. The dogs of war.
2. It was Greek to me.
3. He is a great observer, and he looks
   Quite through the deeds of men.
4. This was the noblest Roman of them all!
5. As proper men as ever trod upon neat's leather.
6. O, what a fall was there, my countrymen!
7. Let me have men about me that are fat,
   Sleek-headed men, and such as sleep o' nights.
8. Beware the ides of March.
9. The choice and master spirits of this age.
10. Now, in the names of all the gods at once,
    Upon what meat does this our Cæsar feed,
    That he is grown so great?
11. A friend should bear his friend's infirmities.
12. We must take the current when it serves,
    Or lose our ventures.
13. Et tu, Brute!
14. Men at some time are masters of their fates.
15. If you have tears, prepare to shed them now.
16. Between the acting of a dreadful thing
    And the first motion, all the interim is
    Like a phantasma, or a hideous dream.
17. I only speak right on.
18. The last of all the Romans, fare thee well!
19. But yesterday the word of Cæsar might
    Have stood against the world; now lies he there
    And none so poor to do him reverence.
20. If we do meet again, why, we shall smile;
    If not, why then this parting was well made.
21. There is a tide in the affairs of men
    Which, taken at the flood, leads on to fortune.

Appendix.

22. Honour is the subject of my story.
23. Yond Cassius has a lean and hungry look;
    He thinks too much: such men are dangerous.
24. Friends, Romans, Countrymen, lend me your ears.
25. The livelong day.
26. I had rather be a dog and bay the moon
    Than such a Roman.
27. This was the most unkindest cut of all.
28. Though last, not least in love.
29. Not that I loved Cæsar less, but that I loved Rome
    more.
30. 'Tis a common proof
    That lowliness is young ambition's ladder.
31. Why, man, he doth bestride the narrow world
    Like a Colossus, and we petty men
    Walk under his huge legs and peep about
    To find ourselves dishonourable graves.
32. I am no orator as Brutus is,
    But, as you know me all, a plain blunt man.
33. O, that a man might know
    The end of this day's business ere it comes.
34. An itching palm.
35. Who is here so base that would be a bondman?
36. Thou art the ruins of the noblest man
    That ever lived in the tide of times.
37. Cowards die many times before their deaths;
    The valiant never taste of death but once.
38. The evil that men do lives after them;
    The good is oft interréd with their bones.
39. Ambition should be made of sterner stuff.
40. A dish fit for the gods.

WHAT WE KNOW ABOUT SHAKESPEARE

The facts that we know with absolute certainty about William Shakespeare can be given in a few meagre paragraphs. Some bare, prosaic records in Stratford and in the Stationers' Register in London, a few signatures, a will, a deed or two, an application for a coat-of-arms, an occasional mention of his name in court proceedings, in lists of actors, and in the works of fellow authors, — this is about all we have as the basis for a life of one of the greatest men that the world has produced. Traditions and quaint fanciful stories exist, as we might expect, in infinite number and variety. Many of these date back to the poet's own time, and therefore may have in them at least an element of truth. By far the greater number, however, gained popularity nearly a century after his death, when the curiosity of an age intensely interested in the drama began to look back and talk about the most marvellous of all the makers of plays. Few of these later traditions can be relied upon. Yet from the few scrappy facts that we have, supplemented by the earlier legends, and above all by a study of the plays themselves, it is possible to make a story of the poet's life, which, though by no means complete, is full enough to give us a fairly clear understanding of his growth in fame and business prosperity, and his development as a dramatist.

It is not strange that we know so little about Shakespeare. His age was not one of biographical writing. To-day a man of not one tenth part of his genius is besought by reporters for interviews concerning his life;

Appendix.

he is persuaded by admiring friends to write his mem-
oirs; as his end approaches, every important newspaper

**Why we
know so
little about
Shake-
speare.**
in the land has an article of several columns
ready to print the instant that word of his death
comes over the wire. Three hundred and fifty
years ago nothing of this kind was possible.
Newspapers and magazines, genealogies and
contemporary history did not exist. Encyclopædias, dic-
tionaries of names, directories, "blue-books," and volumes
of "Who's Who" had not been dreamed of. Personal cor-
respondence was meagre, and what few letters were written
seldom were preserved. Above all, a taste for reading the
lives of men had not been formed. In fact, it was not until
fifty years after Shakespeare's time that the art of biographical writing in England was really born. When we remember, in addition to these facts, that actors and playwrights
then held a distinctly inferior position in society, and by
the growing body of Puritans were looked upon with contempt and extreme disfavor, it is not surprising that no
special heed was paid to the life of Shakespeare. On the
contrary, it is astonishing that we know as much as we do
about him, — fully as much as we know about most of the
writers of his time, and even of many who lived much
later.

In the records of the 16th century there are numerous references to Shakespeares living in the midland

**The poet's
father, John
Shake-
speare.**
counties of England, especially in Warwickshire. For the most part, they seem to have
been substantial yeomen and plain farmers of
sound practical sense rather than men of learning or culture. Some of them owned land and prospered.
Such a one was John Shakespeare, who moved to Strat-

ford-on-Avon about 1550 and became a dealer in malt and corn, meat, wool, and leather. He is referred to sometimes as a glover and a butcher. Probably he was both, and dealt besides in all the staples that farmers about the village produced and brought to market to sell. The fact that he could not write, which was nothing unusual among men of his station in the 16th century, did not prevent his prospering in business. For more than twenty years after the earliest mention of his name in the Stratford records, he is spoken of frequently and always in a way to show us that his financial standing in the community was steadily increasing. He seems also to have been a man of affairs. From one office to another he rose until in 1568 he held the position of High Bailiff, or Mayor of Stratford. Eleven years earlier his fortunes had been increased by his marriage to Mary Arden, the daughter of a prosperous farmer of the neighboring village of Wilmcote, who bequeathed to his daughter a house, with fifty acres of land, and a considerable sum of money. It is not fair, therefore, to speak of the father of William Shakespeare, as some have done, as "an uneducated peasant," or as "a provincial shopkeeper." At the time of the birth of his illustrious son he was one of the most prominent men in Stratford, decidedly well-to-do, respected and trusted by all.

The year before John Shakespeare brought his bride from Wilmcote to Stratford-on-Avon, he had purchased a house in Henley Street, and there he and his wife were living when their children were born. It was a cottage two stories high, with dormer windows, and of timber and plaster construction. Though frequently repaired and built over during the three hundred and fifty years that

The house in which Shakespeare was born.

Appendix.

have passed, it still remains in general appearance much the same as it looked in 1556. Simple, crude, plain, — it is nevertheless the most famous house in England, if not in the world. Noted men and women from all parts of the earth have visited Stratford to see it. Essays, stories, and poems have been written about it. Preserved in the care of the Memorial Society, it is the shrine of the literary pilgrim and the Mecca of tourists who flock during the summer to the quaint old village on the Avon. For here, in a small bare room on the second floor, William Shakespeare was born.

How little we know of Shakespeare, compared with even a minor poet of the 19th century, is shown by the

Date of the poet's birth, April 23, 1564. fact that we are not certain of the exact date on which the greatest of all poets was born. The records of Holy Trinity Church in Stratford show that the child was baptized on April 26, 1564, and since it was the custom at that time for the baptism of children to take place on the third day after birth, it has been generally agreed that William was born on April 23, and that date is celebrated as his birthday. Tradition tells us, and probably truthfully, that it was also on this date, April 23, in 1616, that he died.

Of the poet's boyhood we know next to nothing. It is a mistake, however, to assume that he lacked educational

Shakespeare's boyhood and schooling, 1571–1577. opportunities. There was in Stratford an excellent free Grammar School such as a bailiff's son would attend, and to which it is reasonable to suppose that the boy was sent. Here he studied chiefly Latin, for education then in England consisted almost entirely of the classics, especially Vergil, Ovid, Horace, and the comedies

SHAKESPEARE'S HOUSE AT STRATFORD-ON-AVON

THE ROOM WHERE SHAKESPEARE WAS BORN

of Plautus and Terence. The comment of Ben Jonson, his fellow dramatist of later years, that Shakespeare had "small Latin and less Greek," should not be taken too literally. Compared with the profound scholarship of a college-trained man like Jonson, the Stratford boy had, to be sure, but little knowledge of the classics. Yet there is every evidence to show that he understood both Latin and French pretty well, and that he knew the Bible thoroughly. It is clear, too, that by nature he was a boy of remarkable powers of observation and keenly retentive memory, who used every opportunity about him for acquiring information and ideas. Whether he went to school or not would have made but little difference to one whose mind possessed rare powers of developing and training itself. Like Burns and Lincoln, he was educated more by people and the world of Nature about him than by books and formal teaching.

Ordinarily a boy of the 16th century would remain at the Grammar School from seven to fourteen, but there is a well-founded tradition that Shakespeare left in 1577, when he was thirteen years old, and never attended school again. About this time the records show that his father's financial difficulties began. Another pair of hands was *Five years in Stratford after leaving school, 1577–1582.* needed at home to help in the support of the family, and William was the oldest son. Just how he was occupied, however, between his fourteenth and eighteenth years we cannot say. Probably he assisted his father in his declining business. One of the bits of Stratford gossip, collected by the antiquarian Aubrey, states that he was "in his younger years a school-master in the country," and another tells us that "when he was a boy he exercised his father's trade. When he killed a calf, he would doe it in a high style and make a speech." It may be, as another reference seems to imply, that he was employed in the office of a lawyer. But we must not put too much confidence in these traditions, which, like all stories passed on by word of mouth, grew and changed as the years went by. As much as we should like to know of his employment, his reading, and all the circumstances that were developing his mind and character during these five important years, we must remember that "there is no reason why anything should have been recorded; he was an obscure boy living in an inland village, before the age of newspapers, and out of relation with people of fashion and culture. During this period as little is known of him as is known of Cromwell during the same period; as little, but no less. This fact gives no occasion either for surprise or scepticism as to his marvellous genius; it was an entirely normal fact concerning boys growing up in unliterary times and in rural communities."[1]

The first really authentic record we have of Shakespeare after his school days is that of the baptism of his daughter Susanna, on May 26, 1583. The previous year, when only eighteen, he had married Anne Hathaway, the daughter of a farmer in the neighboring village of Shottery. This picturesque hamlet was reached then from Stratford, as it is to-day, by a delightful foot-path through the wide and fertile fields of Warwickshire. Perhaps no other spot connected with the poet's life, except the house in which he was born, is dearer to people's hearts than the quaint old thatched-

His marriage to Anne Hathaway, 1582.

[1] H. W. Mabie: "William Shakespeare, Poet, Dramatist, and Man," page 51.

ANNE HATHAWAY'S COTTAGE AT SHOTTERY

INTERIOR OF ANNE HATHAWAY'S COTTAGE

roof building known as "Anne Hathaway's cottage"; for it still stands, at least in part, as it was when the "youthful lover went courting through the meadows, past the 'bank where the wild thyme blows,' to Shottery." In February, 1585, two years after the birth of Susanna, twins were born, and soon after the youthful husband and father left his native town to seek his fortunes in London.

It would be most interesting to know when and how and just why Shakespeare left Stratford, but no documents have been found that throw any certain light upon this portion of his life. It has generally been assumed that he found his way to the metropolis soon after the birth of his twins. Probably he walked by the highway through Oxford and Wycombe, or if he rode it was on horseback, purchasing a saddle-horse at the beginning of his journey, as was the custom then, and selling it upon his arrival in the city. There is an old tradition that, with other young men of the village, he had been involved in a poaching escapade upon the estate of Sir Thomas Lucy. In the first regular biography of Shakespeare written by Nicholas Rowe in 1709, nearly a hundred years after the poet's death, the story of this adventure is given as an actual fact. "He had, by a misfortune common enough among young fellows, fallen into ill company, and among them some that made a frequent practice of deer-stealing, engaged him with them more than once in robbing a park that belonged to Sir Thomas Lucy of Charlecote, near Stratford. For this he was prosecuted by that gentleman, as he thought, somewhat too severely; and, in order to revenge that ill-usage, he made a ballad upon him, and though this, probably the first essay of his poetry, be lost,

Reasons for leaving Stratford: the poaching tradition.

125

yet it is said to have been so very bitter that it redoubled the prosecution against him to that degree that he was obliged to leave his business and family in Warwickshire and shelter himself in London." No trace of this ballad has been found; indeed, the whole story rests on gossip, and must not be taken too literally. It is supported, in a way, by the fact that Justice Shallow in "The Merry Wives of Windsor" is unquestionably a humorous sketch, or caricature, of Sir Thomas Lucy of Charlecote Hall, thus suggesting that whether he had been prosecuted and harried out of town by his wealthy neighbor or not, the youthful poet had some personal reasons for ridiculing the head of the Lucy family.

Still another account explains Shakespeare's departure from Stratford by stating that he joined a company of strolling players. Though this may possibly have been the means of his finding congenial travelling companions, it seems more natural to suppose that he left his native village much as a boy to-day leaves a remote country town and goes to the city to seek his fortune. His father's affairs, we know, had been steadily declining; his own family was growing; business in many trades through the midland counties was poor; any ambitious and high-spirited youth would have become restless and discontented. What was more natural, under these circumstances, than the breaking of home-ties and moving to London for its larger opportunities?

Stratford too narrow a field for Shakespeare.

The traditions that Shakespeare, upon his arrival in the capital about 1585, was employed in a printer's shop and a lawyer's office, are extremely doubtful. It seems much more likely that he became connected with the theatre at once, either as a call-boy in the building itself, or as one of those who held the horses on which gallants of the city rode to the play-house. That he should have turned to the theatre rather than to business to get a foothold in London is not strange. Companies of players had frequently visited Stratford in his boyhood. Indeed, the people of his native town seem to have been exceptionally fond of the drama, a fact, as Mr. Mabie has pointed out, "of very obvious bearing on the education of Shakespeare's imagination and the bent of his mind toward a vocation." As a lad of eleven he probably saw the pageant at Kenilworth Castle, in honor of Queen Elizabeth's visit to the Earl of Leicester. The processions and gorgeous costumes of this occasion, the tableaux and scenes set forth by the actors from the city must have made a profound impression on the mind of the imaginative boy. Moreover, it was a time of widespread interest in everything dramatic. When Shakespeare was born in 1564, there was not a single building in London devoted to the presentation of plays. At the time of his death, fifty-two years later, there were at least nine. The development of the drama from simple morality plays and historical pageants given in tavern-yards and on village greens, to "Julius Cæsar" and "Hamlet," covered the period of the poet's youth; so that when he arrived in London, more than ever before or since in English history, the theatre was of compelling interest and attraction.

The six years after his arrival in London are a blank. We must imagine him rapidly rising through various positions at the Rose or the Curtain, for a young man of his genius and enterprise would not long remain obscure.

Appendix.

It is certain that he became an actor before he wrote for the stage. By 1592, however, he had evidently earned sufficient fame as a playwright to stir the jealousy of Robert Greene, a rival author, who in that year refers bitterly to him as "in his owne conceit the only *Shakes-scene* in a countrie," and then parodies a line from an early play that is attributed to Shakespeare. While as an actor he was learning stagecraft in the best possible school, he was undoubtedly trying his prentice hand by mending old plays and contributing bits to the work of his older companions. These earliest dramatic writings may have been numerous, but they are either entirely lost or hidden in plays credited to other men. His progress from a clerk in a country store to a writer of drama is thus admirably described by Sidney Lee: "A young man of two-and-twenty, burdened with a wife and children, he had left his home in the little country town of Stratford-on-Avon in 1586 to seek his fortune in London. Without friends, without money, he had, like any other stage-struck youth, set his heart on becoming an actor in the metropolis. Fortune favoured him. He sought and won the humble office of call-boy in a London playhouse; but no sooner had his foot touched the lowest rung of the theatrical ladder than his genius taught him that the topmost rung was within his reach. He tried his hand on the revision of an old play, and the manager was not slow to recognize an unmatched gift for dramatic writing.[1]

It was not until 1593, when Shakespeare was twenty-nine, that he appeared openly in the field of authorship. On April 18 of that year his long poem "Venus and

His earliest work as actor and playwright.

[1] Sidney Lee: "Shakespeare and the Elizabethan Playgoer," page 32.

Adonis" was entered at Stationers' Hall for publication. It was printed by Richard Field, a Stratford man who had come to London somewhat earlier than the poet, and though published without a name on the title-page, the dedication to the Earl of Southampton was signed "William Shakespeare." The same is true of "Lucrece,"

The first books published under his name.

which was registered in May of 1594. These two long poems must have had wide popularity, for they are often praised by critics of the day, and in the poet's own lifetime several editions of both were issued. They were the means by which Shakespeare became known as an author, for though some of his dramatic work may have been printed before this, plays were not regarded then as literature to be read, whereas these poems were issued under the poet's supervision for the reading public, and were thus "the first fruits of his conscious artistic life."

Both as actor and playwright, Shakespeare's fame rapidly increased after 1594; in fact, the eight years that followed saw him rise to the height of his powers. His name stands first on the list of "principal Comedians" who acted Jonson's "Every Man in his Humour" in 1598. Francis

Progress in fame and fortune.

Meres in his "Palladis Tamia," published in the same year, speaks of the "mellifluous and honey-tongued Shakespeare," and then proceeds to name twelve of his plays and compare him favorably with the Roman dramatists Seneca and Plautus. Even if this list is incomplete we see that already before 1598 he had written three of his most charming comedies, one of them "The Merchant of Venice," and at least one of the tragedies that ranks among his very greatest. From then until his retirement to Stratford fourteen years later, there are frequent references to his plays which appeared with astonishing rapidity. The dates when they were written and first acted are often uncertain, but before 1612 he had produced more than twenty dramas which together constitute the most marvelous body of literary work that ever came from a human mind.

As an actor he did not continue to excel. If we may trust the sentiments of the sonnets, it is clear that he thoroughly disliked this part of his profession. Probably after 1604 he ceased to appear on the stage altogether. Financially it is certain that he was prosperous. We know, for one thing, that he owned shares in several London theatres, notably the Globe, where many of his own plays were first presented to enthusiastic London audiences. Then his successful application to the College of Heralds in 1599, on behalf of his father, for a grant of coat-of-arms; his purchase of several pieces of property in his native town; the records of lawsuits to recover debts which were owed him; numerous references which show us that he was looked upon as a man of means and standing; his friendship with Ben Jonson and other learned men of his day, — these facts, with the traditions of later generations, all convince us that the author of "Hamlet" and "Macbeth" was a successful man of affairs, as well as one of the most prominent and best-loved dramatists of his time.

Although Shakespeare made London his home after 1584 or 1585, it is probable that he often visited Stratford where his family continued to reside. An old legend states that he frequently put up at the Crown Inn in Oxford on his way to and fro. Documents exist, moreover, which

HOLY TRINITY PARISH CHURCH, STRATFORD-ON-AVON

GOOD FREND FOR IESVS SAKE FORBEARE,
TO DIGG THE DVST ENCLOASED HEARE:
BLESE BE Y MAN Y SPARES THES STONES,
AND CVRST BE HE Y MOVES MY BONES.

INSCRIPTION ON SHAKESPEARE'S TOMB

IVDICIO PYLIVM, GENIO SOCRATEM, ARTE MARONEM
TERRA TEGIT, POPVLVS MÆRET, OLYMPVS HABET

STAY PASSENGER, WHY GOEST THOV BY SO FAST,
READ IF THOV CANST, WHOM ENVIOVS DEATH HATH PLAST,
WITH IN THIS MONVMENT SHAKSPEARE: WITH WHOME,
QVICK NATVRE DIDE: WHOSE NAME, DOTH DECK Y TOMBE,
FAR MORE, THEN COST: SIEH ALL, Y HE HATH WRITT,
LEAVES LIVING ART, BVT PAGE, TO SERVE HIS WITT.

OBIIT AÑO DO 1616
ÆTATIS 53 DIE 23 AP.

INSCRIPTION ON SHAKESPEARE'S MONUMENT, TRINITY CHURCH,
STRATFORD-ON-AVON

show that he was constantly investing money in real estate in his native village, to which he seems to have looked forward as a pleasant retreat after the strenuous days of actor, theatre-manager, and playwright were over. Probably the breaking **Retirement from London, 1612.** off of London ties was gradual; but it is doubtful whether he was much in the city after 1612, the year in which "Henry VIII," the last of his plays, was written. He now appears in the records as "William Shakespeare, Gent., of Stratford-on-Avon"; and there he lived with his well-won honors, respected and loved, for four years.

In the early spring of 1616, Shakespeare's youngest daughter, Judith, was married. A month later he made his will, and on April 25 the register of Christ Church in Stratford shows that he was buried. **Death in Stratford, April 23, 1616.** According to the lettering on the monument he died on April 23, and that date, the date of his birth fifty-two years before, has been generally accepted as the day of his death. He was buried in the chancel of the fine old church, not far from the spot where he had been christened, and over the place where he lies may still be seen the quaint lines which tradition tells us he himself wrote to be inscribed above him:—

GOOD FREND FOR IESUS SAKE FORBEARE,
TO DIGG THE DUST ENCLOASED HEARE:
BLEST BE Yᵉ MAN Yᵗ SPARES THES STONES,
AND CURST BE HE Yᵗ MOVES MY BONES.

Whether the poet wrote these threatening words or not, no sexton has disturbed his remains, and the grave of William Shakespeare in the beautiful church by the river he loved has remained unopened.

SHAKESPEARE'S PLAYS AND POEMS

One of the problems of Shakespearean scholars for more than a century has been to determine the exact

Difficulties of determining the dates of the plays. years in which the various plays were written. For just as we have no details of the poet's life, so are the records of his work either extremely meagre or entirely lacking. Not a single manuscript of anything that Shakespeare wrote has been preserved. The fire which burned the Globe theatre to the ground in 1613 may have destroyed the original pages of all the dramas: and yet, interesting and precious as they would be to us to-day, it is doubtful whether we can attribute to their loss our lack of knowledge as to just when each was written. We must remember that in Elizabethan times plays were not considered literature to be read. After they had served their purpose on the stage and passed out of popular favor, they were set aside and wholly neglected. As long as there was the slightest chance of their being in demand at the theatre, the author and companies of actors did their best to keep them out of print altogether, apparently in the belief that attendance at the playhouse would suffer if the drama in book form was in the hands of the people. Moreover, among the most cultivated men of the day, and especially among the growing body of Puritans, there was a strong prejudice against the whole theatrical business. By them, actors were held in low esteem, and plays were looked upon as things of light, or even questionable, character. The modern conception that regards the drama as a high and artistic form of literature had not been born.

Under these circumstances it is not surprising that during his own lifetime only sixteen of Shakespeare's thirty-seven plays appeared in print. These editions, which are known to-day as the Quartos, were small, cheaply-made, paper-bound pamphlets usually sold for a sixpence each. It is generally believed that they were issued without the poet's consent, and probably even against his wishes. Several of them were undoubtedly printed from shorthand notes taken slyly at a performance in the theatre. Others may have been set up from the soiled and tattered copies of a needy actor who had been secretly bribed to part with them. The confusion and strange blunders in the text show us that these Quartos were the careless and hasty work of piratical printers; indeed, it is almost certain that Shakespeare himself did not revise or in any way prepare a single one of them for the press.

The Quarto editions of the plays.

Inexact and inadequate as are the pirated Quarto editions, they would probably be the only plays of Shakespeare known to us to-day had it not been for a remarkable book that appeared seven years after his death. In 1623 two of the poet's friends put forth in a single volume his complete dramatic works. These men, John Heminge and Henry Condell, — names which are forever linked with Shakespeare's, — were actors in the same company with him, and, with Burbage, were joint owners of the Globe Theatre. The great dramatist, as a token of lifelong friendship, in his will bequeathed to them and to Burbage the sum of twenty-six shillings and eight pence to buy rings; and they in turn collected and edited his plays "to keepe the memory of so worthy a friend and fellow

The First Folio edition of the plays.

alive." It is a large volume of 901 pages in two columns of fine print, and on the title-page, besides a crude engraving of the poet, are these words:

Mr. William

SHAKESPEARES

COMEDIES,

HISTORIES, &

TRAGEDIES

Published according to the True Original Copies.

LONDON

Printed by Isaac Iaggard, and Ed. Blount.   1623.

This is perhaps the most important volume in the whole range of English literature, for in it appeared for the first time in print twenty of Shakespeare's plays, among them "The Tempest," "Twelfth Night," "Julius Cæsar," "Macbeth," "Cymbeline," and others of the dramatist's masterpieces.   Heminge and Condell had access to stage copies of these plays which in another generation might have been lost or destroyed by fire; so that their work, coming when it did, saved for us a large portion of the finest poetry and deepest wisdom of Shakespeare's mind. It is no wonder that the 156 extant copies of this notable book are preserved as priceless treasures; for no other single volume ever did a greater service to literature than this Folio of 1623.

Although Heminge and Condell must have known in many cases the exact years in which Shakespeare was at work upon his various plays, they did not consider such information of sufficient interest to include it in their edition. Well might we spare some of the tiresome eulogies, which they printed in their preface, for a page or two of facts that they so easily might have included. As it stands, however, the First Folio helps but little in arranging the chronology of the comedies and tragedies. And yet, in spite of all difficulties, by painstaking research scholars have come to a pretty general agreement upon the dates of composition of most of the plays. The evidence which they have used may be divided into two kinds, external and internal, — that is, evidence found outside of the plays, and evidence found within the works themselves. External evidence consists of such information as has been obtained from records of performances

Dates of composition: external evidence.

in diaries and letters; quotations and allusions in other books; entries in the register of the Stationers' Company, which for nearly three hundred years regulated the publication of all books in England; records of the Master of Revels at Court, and of course the dates on the title-pages of the Quartos themselves. A good illustration of this sort of evidence is the journal of a certain Dr. Simon Forman, in which he mentions the fact that in 1610 and 1611 he witnessed performances of "Macbeth," "Cymbeline," and "The Winter's Tale" at the Globe. Another is the celebrated passage in the "Palladis Tamia," or "Wit's Treasury," of Francis Meres, which was published in 1598 "As *Plautus* and *Seneca* are accounted the best for Comedy and Tragedy among the Latines, so *Shakespeare* among yᵉ English is the most excellent in both kinds for the stage; for Comedy, witness his *Gētlemē of Verona*, his *Errors*, his *Love labors lost*, his *Love*

Appendix.

labours wonne, his *Midsummers night dreame*, & his *Merchant of Venice:* for Tragedy, his *Richard the 2, Richard the 3, Henry the 4, King John, Titus Andronicus,* and his *Romeo and Iuliet."* Such references as these give a definite year, later than which the plays referred to could not have been written. With a starting point thus settled, it is often possible to work backward and fix definitely the date of composition.

Internal evidence, though seldom as exact as external, and therefore more difficult to interpret, is much more

Dates of composition: internal evidence. abundant. It may be nothing more than a reference in the mouth of an actor to events or books the dates of which are known, such as the words in the Prologue to " Henry V " that refer to the expedition of the Earl of Essex to Ireland in 1599. More often it deals with considerations of the metre, language, and form of the work itself. By studying such matters as classical allusions, the use of Latin words, kinds of figures of speech, puns, variations of verse and prose, and many other changing peculiarities of the poet's method, scholars have been able to trace the development of Shakespeare as a writer, and thus assign many of his plays to their probable year on no other evidence than their style. For instance, the date of " Julius Cæsar " is generally agreed to be not earlier than 1601 from the poet's use of the word " eternal " in the phrase " the eternal devil." As late as 1600 Shakespeare was using " infernal " in such expressions, but after that year he began to use " eternal," owing probably to the increasing objection among Puritans of London to the use of profanity on the stage. Even such a simple matter as the number of rhyming lines in a play may help to place it approximately. In "Love's Labour's Lost," the earliest of the comedies, there are 1028 rhymes; whereas in "The Winter's Tale" and "The Tempest," written twenty years later, there are none and two respectively. It is therefore safe to assume that as Shakespeare's style developed he used rhyme less and less, so that tragedies with but few rhyming lines, such as "Antony and Cleopatra" and "Coriolanus," may be assigned, if on no other ground, to the later years of his life. Such matters of structure and style are by no means always certain. They are delicate to handle and require sound judgment and long experience. Yet it is by this sort of internal evidence, rather than by external facts, that the chronology of the plays has been determined.

The following table gives the result of research and comparison, of proof and conjecture, on the part of Shakespearean scholars. There still remain, of course, many differences of opinion; some of **Probable** the dates are less certain than others; a few **dates of the** are almost entirely the result of guesswork. **plays.** Yet when we consider the meagre data upon which students have built their conclusions, their lack of agreement seems remarkably slight and insignificant.

Of the thirty-seven plays in the following table, the sixteen which appeared in Quarto editions during the poet's life were "Titus Andronicus," 1594; **Plays** "Richard II.," "Richard III.," and "Romeo **printed** and Juliet," 1597; "1 Henry IV" and "Love's **before** Labour's Lost," 1598; "The Merchant of **1623.** Venice," "Henry V.," "Much Ado About Nothing," "2 Henry IV," and "A Midsummer Night's Dream," 1600; "The Merry Wives of Windsor," 1602; "Hamlet,"

CHRONOLOGICAL TABLE OF SHAKESPEARE'S PLAYS AND POEMS

PERIOD	YEAR	POEMS	COMEDIES	HISTORIES	TRAGEDIES
I	1590		Love's Labour's Lost	1 Henry VI	
	1591		Comedy of Errors	2 Henry VI; 3 Henry VI	
	1592		Two Gentlemen of Verona	Richard III	Romeo and Juliet
	1593	Venus and Adonis		King John	Titus Andronicus
	1594	Lucrece	A Midsummer Night's Dream		
	1595		Taming of the Shrew	Richard II	
	1596		Merchant of Venice		
II	1597		Merry Wives of Windsor	1 Henry IV	
	1598		Much Ado About Nothing	2 Henry IV	
	1599	Passionate Pilgrim?	As You Like It	Henry V	
	1600		Twelfth Night		

	Year	Poems	Comedies & Romances	Henry VIII	Tragedies
III	1601	Phoenix and the Turtle?	Troilus and Cressida		Julius Caesar
	1602		All's Well that Ends Well		Hamlet
	1603		Measure for Measure		
	1604				Othello
	1605				King Lear
	1606				Macbeth
	1607				Timon of Athens
	1608	A Lover's Complaint?	Pericles		Antony and Cleopatra
	1609	Sonnets (Printed)			Coriolanus
IV	1610		Cymbeline		
	1611		Winter's Tale; Tempest		
	1612			Henry VIII	

139

1603; "King Lear," 1608; "Troilus and Cressida," and "Pericles," 1609. In addition to these, a Quarto of "Othello" was printed in 1622. The other twenty plays were not published, so far as we know, until 1623, when Heminge and Condell included them in the First Folio.

The periods shown in the table are, of course, wholly artificial. Shakespeare himself had no such division of **Periods of Shakespeare's development.** his works in mind, and it is dangerous for us to-day to press very far the suggestion of clearly defined compartments for the plays. The development of the dramatist, like that of any artist, was gradual. Changes in style, in method, in views of life took place not in a single year, but were the result of slowly expanding power and growth of character. In that growth there were no sudden breaks or unaccountable transformations. The mind that created "Hamlet" in 1602 was the same mind that created "Twelfth Night" in 1600, no matter how black the line that separates them into two different periods. Yet a glance at the divisions in the table reveals two or three interesting facts.

When Shakespeare has gained a foothold in the London theatres he first turns his hand to old plays, touching them **The years of experiment, 1590–1593.** up, remodelling, and improving. This is his natural work as an apprentice playwright. As he gains confidence and strikes out for himself, he experiments with all the forms of play-writing that then are known. Thus in "Love's Labour's Lost" we find one of the very few works the plot of which is his own invention; in "The Comedy of Errors" and "The Two Gentlemen of Verona" he imitates the Latin comedies of Plautus; in "Richard III" and "King John" he attempts historical tragedy, and in " Romeo and Juliet " he gives us tragedy, full of romance and passion, drawn from Italy whence so many of his stories of later years are to come. The four years from 1590 to 1593 are evidently years of feeling about, testing himself, and experimenting. Naturally he writes with great rapidity: he is full of enthusiasm and the impetuous rush of youth. All that he does shows signs of a beginner and an unsettled purpose. We therefore do not expect to find highly finished work. As a matter of fact, with the exception of " Romeo and Juliet " and " Richard III," none of the plays of this early period are acted on the stage to-day or often read.

It is now that Shakespeare writes his two long story poems, — " Venus and Adonis " in 1593 and " Lucrece " in 1594. In them he retells classical legends taken chiefly from the Roman poet Ovid. **The poems.** Their elaborate and florid language reminds us of similar narrative poems of the period. In their spirit and style they resemble the early plays, but in one important respect they differ: they are published with their author's name on the title-page. Unlike the Quartos of the dramas, Shakespeare prepares these poems for the press. Their popularity surpasses even that of the comedies. Seven editions of " Venus and Adonis " are issued between 1593 and 1602, and five of " Lucrece " between 1594 and 1616. Among the reading public of his day he becomes more widely known by them than by his work for the stage. He is now, in the eyes of the learned world, an author and creator of real literature.

By 1594 the years of apprenticeship are over; Shakespeare has found where his powers lie. He is still young

and ardent; the sadder and more serious things of
life have not yet come to him; he sympathizes with the

**The great
comedies,
1594-1600.**
demands of the London populace to be amused.
The results are the last of the histories and
seven years of comedies, — the fullest, and
we may well believe, the happiest time of his life as a
dramatist. His power of expression, his skill in con-
structing a play, — above all, his keen insight into human
nature, — develop with astonishing rapidity, until he is
the favorite playwright of his day. In wit and enthusiasm, in pure poetry and "gusto," in creation of interesting
and delightful character, the plays from "A Midsummer
Night's Dream" to "Twelfth Night" stand unmatched.
Not one of them has faded after three hundred years;
they still are acted and read with profit and pleasure.
Together they form "the rich period of unsurpassable
comedy."

But youth and rollicking fun, high spirits and unbroken
happiness, do not last. With the end of the century comes

**The great
tragedies,
1601-1609.**
a turning-point in Shakespeare's life. Perhaps it is personal grief and suffering; possibly it is poor health and for the first time the
thought that his own death may not be far away; possibly it is disappointment in his friends or his ambitions;
or it may be simply a deeper wisdom coming with maturer
years that now begins to make him think more and more
of the greater and more serious things of life. The passions, the temptations, the moral struggles of mankind
now absorb his interest. Naturally, comedy and history
are inadequate for the expression of these deeper thoughts
and emotions. With "Julius Cæsar" begin the great
tragedies, that "series of spectacles of the pity and terror

of human suffering and human sin without parallel in the modern world."[1] Even the three comedies of these years are comedies only in name. Throughout them there is the atmosphere of suffering and sin. Their theme and spirit are more in keeping with "Hamlet" and "King Lear" than with the merrymaking and joyous fun of "As You Like It" and "A Midsummer Night's Dream." Thus every play of this period has a tragic motive, for during its nine years the mind and heart of the poet are concerned with the saddest and deepest things of human life.

In 1609, toward the close of this period of tragedy, Shakespeare prints his volume of sonnets, one hundred and fifty-four in number. Some of them must have been written much earlier. Their style **The sonnets.** and youthful spirit show that; but besides, as early as 1598, Francis Meres spoke of Shakespeare's "sugred Sonnets among his private friends." Yet many of them show such power, such masterful handling of profound thought, such noble poetic form, that they seem to come from the years that produced "Hamlet" and "Othello." Probably the poet has been writing them off and on ever since he came to London, and now in 1609 he puts them at last into book form. It is well that he does so; for to-day every one who enjoys poetry reads them with delight. Unlike "Venus and Adonis" and "Lucrece" they do not fade; they are among the most perfect sonnets in our language, and they contain some of the finest lines that ever came from Shakespeare's pen. Here are two of the most admired:

[1] "The Facts about Shakespeare," Neilson and Thorndike. The Macmillan Company. 1915.

Appendix.

29.

When, in disgrace with fortune and men's eyes,
I all alone beweep my outcast state
And trouble deaf heaven with my bootless cries
And look upon myself and curse my fate,
Wishing me like to one more rich in hope,
Featured like him, like him with friends possess'd,
Desiring this man's art and that man's scope,
With what I most enjoy contented least;
Yet in these thoughts myself almost despising,
Haply I think on thee, and then my state,
Like to the lark at break of day arising
From sullen earth, sings hymns at heaven's gate;
   For thy sweet love remember'd such wealth brings
   That then I scorn to change my state with kings.

116.

Let me not to the marriage of true minds
Admit impediments.   Love is not love
Which alters when it alteration finds,
Or bends with the remover to remove:
O, no! it is an ever-fixèd mark
That looks on tempests and is never shaken;
It is the star to every wandering bark,
Whose worth's unknown, although his height be taken;
Love's not Time's fool, though rosy lips and cheeks
Within his bending sickle's compass come;
Love alters not with his brief hours and weeks,
But bears it out even to the edge of doom.
   If this be error and upon me proved,
   I never writ, nor no man ever loved.

The storm and stress of tragedy, however, does not continue to the end. In the last years Shakespeare turns away from the bitterness and sorrow of life, and leaves us as his final message three romantic comedies of delightful charm. The calm and quiet humor of **The later** these plays is very different from the boisterous **comedies,** farce of "The Merry Wives of Windsor" and **1610–1612.** the buffoonery of the clowns in the earlier dramas; but their beauty and sweetness and idealism make a happy and fitting close to the poet's work. In "Henry VIII," which shows brilliant flashes of his genius, and in "The Two Noble Kinsmen," which is not generally included among his plays, he writes in collaboration with John Fletcher, or with some other of the younger dramatists of these later years. He has made his fortune; he knows that his work is done; he is looking fondly toward his Stratford home, and so he turns over his place to other men.

First,— imitating, feeling his way, experimenting, rapidly and eagerly trying everything about him; then seven full years of whole-souled joy of living, enthu- **Summary.** siasm, laughter, and fun; then deeper emotions and profound thought upon the saddest and most serious things of life; then a happier time of calm reflection and repose, followed by retirement from active work in London to the peaceful village home on the Avon; then, after four quiet years, the end. Thus, in a way, we begin to understand the development of Shakespeare's mind and character by a study of the years in which he wrote his plays and poems.

SHAKESPEARE'S POPULARITY IN HIS OWN DAY

There somehow exists a quite general feeling that Shakespeare's genius was not properly appreciated in his own time; that dramatists, now ranked far below him, were more popular with audiences in the days of Queen Elizabeth and King James I. Whether this notion comes from the scarcity of facts which we have concerning the poet's life, it is hard to say. Certainly such a belief must be ranked among the most unfortunate of popular errors. There is ample evidence to show that he was not only popular with uneducated London tradesmen and apprentices who thronged the pit of the Globe, but in the best critical judgment of the day he was considered the first of poets and dramatists. "Throughout his lifetime," says Sidney Lee, "and for a generation afterwards, his plays drew crowds to pit, boxes, and gallery alike. It is true that he was one of a number of popular dramatists, many of whom had rare gifts, and all of whom glowed with a spark of genuine literary fire. But Shakespeare was the sun in the firmament: when his light shone, the fires of all contemporaries paled in the playgoer's eye."[1]

Shakespeare widely appreciated in his own lifetime.

Many bits of evidence have come down to us that show how high a place in people's hearts the plays of Shakespeare held in their author's lifetime. For instance, when he had been in London but ten years he was summoned by Queen Elizabeth to play before her and the court at Greenwich in the

Evidences of his popularity.

[1] Sidney Lee: "Shakespeare and the Elizabethan Playgoer."

Christmas holidays. The favor which King James showed his tragedies is well known. "Hamlet" was acted several times in the first year of its production, both in London and at Oxford and Cambridge. Four editions were printed in eight years,—an unusual demand for those times. Moreover, the name of Shakespeare appears in the works of contemporary authors more than that of any other dramatist, and almost invariably it is coupled with praise and admiration. He is the "mellifluous" and "honey-tongued" poet. One sets him above Plautus and Seneca; another prefers him to Chaucer, Gower, and Spenser; another declares that "he puts them all down, ay, and Ben Jonson, too." In the preface of the first complete edition of his plays, published seven years after his death, the compilers, who were his fellow-actors and friends, wrote of him that he was one "who as he was a happie imitator of Nature, was a most gentle expresser of it. His mind and hand went together; and what he thought, he uttered with that easinesse that wee have scarce received from him a blot in his papers. But it is not our province, who onely gather his works and give them you, to praise him. It is yours that reade him. And there we hope, to your divers capacities, you will finde enough both to draw and hold you; for his wit can no more lie hid than it could be lost. Reade him, therefore; and againe and againe; and if then you doe not like him, surely you are in some manifest danger not to understand him."

A part of the introductory material of this First Folio edition of the plays consists of poems of praise contributed by the poet's admirers. Among the most famous are the noble lines

Ben Jonson's praise of Shakespeare.

147

of Ben Jonson, scholar, poet, and dramatist. Here are the words of a thoughtful critic who knew the theatre from the stage and from the audience, — a man who had been associated with Shakespeare throughout his London career and who understood, better than any other, his place in the hearts of English people.

TO THE MEMORY OF MY BELOVED MASTER WILLIAM SHAKESPEARE AND WHAT HE HATH LEFT US

To draw no envy, Shakespeare, on thy name,
Am I thus ample to thy book and fame ;
While I confess thy writings to be such,
As neither Man nor Muse can praise too much.

* * * * * * * *

Soul of the age !
The applause, delight, the wonder of our stage !
My SHAKESPEARE, rise ! I will not lodge thee by
Chaucer, or Spenser, or bid Beaumont lie
A little further to make thee a room :
Thou art a monument without a tomb,
And art alive still while thy book doth live,
And we have wits to read, and praise to give.
That I not mix thee so my brain excuses, —
I mean with great, but disproportioned Muses ;
For if I thought my judgment were of years,
I should commit thee surely with thy peers,
And tell how far thou didst our Lyly outshine,
Or sporting Kyd, or Marlowe's mighty line.
And though thou hadst small Latin and less Greek
From thence to honour thee I would not seek

For names, but call forth thund'ring Æschylus,
Euripides and Sophocles to us,
Pacuvius, Accius, him of Cordova dead,
To life again to hear thy buskin tread,
And shake a stage; or when thy socks were on,
Leave thee alone for a comparison
Of all that insolent Greece or haughty Rome
Sent forth, or since did from their ashes come.
Triumph, my Britain, thou hast one to show,
To whom all scenes of Europe homage owe.
He was not of an age, but for all time!
And all the Muses still were in their prime,
When, like Apollo, he came forth to warm
Our ears, or like a Mercury to charm!
Nature herself was proud of his designs,
And joyed to wear the dressing of his lines,
Which were so richly spun, and woven so fit,
As, since, she will vouchsafe no other wit.
The merry Greek, tart Aristophanes,
Neat Terence, witty Plautus, now not please;
But antiquated and deserted lie,
As they were not of Nature's family.
Yet must I not give Nature all; thy Art,
My gentle Shakespeare, must enjoy a part.
For though the poet's matter nature be,
His art doth give the fashion; and that he
Who casts to write a living line, must sweat
(Such as thine are) and strike the second heat
Upon the Muses' anvil, turn the same,
And himself with it, that he thinks to frame;
Or for the laurel he may gain to scorn;
For a good poet's made, as well as born.

Appendix.

And such wert thou!   Look how the father's face
Lives in his issue, even so the race
Of Shakespeare's mind and manners brightly shines
In his well turnèd and true filèd lines,
In each of which he seems to shake a lance,
As brandished at the eyes of ignorance.
Sweet Swan of Avon! what a sight it were
To see thee in our waters yet appear,
And make those flights upon the banks of Thames,
That so did take Eliza and our James!
But stay, I see thee in the hemisphere
Advanced, and made a constellation there!
Shine forth, thou Star of Poets, and with rage
Or influence chide or cheer the drooping stage,
Which, since thy flight from hence, hath mourned like
    night,
And despairs day but for thy volume's light.

Even without these lines and numerous other bits of
unqualified praise from contemporary pens, the fact that
the plays were financially successful, and that from them
their author made for those times a small fortune, shows
us that Shakespeare was truly appreciated by all sorts of
people in his own day.   Before his death he had taken
the place which he now holds, — that of the foremost of
English poets and dramatists.

SHAKESPEARE'S FAME SINCE HIS DEATH

During the three hundred years since Shakespeare's death the popularity of his plays on the stage has naturally varied somewhat with the changing taste of the times. Toward the end of his life a decline in the drama had begun, so that the generation which followed was more pleased **Shakespeare on the stage since 1616.** by the coarse blood-and-thunder tragedies of Webster, Ford, and Massinger than by the more profound and more artistic work of Shakespeare. Certain ones of the plays that very early ceased to be popular on the stage have never since come into favor. Most of the histories, two or three of the earliest comedies, "All's Well That Ends Well," "Measure for Measure," "Pericles," "Timon of Athens," "Troilus and Cressida," and "Coriolanus" have seldom been acted since they were first produced. The subjects of some of these are not suitable to present in a modern theatre; in others, as in the histories, there is not enough action or dialogue to satisfy an audience to-day. Yet these make but a small portion of the poet's work. With the exception of the twenty years, 1640–1660, when all theatres in England were closed under the censorship of Cromwell's Puritan Government, there never has been an age that has not had the opportunity to see its foremost actors in the greater comedies and tragedies that came from Shakespeare's pen.

During the reign of Charles II, in the period known as the Restoration, and for the forty years that followed, literary taste was at its lowest mark. Naturally Shakespeare suffered at a time when the coarse and artificial

Appendix.

plays of Wycherley, Vanbrugh, and Farquhar fascinated both the nobility and the common people of London.

The feeling for Shakespeare during the Restoration, 1660–1740. His dramas, to be sure, were still presented on the stage, but they were generally worked over, or even rewritten, to suit the strange fancies of the age. With music, new scenes, and new characters they were mutilated almost beyond recognition. From one point of view they were spoiled; yet it is significant that even to the theatre-goers of 1680 they still had enough vitality and imaginative power to be made the foundation of popular and successful entertainments. Dryden, the chief poet of the time, admired the genius of their author, and wrote prefaces for them in their renovated form. Betterton, the greatest actor of the age, was regarded at his best as the Prince in "Hamlet," a part which he played on many occasions, and always to enthusiastic houses. Samuel Pepys, who kept a remarkable diary between 1661 and 1669, records in his journal three hundred and fifty-one visits to the London theatres during these eight years. On forty-one of these occasions he saw plays by Shakespeare, or plays based upon them. Though Pepys was entirely unable to appreciate the poetry and all the finer qualities of what he heard, — he speaks in especially slighting terms of the comedies, — still it is interesting to know that he had even the opportunity, in eight short years, to witness fourteen different works of the great Elizabethan dramatist. This, too, in England's darkest age of literary appreciation!

The middle of the eighteenth century saw a new and genuine enthusiasm for Shakespeare. Scholars began to study his life and his work. New editions were published, with notes and comment. The plays were revived on the stage in their original and true form. A great interest in all that he had said and thought was born,— an interest which grew through the years that followed, and still is growing. The foremost actors of all times have turned to him for their most ambitious work, and the crowning of their professional achievement. Perhaps the greatest of them all was David Garrick. "From his first triumph in Richard III, in 1741, to his farewell performance of Lear in 1776, he won a series of signal successes in both tragedy and comedy, in Hamlet, Lear, Macbeth, Richard III, Falconbridge, Romeo, Hotspur, Iago, Leontes, Posthumus, Benedick, and Antony. Garrick's services to Shakespeare extended beyond the parts which he impersonated. He revived many plays, and though he garbled the texts freely, yet in comparison with earlier practice he really had some right to boast that he had restored the text of Shakespeare to the stage. Further, his example led to an increased popularity of Shakespeare in the theatre and afforded new incentives for other actors. Mrs. Clive, Mrs. Cibber, and Mrs. Pritchard were among the women who acted with Garrick. Macklin, by his revival of Shylock as a tragic character, Henderson, by his impersonation of Falstaff, and John Palmer in secondary characters, as Iago, Mercutio, Touchstone, and Sir Tobey, were his contemporaries most famous in their day."[1] After Garrick came Mrs. Kemble, Edmund Kean, Mrs. Siddons, Macready, and Booth,— names remembered to-day chiefly in connection with the Shakespearean rôles which they nobly played.

The great actors in Shakespeare's plays.

[1] Neilson and Thorndike: "The Facts about Shakespeare," page 174.

Appendix.

Conditions have not changed in our own time. The greatest actors of our own generation, Sir Henry Irving,

Shake-
speare on
the stage
to-day. Ellen Terry, Helena Modjeska, Ada Rehan, Forbes Robertson, Beerbohm Tree, Julia Marlowe, and Edward Sothern, have been seen at their best in the comedies and tragedies of Shakespeare. Even in the twentieth century, with musical comedies, vaudeville, and moving-pictures to contend with, his plays are presented in greater number than are the plays of any other man who has ever lived. Nor are they revived merely for the sake of sentiment. They draw large audiences of all sorts of people. They still pay as purely business undertakings. "The Merchant of Venice," "Julius Cæsar," "Hamlet," "Macbeth," "Twelfth Night," "As You Like It," "A Midsummer Night's Dream," "Romeo and Juliet," "The Taming of the Shrew," and "The Merry Wives of Windsor" still earn money for actors and theatre-managers as they did three centuries ago. What is far more important, they still give pleasure and amusement, they still stir laughter and tears and awaken the imagination as they did at the Globe in London in the lifetime of their creator.

Shakespeare, we know, wrote his plays to be acted: to him they were distinctly stage productions to be seen and

Shake-
speare's
plays read,
as well as
acted. heard at the theatre. So little did he think of their being read that he apparently had no concern about them in their book form. To-day, on the contrary, though they still are presented on the stage, it is in school and college classrooms, in libraries, and in homes that they are chiefly known. New editions are constantly appearing. Plays and novels that were popular twenty years ago are out of print and difficult to find; the works of Shakespeare, in a dozen different forms, are in every book-store of England and America. Quite apart from their acting qualities, they have come to be regarded as the highest type of literature in our language.

This is not the place to give an extensive criticism of Shakespeare's works, nor a full analysis of the reasons why the world regards them so highly apart from **Why Shake-** their value as stage performances. It will be **speare** enough to remind the student that in nothing **lives.** that has ever been written do we find a clearer or more faithful portrayal of all the varying moods and emotions of human nature. The characters which Shakespeare has created live in our minds both as individuals and as types of the ideal. He strips away the petty things from life and shows us the eternal elements underneath. He has that wonderful and rare quality called universality; for he expresses the thoughts and feelings of us all, — the things which we know to be great and true. Somewhere in his plays everyone finds himself, and the discovery, though he may not realize it at the time, makes a lasting impression. For Shakespeare is the supreme teacher: he suggests, but does not preach, the art of living. Other men have done all this. But Shakespeare has left us his wisdom and his interpretation of life in a more beautiful and stately diction, in phrasing more apt and pleasing, in poetry of greater imaginative power, than has ever come from the mind of man.

More books have been written about Shakespeare than about any other person who ever lived.[1] This is not surpris-

1 For titles of those books on Shakespeare most interesting to students and teachers, see page 182.

ing when we consider that the interest in his plays, which has existed now for three centuries, is world-wide, and when we remember that the language in which he wrote often needs explanation and comment to make it perfectly clear to the average reader to-day. Almost every English and American poet of note has left a tribute to the greatest of all poets. Perhaps the best known are Milton's famous Epitaph, printed on page vii of this volume, and Ben Jonson's lines contributed to the First Folio in 1623, which are given on page 148. Here are a few other short poems or selections from poems, which give honor and praise to those characteristics that have made Shakespeare the inspiration and the guiding-star of poets since Elizabethan times.

JAMES THOMSON

FOR lofty sense,
Creative fancy, and inspection keen
Through the deep windings of the human heart,
Is not wild Shakespeare thine and Nature's boast?

Summer — 1727.

WILLIAM COLLINS

THE temper of our isle, though cold, is clear;
And such our genius, noble though severe.
Our Shakespeare scorn'd the trifling rules of art,
But knew to conquer and surprise the heart!
In magic chains the captive thought to bind,
And fathom all the depths of human kind!

On our Late Taste in Music — 1747.

THOMAS GRAY

FAR from the sun and summer gale
In thy green lap was Nature's Darling laid,
What time, where lucid Avon stray'd,
   To him the mighty mother did unveil
Her awful face: the dauntless child
Stretch'd forth his little arms and smiled.
" This pencil take (she said), whose colours clear
Richly paint the vernal year:
Thine too these golden keys, immortal boy!
This can unlock the gates of joy;
Of horror that, and thrilling fears,
Or ope the sacred source of sympathetic tears."

The Progress of Poesy — 1757.

HENRY ALFORD

WE stood upon the tomb of him whose praise,
   Time, nor oblivious thrift, nor envy chill,
Nor war, nor ocean with her severing space,
   Shall hinder from the peopled world to fill;
And thus, in fulness of our heart, we cried:
   God's works are wonderful — the circling sky,
The rivers that with noiseless footing glide,
   Man's firm-built strength, and woman's liquid eye;
But the high spirit that sleepeth here below,
   More than all beautiful and stately things,
Glory to God the mighty Maker brings;
   To whom alone 'twas given the bounds to know
Of human action, and the secret springs
   Whence the deep streams of joy and sorrow flow.

Stratford-upon-Avon — 1837.

157

Appendix.

ELIZABETH BARRETT BROWNING

THERE Shakespeare, on whose forehead climb
The crowns o' the world : O eyes sublime
With tears and laughter for all time !

A Vision of Poets — 1844.

LEIGH HUNT

. . . HUMANITY's divinest son,
That sprightliest, gravest, wisest, kindest one . . .

Thoughts of the Avon — 1844.

ROBERT BROWNING

— I DECLARE our Poet, him
Whose insight makes all others dim :
A thousand Poets pried at life,
And only one amid the strife
Rose to be Shakespeare.

Christmas Eve and Easter Day — 1850.

HARTLEY COLERIDGE

GREAT poet, 'twas thy art
To know thyself, and in thyself to be
Whate'er love, hate, ambition, destiny,
Or the firm, fatal purpose of the heart,
Can make of Man.   Yet thou wert still the same,
Serene of thought, unhurt by thy own flame.

To Shakespeare — 1851.

WILLIAM WETMORE STORY

. . . SHAKESPEARE, whose strong soul could climb
Steeps of sheer terror, sound the ocean grand
Of Passion's deeps, or over Fancy's strand
Trip with his fairies, keeping step and time.
His, too, the power to laugh out full and clear,
With unembittered joyance, and to move
Along the silent, shadowy paths of love
As tenderly as Dante, whose austere,
Stern spirit through the worlds below, above,
Unsmiling strode, to tell their tidings here.

The Mighty Makers, II — 1851.

MATTHEW ARNOLD

OTHERS abide our question.   Thou art free.
We ask and ask — thou smilest and art still,
Out-topping knowledge.   For the loftiest hill,
Who to the stars uncrowns his majesty,
Planting his steadfast footsteps in the sea,
Making the heaven of heavens his dwelling-place,
Spares but the cloudy border of his base
To the foil'd searching of mortality ;

And thou, who didst the stars and sunbeams know,
Self-school'd, self-scann'd, self-honour'd, self-secure
Didst tread on earth unguess'd at. — Better so !

All pains the immortal spirit must endure,
All weakness which impairs, all griefs which bow,
Find their sole speech in that victorious brow.

Shakespeare — 1867.

159

THE THEATRE OF SHAKESPEARE'S DAY

When Shakespeare left Stratford and went to London theatres were in their infancy. The first one had been **Popularity of the first theatres.** built in 1576, when he was a lad of twelve, and on his arrival in the city there were but three small wooden structures devoted to the production of plays. Enthusiasm for the drama, however, was aglow. With the sanction of Queen Elizabeth, herself a lover of pageants and revels, and under the patronage of the powerful Earls of Leicester, Southampton, and Rutland, the popular demand for this form of amusement grew with amazing rapidity. Theatres shot up one after another until in 1633 there were at least nineteen in London, " a number," says Brandes, " which no modern town of 300,000 inhabitants can equal." Poets, courtiers, scholars, — everyone who could write, — turned to the making of plays. The art which Shakespeare found in its crude and humble beginnings, in the short period of his active life, that is, between 1585 and 1610, developed through every stage to its highest form, so that never in the three hundred years that have since elapsed has the drama of the Elizabethan days been surpassed. In this development Shakespeare was " a pioneer — almost the creator or first designer — as well as the practised workman in unmatched perfection." [1]

Though the first theatre in England was not erected until Shakespeare was twelve years old, long before his time there had been many different kinds of simple plays. The instinct to act out a story had existed from the child-

[1] Sidney Lee: "Shakespeare and the Elizabethan Playgoer."

hood of the race. With the earliest telling of legends and folktales by minstrels and bards there had often been occasion for dramatic recital, dialogue, and action. For centuries, too, there had been the solemn mysteries and quaint old moralities. Mummers and bands of strolling players had **Plays before theatres were built.** wandered over Europe throughout the Middle Ages. The drama, therefore, which flowered in the last half of the sixteenth century, was not a new and sudden birth, but rather came as the natural outgrowth of centuries of crude and humble plays. In the beginning these had been closely connected with the service of the church; in fact, they had been a means of religious instruction rather than a form of amusement. To understand this more clearly, let us compare their origin with that of the Greek drama in earlier ages still.

Many, many centuries before Shakespeare was born,—five or six hundred years B.C.,—the God Dionysus, or Bacchus, was worshipped in Greece at country festivals by boisterous groups of men who chanted and marched and exchanged bantering jests as they danced about the altar and acted out legends connected with the god. These actors, who represented the satyr followers of Dionysus, generally were clad in goatskins, whence we have our word "tragedy," from the Greek *tragos*, a goat, and *tragodia*, a goat-song. From these simple beginnings sprang the drama of Greece, **The religious origin of the Greek drama.** which produced Æschylus, Sophocles, and Euripides. The religious element persisted in ancient times much longer than in England, for the plays of the Greek dramatists who correspond to Shakespeare were still a form of worship. In the center of the orchestra

Appendix.

stood the altar of Dionysus, about which the chorus moved in solemn procession, chanting and reciting; before the performance began there were sacrifices to the god, and the plays were given in the spring on the days of the Dionysian festival. Greek tragedy was therefore not merely an entertainment, but a serious religious function. Beginning as a popular form of Nature worship, it finally became a means of expression for the most serious and finest of Greek thought and wisdom. As it spread from Athens to other towns, little by little it ceased to be a religious affair, until at last, as it gradually lost its vitality and splendor, its relation to the worship of Dionysus entirely disappeared. In similar fashion, comedy (from *comos*, a band of revellers, and *odé*, a song) developed from the ruder, more rustic elements in the worship of the same god, though here, as we might expect, the religious element did not persist as long as it did in its greater and more serious cousin, tragedy.

More than eighteen hundred years later, in England, we find the beginnings of the drama again closely related to **English drama begins in the Church.** worship. At a time when few of the common people could read, the priests in the churches found no method of teaching their congregations the stories of the Bible so effective as the use of objects and pictures which appealed to the eye. The effectiveness of their teaching was enormously increased when they added movement, action, and talk to their picture lessons. Indeed, it was but a step from the impressive and beautiful service of the Mass to a dramatic presentation, in simple form, of the most solemn scenes in religious history. " In this manner the people not only *heard* the story of the Adoration of the Magi and of the

Marriage in Cana, but *saw* the story in tableau. In course of time the persons in these tableaux spoke and moved, and then it was but a logical step to the representation dramatically, by the priests before the altar, of the striking or significant events in the life of Christ."[1]

Thus in the services of the church at Christmas, Good Friday, and Easter were laid the foundations of our modern drama. These earliest performances, which were called Mysteries, dealt wholly with Bible stories, from the Creation to the Day of Judgment, and with the life of Christ; but **The Mysteries and Miracle Plays.** as they became more and more popular with the masses, a broader field of subjects was sought, and lives of saints were used for dramatic material in the Miracle Plays of a century later. Not only were the priests the authors of both these simple forms of drama, but with the choir boys they were also the actors. For many years these plays were given on Holy Days and Saints' Days, either at the altar in the church itself, or in the enclosure just outside its walls. Their object continued to be largely religious instruction. In the Miracle plays, however, there were opportunities for a good deal of grotesque amusement. Incidents in the lives of the saints were not always serious or spiritual. The Devil gradually became more or less of a comic character. As the performances grew less solemn and awe-inspiring, the attitude of the people toward them changed. No longer did they attend them to worship, but rather to see a show and be amused. Gradually, therefore, they became separated from the service of the church, until finally they were banished once for all from the sacred walls, and but a few years after they had been

[1] W. H. Mabie: " William Shakespeare: Poet, Dramatist, and Man."

given at the altar they were being denounced by the priests as base and wicked things. Indeed, the feeling that plays are devices and temptations of Satan, which still exists, may be traced to the time, four centuries ago, when the drama lost favor with the Church.

The Mysteries and Miracle Plays did not decline in popularity when they were abandoned by the various re-
Trade- ligious orders. On the contrary, with the
Guilds and greater freedom and larger opportunity which
the plays. separation from the church gave them, they increased rapidly in the people's favor. They were now taken up by the trade-guilds which, by the fifteenth century, developed elaborate and systematic methods of presenting them. Often different groups of tradesmen, such as the weavers' guild or the goldsmiths' guild, would unite, each band or " company " presenting an act or scene in the play to be undertaken. Huge, two-story covered wagons, somewhat like our large moving-vans to-day, took the place of stage and property-rooms. The actors dressed in the enclosed part of the vehicle, and then mounted a ladder or some rough stairs to the top story, or roof, where they performed their parts. Announced by heralds, — sometimes even by proclamation of the Mayor, — these pageants, as they were called, were drawn through the town on holidays and occasions of special festival. In the course of its progress the moving-stage would stop several times, — at the corners of the principal streets, in a public square, often at the doors of a church or cathedral. Then the crowd which had been following in its wake gathered about it to witness again the drama of Adam and Eve and the Garden of Eden, of Noah, the flood and the ark, of Pilate and Herod, or one of the

numberless other stories with which they had been familiar from childhood.

Miracle Plays and Mysteries were followed by the Moralities in which abstract qualities such as Pleasure, Slander, Rage, Perseverance, and the Seven Deadly Sins took the place of characters from the Bible. This was a long stride forward. **The Moralities.** Now the field of subjects was greatly enlarged. Originality both in writing plays and in producing them was now first in demand. Opportunity had come at last for the creation of character, and for the use of everyday life on the stage. "Everyman," which has often been acted in our time, is a good example of what the Moralities at their best could be. Like the Miracle plays they were generally given by the guilds in marketplaces, enclosures of castles, and inn-yards where people could watch them from windows and balconies, as well as from the ground about the portable stage. Heavy, crude, and dull as these old plays now seem to us, they were intensely enjoyed by the populace of those far-away simpler times. From the eagerness and excitement with which they awaited their coming to town, or travelled long distances to see them, it is evident that a love of acting was inborn in the hearts of the people which sooner or later would develop a more finished and artistic drama.

None of the performers in the Mysteries or Miracle Plays had been professional actors; but now with the Moralities came the opportunity for men to make a business of acting. As religious subjects gradually disappeared from the pageant stage, actors by profession came into existence. Wandering minstrels and story-tellers, mummers **Acting as a profession; companies of actors.**

Appendix.

and strolling players, began to join together in troops for protection and companionship. "From the days of Henry VI onwards, members of the nobility began to entertain these companies of actors, and Henry VII and Henry VIII had their own private comedians. A 'Master of the Revels' was appointed to superintend musical and dramatic entertainments at court." A little later a statute of Parliament declared that "all actors who were not attached to the service of a nobleman should be treated as rogues and vagabonds, or in other words, might be whipped out of any town in which they appeared. This decree, of course, compelled all actors to enter the service of one great man or other, and we see that the aristocracy felt bound to protect their art. A large number of the first men in the kingdom, during Elizabeth's reign, had each his company of actors. The player received from the nobleman, whose 'servant' he was, a cloak bearing the arms of the family. On the other hand, he received no salary, but was simply paid for each performance given before his patron. We must thus conceive Shakespeare as bearing on his cloak the arms of Leicester, and afterwards of the Lord Chamberlain, until about his fortieth year. From 1604 onwards, when the company was promoted by James I to be His Majesty's Servants, it was the Royal arms that he wore."[1]

For many years these companies of professional actors had no regular buildings in which to give their perform-**The first theatres in London.** ances. Their plays were presented before their noble patrons in the great halls of their castles, and occasionally at court for the amusement of the king or queen. As late as Shake-

1 Georg Brandes: "William Shakespeare," page 99.

speare's boyhood they were witnessed by the common people in the yards of taverns, in the open streets, or on village greens. If the actors played in London, either in the guild-halls or out of doors, they first had to obtain a license from the Lord Mayor for each performance, and then they were obliged to surrender half of their receipts to the city treasury. These trying conditions, with the growing popularity of the drama among all classes, finally led in 1576 to the erection of the first building for acting purposes. This was called the Theatre. The following year the Curtain was erected; in 1587, the Rose; in 1594, the Swan; and in 1599, the Globe. Once begun they shot up with wonderful rapidity. When Shakespeare arrived in the city there were but three playhouses; in 1611, when he retired to Stratford, there were probably ten or twelve.

In one sense London even then did not possess a theatre, for the early playhouses were not in the city at all. They were built on a tract of open land The loca-
across the Thames, at the further end of Lon- tion of
don Bridge, outside the walls and well beyond the first
the jurisdiction of the Mayor. The capital theatres.
was then a town of small dimensions, barely a mile square, with a population of nearly 200,000 crowded together in houses which were constructed largely of wood. The streets were narrow, crooked, and muddy. Adequate means of fighting fire and disease did not exist. The Corporation was therefore strongly opposed to the erection of dangerous and inflammable structures upon the few vacant spaces within the walls. Moreover, among the Puritans, who were coming to be a large and influential body, opposition to the drama was growing more marked

and open; so that the companies of actors were obliged to put up their theatres well beyond the reach of the city's laws.

Let us now pay a visit to the Globe, to us the most interesting of all the theatres, for it is here that Shakespeare's company acts, and here many of his **The Globe Theatre: its external appearance.** plays are first seen on the stage. We cross the Thames by London Bridge with its lines of crowded booths and shops and throngs of bustling tradesmen; or if it is fine weather we take a small boat and are rowed over the river to the southern shores. Here on the Bankside, in the part of London now called Southwark, beyond the end of the bridge, and in the open fields near the Bear Garden, stands a roundish, three-story wooden building, so high for its size that it looks more like a clumsy, squatty tower than a theatre. As we draw nearer we see that it is not exactly round after all, but is somewhat hexagonal in shape. The walls seem to slant a little inward, giving it the appearance of a huge thimble, or cocked hat, with six flattened sides instead of a circular surface. There are but few small windows and two low shabby entrances. The whole structure is so dingy and unattractive that we stand before it in wonder. Can this be the place where "Hamlet," "The Merchant of Venice," and "Julius Cæsar" are put on the stage!

Our amazement on stepping inside is even greater. The first thing that astonishes us is the blue sky over our **The Globe Theatre: the interior.** heads. The building has no roof except a narrow strip around the edge and a covering at the rear over the back part of the stage. The front of the stage and the whole center of the theatre is open to the air. Now we see how the in-

THE GLOBE THEATRE

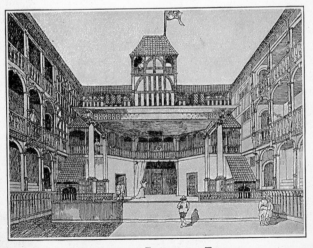

INTERIOR OF AN ELIZABETHAN THEATRE

Godfrey's reconstruction of the Fortune Theatre

terior is lighted, though with the sunshine must often come rain and sleet and London fog. Looking up and out at the clouds floating by, we notice that a flag is flying from a short pole on the roof over the stage. This is most important, for it is announcing to the city across the river that this afternoon there is to be a play. It is bill-board, newspaper notice, and advertisement in one: and we may imagine the eagerness with which it is looked for among the theatre-loving populace of these later Elizabethan years. When the performance begins the flag will be lowered to proclaim to all that "the play is on."

Where, now, shall we sit? Before us on the ground level is a large open space, which corresponds to the orchestra circle on the floor of a modern play-house. But here there is only the flat bare earth, trodden down hard, with rushes and straw scattered over it. There is not a sign of a seat! This is the "yard," or, as it is sometimes called, "the pit," where, by paying a penny or two, London apprentices, sailors, laborers, and the mixed crowd from the streets may stand jostling together. Some of the more enterprising ones may possibly sit on boxes and stools which they bring into the building with them. Among these "groundlings" there will surely be bustling confusion, noisy wrangling, and plenty of danger from pickpockets; so we look about us to find a more comfortable place from which to watch the performance.

Seating arrangements in the theatre: the pit.

On three sides of us, and extending well around the stage, are three tiers of narrow balconies. In some places these are divided into compartments, or boxes. The prices here are higher, varying from a few pennies to half a crown, according to

The balconies and boxes.

Appendix.

the location. By putting our money into a box held out to us, — there are no tickets, — we are allowed to climb the crooked wooden stairs to one of these compartments. Here we find rough benches and chairs, and above all a little seclusion from the throng of men and boys below. Along the edge of the stage we observe that there are stools, but these places, elevated and facing the audience, seem rather conspicuous, and besides the prices are high. They will be taken by the young gallants and men of fashion of London, in brave and brilliant clothes, with light swords at their belts, wide ruffled collars about their necks, and gay plumes in their hats. It will be amusing to see them show off their fine apparel, and display their wit at the expense of the groundlings in the pit, and even of the actors themselves. We are safer, however, and much more comfortable here in the balcony among the more sober, quiet gentlemen of London, who with me-chanics, tradesmen, nobles, and shop-keepers have come to see the play.

The moment we entered the theatre we were impressed by the size of the stage. Looking down upon it from the balcony, it seems even larger and very near us.

The stage. If it is like the stage of the Fortune it is square, as shown in the illustration facing page 168. Here in the Globe it is probably narrower at the front than at the back, tapering from the rear wall almost to a point. Whatever its shape, it is only a roughly-built, high platform, open on three sides, and extending halfway into the "yard." Though a low railing runs about its edge, there are no footlights, — all performances are in the afternoon by the light of day which streams down through the open top, — and strangest of all there is no curtain. At each side of the rear we can see a door that leads to the "tiring-rooms," where the actors dress, and from which they make their entrances. These are the "green-rooms" and wings of our theatre to-day. Between the doors is a curtain that now before the play begins is drawn together. Later when it is pulled aside, — not *upward* as curtains usually are now, — we shall see a shallow recess or alcove which serves as a secondary, or inner stage. Over this extends a narrow balcony covered by a roof which is supported at the front corners by two columns that stand well out from the wall. Still higher up, over the inner stage, is a sort of tower, sometimes called the "hut," and from a pole on this the flag is flying which summons the London populace from across the Thames. Rushes are strewn over the floor; there are no drops or wings or walls of painted scenery. In its simplicity and bareness it reminds us of the rude stage of the strolling players. Indeed, the whole interior of the building seems to be but an adaptation of the tavern-yard and village-green.

How, we wonder, can a play like "Julius Cæsar" or "The Merchant of Venice" be staged on such a crude affair as this! What are the various parts of it for? Practically all acting is done, we shall see, on the front of the platform well out **Use of the main stage.** among the crowd in the pit, with the audience on three sides of the performers. All out-of-door scenes will be acted here, from a conversation in the streets of Venice or a dialogue in a garden, to a battle, a procession, or a banquet in the Forest of Arden. Here, too, with but the slightest alteration, or even with no change at all, interior scenes will be presented. With the "groundlings" crowded close up to its edges, and with young gallants

Appendix.

sitting on its sides, this outer stage comes close to the people. On it will be all the main action of the drama: the various arrangements at the rear are for supplementary purposes and certain important effects.

The inner stage, or alcove beyond the curtain, is used in many ways. It may serve for any room somewhat removed from the scene of action, such as a **Uses of the inner stage.** passage-way or a study. It often is made to represent a cave, a shop, or a prison. Here Othello, in a frenzy of jealous passion, strangles Desdemona as she lies in bed; here probably the ghost of Caesar appears to Brutus in his tent on the plains of Philippi; here stand the three fateful caskets in the mansion at Belmont, as we see by Portia's words,

> "Go, *draw aside the curtains*, and discover
> The several caskets to this noble Prince."

Tableaux and scenes within scenes, such as the short play in "Hamlet" by which the prince "catches the conscience of the king," are acted in this recess. But the most important use is to give the effect of a change of scene. By drawing apart and closing the curtain, with a few simple changes of properties in this inner compartment, a different background is possible. By such a slight variation of setting at the rear, the platform in the pit is transformed, by the quick imagination of the spectators, from a field or a street to a castle hall or a wood. Thus, the whole stage becomes the Forest of Arden by the use of a little greenery in the distance. Similarly, a few trees and shrubs at the rear of the inner stage, when the curtain is thrown aside, will change the setting from the court-room in the fourth act of "The Merchant of Venice," to the scene in the garden at Belmont which immediately follows.

The balcony over the inner stage serves an important purpose, too. With the windows, which are often just over the doors leading to the tiring-rooms, it gives the effect of an upper story in a house, of walls in a castle, a tower, or any elevated position. This is the place, of course, where Juliet comes to greet Romeo who is in the garden below. In "Julius Cæsar" when Cassius says,

Uses of the balcony over the stage.

> "Go Pindarus, *get higher on that hill;*
>
> *   *   *   *   *   *
>
> And tell me what thou notest about the field,"

the soldier undoubtedly climbs to the balcony, for a moment later, looking abroad over the field of battle, he reports to Cassius what he sees from his elevation. Here Jessica appears when Lorenzo calls under Shylock's windows, "Ho! who's within?" and on this balcony she is standing when she throws down to her lover a box of her father's jewels. "Here, catch this casket; it is worth the pains," she says, and retires into the house, appearing below a moment later to run away with Lorenzo and his masquerading companions.

Besides these simple devices, if we look closely enough we shall see a trap-door, or perhaps two, in the platform. These are for the entrance of apparitions and demons. They correspond, in a way, to the balcony by giving the effect of a place lower than the stage level. Thus in the first scene of "The Tempest," which takes place in a storm at sea, the notion of a ship may be suggested to the audience by sailors

Other stage devices.

Appendix.

entering from the trap-door, as they might come up a hatchway to a deck. If it is a play with gods and goddesses and spirits, we may be startled to see them appear and disappear through the air. Evidently there is machinery of some sort in the hut over the balcony which can be used for lowering and raising deities and creatures that live above the earth. On each side of the stage is a flight of steps leading to the balcony. These are often covered, as plainly shown by Mr. Godfrey's reconstruction of the Fortune Theatre facing page 168. Here sit councils, senates, and princes with their courts. Macbeth uses them to give the impression of ascending to an upper chamber when he goes to kill the king, and down them he rushes to his wife after he has committed the fearful murder.

What astonishes us most, however, is the absence of scenery. To be sure, some slight attempt has been made to create scenic illusion. There are, perhaps, a few trees and boulders, a table, a chair or two, and pasteboard dishes of food. But there is little more. In the only drawing of the interior of an Elizabethan theatre that has been preserved, — a sketch of the Swan made in 1596, — the stage has absolutely no furniture except one plain bench on which one of the actors is sitting. Here before us in the Globe the walls may be covered with loose tapestries, black if the play is to be a tragedy, blue if a comedy ; but it is quite possible that they are entirely bare. A placard on one of the pillars announces that the stage is now a street in Venice, now a courtroom, now the hall of a stately mansion. It may be that the Prologue, or even the actors themselves, will tell us at the opening of an act just where the scene is laid and what we are to imagine the platform to represent.

Scenery on the stage.

In "Henry V," for instance, the Prologue at the beginning not only explains the setting of the play, but asks
forgiveness of the audience for attempting to put on the
stage armies and battles and the "vasty fields of France."

> " But pardon, gentles all,
> The flat unraiséd spirit that hath dared
> On this unworthy scaffold to bring forth
> So great an object. Can this cockpit hold
> The vasty fields of France? or may we cram
> Within *this wooden O* the very casques
> That did affright the air at Agincourt?
> O, pardon! since a crooked figure may
> Attest in little place a million;
> And let us, ciphers to this great accompt,
> On your imaginary forces work.
> Suppose within the girdle of these walls
> Are now confined two mighty monarchies,
> Whose high-uprearéd and abutting fronts
> The perilous, narrow ocean parts asunder.
> Piece out our imperfections with your thoughts;
> Into a thousand parts divide one man,
> And make imaginary puissance.
> Think, when we talk of horses, that you see them
> Printing their proud hoofs i' the receiving earth,
> For 'tis your thoughts that now must deck our kings,
> Carry them here and there, jumping o'er times,
> Turning the accomplishment of many years
> Into an hour-glass."

In "As You Like It" it is an actor who tells us at the
opening of the second act that we are now to imagine the
Forest of Arden before us. In the first sentence which

the banished Duke speaks, he says, " Are not *these woods* more free from peril than the envious court ? " and a moment later, when Touchstone and the runaway maidens first enter the woods, Rosalind exclaims, " Well, this is the Forest of Arden ! " A hint, a reference, a few simple contrivances, a placard or two, — these are enough. " Imaginary forces " are here in the audience keenly alive, and they will do the rest. By means of them, without the illusion of scenery, the bare wooden stage will become a ship, a garden, a palace, a London tavern. Whole armies will enter and retire by a single door. Battles will rage, royal processions pass in and out, graves will be dug, lovers will woo, — and all with hardly an important alteration of the setting. Lack of scenery does not limit the type of scenes that can be presented. On the contrary, it gives almost unlimited opportunities to the dramatist, for the spectators, in the force and freshness of their imagination, are children who willingly " play " that the stage is anything the author suggests. Their youthful enthusiasm, their simple tastes, above all their lack of knowledge of anything different, give them the enviable power of imagining the grandest, most beautiful, and most varied scenes on the same bare, unadorned boards. Apparently they are well satisfied with their stage ; for it is not until nearly fifty years after Shakespeare's death that movable scenery is used in an English theatre.

It is now three o'clock and time for the performance to begin. Among the motley crowd of men and boys in the **The performance of a play.** yard there is no longer room for another box or stool. They are evidently growing impatient and jostle together in noisy confusion. Suddenly three long blasts on a trumpet sound. The mutterings in the pit subside, and all eyes turn toward the stage. First an actor, clothed in a black mantle and wearing a laurel wreath on his head, comes from behind the curtain and recites the prologue. From it we learn something of the story of the play to follow, and possibly a little about the scene of action. This is all very welcome, for we have no programs and the plot of the drama is unfamiliar. In a minute or two the Prologue retires and the actors of the first scene enter. We are soon impressed by the rapidity with which the play moves on. There is little stage "business"; though there may be some music between the acts, still there are no long waits; one scene follows another as quickly as the actors can make their exits and entrances. The whole play, there. fore, does not last much over two hours. At the close there is an epilogue, spoken by one of the actors, after which the players kneel and join in a prayer for the queen. Then comes a final bit of amusement for the groundlings: the clown, or some other comic character of the company, sings a popular song, dances a brisk and boisterous jig, and the performance of the day is done.

During our novel experience this afternoon at the Globe, nothing has probably surprised us more than the elaborate and gorgeous costumes of the actors. **Costumes** At a time when so little attention is paid to **of the** scenery we naturally expect to find the dress **actors.** of the players equally simple and plain. But we are mistaken. The costumes, to be sure, make little or no pretension to fit the period or place of action. Cæsar appears in clothes such as are worn by a duke or an earl in 1601. "They are the ordinary dresses of various classes of the day, but they are often of rich material, and

177

in the height of current fashion. False hair and beards, crowns and sceptres, mitres and croziers, armour, helmets, shields, vizors, and weapons of war, hoods, bands, and cassocks, are relied on to indicate among the characters differences of rank or profession. The foreign observer, Thomas Platter of Basle, was impressed by the splendor of the actors' costumes. 'The players wear the most costly and beautiful dresses, for it is the custom in England, that when noblemen or knights die, they leave their finest clothes to their servants, who, since it would not be fitting for them to wear such splendid garments, sell them soon afterwards to the players for a small sum.'"[1] But no money is spared to secure the fitting garment for an important part. Indeed, it is quite probable that more is paid for a king's velvet robe or a prince's silken doublet than is given to the author for the play itself. Whether the elaborate costumes are appropriate or not, their general effect is pleasing, for they give variety and brilliant color to the bare and unattractive stage.

If we are happily surprised by the costuming of the play, what shall we say of the actors who take the female **Female parts taken by boys.** parts! They are very evidently not women, or even girls, but boys whose voices have not changed, dressed, tricked out, and trained to appear as feminine as possible. It is considered unseemly for a woman to appear on a public stage, — indeed, the professional actress does not exist and will not be seen in an English theatre for nearly a century. Meanwhile plays are written with few female parts (remember "The Merchant of Venice," "Julius Cæsar," and "Macbeth") and young boys are trained to take these

[1] Sidney Lee: "Shakespeare and the Modern Stage," page 41.

rôles. The theatregoers seem to enjoy the performance just as much as we do to-day with mature and accomplished actresses on the stage. Shakespeare and his fellow dramatists treated the situation with good grace or indifference. Thus in the epilogue of "As You Like It" Rosalind says to the audience, "*If I were a woman* I would kiss as many of you as had beards that pleased me." The jest, of course, consists in the fact that she is *not* a woman at all, but a stripling. In a more tragic vein Cleopatra, before she dies, complains that "the quick comedians . . . will stage us, . . . and I shall see some *squeaking Cleopatra boy my* greatness." It may be that the boys who take the women's parts this afternoon wear masks to make them seem less masculine, though how that can improve the situation it is difficult to understand. There is an amusing reference to this practice in "A Midsummer Night's Dream." When Flute, the bellows-mender, is assigned a part in the drama which the mechanics of Athens are rehearsing, he exclaims, "Nay, faith, let me not play a woman; I have a beard coming"; to which protest Quince replies, "That's all one: you shall play it *in a mask*, and you may speak as small as you will."

Though rapid action, brilliant costumes, and, above all, the force and beauty of the lines, may lead us to forget that the heroine is only a boy, it is more difficult to keep our attention from being distracted by the audience around us. It surprises us that there are so few women present. We notice, too, that many of those who have come wear a mask of silk or velvet over their faces. Evidently it is hardly the proper thing for a respectable woman to be seen in a public theatre. The people in the balconies are fairly orderly, but below in the pit the crowd is restless, noisy, and at times even boisterous. Bricklayers, dock-laborers, apprentices, serving-men, and idlers stand in jostling confusion. There are no police and no laws that are enforced. Pickpockets ply an active trade. One, we see, has been caught and is bound to the railing at the edge of the stage where he is an object of coarse jests and ridicule. Refreshment-sellers push about in the throng with apples and sausages, nuts and ale. There is much eating and drinking and plenty of smoking. On the stage the gallants are a constant source of bother to the players. They interrupt the Prologue, criticise the dress of the hero, banter the heroine, and joke with the clown. Even here in the gallery we can hear their comments — far from flattering — upon a scene that does not please them; when a little later they applaud, their praises are just as vigorous. Once it seems as though the play is going to be brought to a standstill by a wrangling quarrel between one of these rakish gentlemen and a group of groundlings near the stage. Their attention, however, is taken by the entrance of the leading actor declaiming a stirring passage, and their differences are soon forgotten. It is, on the whole, a good-natured rough crowd of the common people, the lower and middle classes from the great city across the river, — more like the crowd one sees to-day at a circus or a professional ball-game than at a theatre of the highest type. They loudly cheer the clown's final song and dance, and then with laughter, shouting, and jesting they pour out of the yard and in a moment the building is empty. The play is over until to-morrow afternoon.

What a contrast it all has been to a play in a theatre of

the twentieth century! When we think of the uncomfortable benches, the flat bare earth of the pit, the lack of scenery, footlights, and drop curtains; when we hear the shrill voices of boys piping the women's parts, and see mist and rain falling on spectator's heads, we are inclined to pity the playgoer of Elizabethan **Conclusions** times. Yet he needs no pity. To him the **to be** theatre of his day was sufficient. The drama **drawn.** enacted there was a source of intense and genuine pleasure. His keen enthusiasm; his fresh, youthful eagerness; above all, his highly imaginative power, — far greater than ours to-day, — gave him an ability to understand and enjoy the poetry and dramatic force of Shakespeare's works, which we, with all the improvements of our palatial theatres, cannot equal. Crude, simple, coarse as they now seem to us, we can look back only with admiration upon the Swan and the Curtain and the Globe; for in them "The Merchant of Venice," "As You Like It," "Julius Cæsar," "Hamlet," and "Macbeth" were received with acclamations of joy and wonder. In them the genius of Shakespeare was recognized and given a place in the drama of England which now, after three centuries have passed, it holds in the theatres and in the literature of all the world.

BOOKS OF INTEREST TO STUDENTS OF SHAKESPEARE

[A bibliography of works on Shakespeare would make a volume of considerable size. Here are a few of the most useful books for students and teachers.]

William Shakespeare : A Critical Study.

GEORGE BRANDES. The Macmillan Co.

A Life of William Shakespeare.

SIDNEY LEE. The Macmillan Co.

The Facts about Shakespeare.

NEILSON AND THORNDIKE. The Macmillan Co.

William Shakespeare : Poet, Dramatist, and Man.

H. W. MABIE. The Macmillan Co.

Shakespeare and the Modern Stage.

SIDNEY LEE. Charles Scribner's Sons.

Introduction to Shakespeare.

EDWARD DOWDEN. Charles Scribner's Sons.

Shakespeare.

WALTER RALEIGH. The Macmillan Co.

William Shakespeare.

JOHN MASEFIELD. Henry Holt & Co.

Shakespeare : The Boy.

W. J. ROLFE. Harper Bros.

Handbook to the Works of Shakespeare.

MORTON LUCE. George Bell & Sons.

Shakespeare: his Life, Art, and Characters.
REV. H. N. HUDSON.   Ginn & Co.

Shakespeare's England.
WILLIAM WINTER.   Moffat, Yard & Co.

Shakespeare Manual.
F. G. FLEAY.   The Macmillan Co.

An interesting story of Shakespeare's times is *Master Skylark*, by JOHN BENNETT, published by The Century Company.

Scott's *Kenilworth* is a story of London and Warwickshire in 1575, and *The Fortunes of Nigel* gives a good picture of London in 1604, the year of "Othello."

EXPLANATORY NOTES

DRAMATIS PERSONÆ = *persons of the drama ; the cast.*

In the folio of 1623, which was the earliest edition of "Julius Cæsar," there is no list of *dramatis personæ*, and the acts are not divided into scenes. These additions, with many of the stage directions, are the work of later editors.

triumvirs. Three men united in public office or authority. In Roman history the alliance of Pompey, Cæsar, and Crassus in 60 B.C. is known as the First Triumvirate. A similar alliance in 43 B.C. of Octavius Cæsar, Antonius, and Lepidus is called the Second Triumvirate, and each member a *triumvir*.

ACT I

The subject of the play, it must be understood from the beginning, is *Marcus Brutus*.

The idea of a conspiracy against Cæsar's life is shown in the first act as originating in the mind of Cassius on grounds of personal enmity, and as finding acceptance in the mind of Brutus on grounds of concern for the public welfare. The deliberate, conscientious meditation of Brutus on the awful step he contemplates as the means of freeing Rome from tyranny, is contrasted with the ardor and the trickery with which Cassius and Casca apply themselves to the furtherance of the plot, and chiefly to the securing of Brutus as its leader. The sum and substance of the act is expressed in the last eight lines of the last scene.

Casca. O, he (*i.e.* Brutus) sits high in all the people's hearts :
    And that which would appear offence in us
    His countenance, like richest alchemy,
    Will change to virtue and to worthiness.

Cas.   Him and his worth and our great need of him
        You have right well conceited. Let us go,
        For it is after midnight; and ere day
        We will awake him and be sure of him.

                               (I, 3, 157-164.)

Scene 1

All the actors in this scene disappear from the play with the end of the scene itself. Tribunes and commoners, they are not *personæ* of the drama at all, but speak their brief parts as types of the social divisions and the political animosities of the Rome of Cæsar's time. What the historian would require pages to tell and explain the poet in a few lines reveals to us as a picture. The commoners are nameless, as they are in the records of history, and have to be distinguished by being numbered; they are witty, good-natured, coarse of speech, incapable of high political principle. But they represent the physical strength of Rome because they are a multitude and will follow devotedly a leader who wins them to his side. Whoever aspires to control Rome must be popular with the commons, and the commons have been won by Cæsar. The tribunes stand by the lost cause of Pompey. The tribunes represent patrician conservatism; they are imperious and full of dignity; their speech is warmed with noble sentiment; they typify Roman patriotism.

Rome. A Street. The scene opens on the feast of the Lupercalia, February 15, in the year 44 B.C. The period of action extends to the battle of Philippi, in the autumn of 42 B.C.

Commoners: common people, tradesmen.

LINE **3. being mechanical**: being mechanics, workmen.

4, 5. the sign of your profession: the regular clothes and badges of your trades. Shakespeare transfers to Rome the customs of the English guilds, or bands of tradesmen, of his day.

5. what trade art thou? "**Of**" is omitted, as again in line 9, and as was "to" in line 3.

1-5. Flavius and Marullus would seem in this passage, lines 1-5, to be enforcing a Roman law; but the existence of such a law is an invention of the poet, who perhaps transfers to Rome a usage of his own country. It must be remembered that Shakespeare got his knowledge of history from very limited reading, and had no conception of nice scholarly scruples about mingling features of ancient and modern times. It may be said, generally, that the plays give evidence of wide observation, but not of exact learning.

9. in respect of: in comparison with.

10. a cobbler: a clumsy workman; a "botcher." The word in Shakespeare's time did not necessarily refer to a mender of shoes. Marullus therefore repeats his question.

11. directly: without evasion, in a straightforward manner.

13. a mender of bad soles. The Second Commoner is a witty fellow, who evidently delights in plaguing Marullus with his puns. Already he has played upon the double meaning of *cobbler*; here he does the same with *soles* (souls), and a moment later he is at it again. Punning was evidently considered a high form of wit in 1600; indeed from its frequent occurrence in Shakespeare's plays and those of his fellow dramatists, it seems to have been a genuine source of amusement to the Elizabethan audience.

14. knave: rascal, rogue.

16. be not out with me: be not at odds or angry with me. Playing upon the word, in the next line the cobbler uses "out" in the sense of "out at the toes."

23. awl. The small, slender tool used by cobblers for making holes in leather. Here, and again in "recover" two lines below, the commoner is teasing Marullus with word quibbles.

26. proper: handsome, goodly. In "The Merchant of Venice" Portia says of Falconbridge, "He is a *proper* man's picture." **neat's-leather:** ox-hide, cow-hide.

32. in his triumph. This was Cæsar's fifth and last triumph, given him in honor of his victory over the sons of Pompey at the battle of Munda in Spain. A Roman "triumph" was a celebration, with processions and religious ceremonies, given to a returning victor.

34. tributaries: persons who pay tribute, dependents. One of the features of a Roman general's "triumph" was the procession of captives, bound to his chariot and dragged through the streets of the capital.

38. Pompey. Three years earlier than this, Cæsar had overthrown Pompey at the battle of Pharsalia.

43. pass the streets. Notice throughout the play the frequent omission of prepositions. (See lines 3 and 5 above.)

46. That: so that, — an ellipsis common in Shakespeare.

47. To hear the replication: at hearing the echo.

48. her concave shores: her hollowed, rounded banks. The Romans personified rivers as masculine: the Tiber to them was "Father Tiber"; but writers of Shakespeare's time more frequently thought of rivers as feminine. So in the next scene we find, "The troubled Tiber, chafing with her shores." The poet uses the neuter possessive "its" only ten times in all his works, and it does not occur once in the King James Bible, translated in 1611.

50. cull out: pick out. "Is this the time to choose for a holiday?"

52. Pompey's blood: Pompey's sons, whom Cæsar had defeated in the battle of Munda. One of them, Cnæus, had been slain.

55. intermit the plague: avert or moderate the pestilence. The fearful plagues which swept over Europe in the Middle Ages, and which lasted well through the seventeenth century, were often regarded as a form of divine punishment for human sins.

56. needs: of necessity. In "The Merchant" Lorenzo says, "I must *needs* tell thee all."

60. till the lowest stream, etc.: "till your tears swell the river from the extreme low-water mark to the extreme high-water mark" (Hudson). This sort of exaggeration, or hyperbole, is not uncommon in the plays.

62. metal: spirit, — a favorite word with Shakespeare in this sense.

65. the images. That is, Cæsar's statues and busts, which were adorned with "ceremonies," or scarfs and decorations.

68. Lupercal. The Lupercalia was a festival celebrated in Rome on February 15, in honor of Lupercus, a god closely identified with the Greek Pan. From another name of Lupercus, *Februus*, comes our word February.

71. the vulgar: the common people, — the original meaning of the word. (LAT. *vulgus*, common people.)

74. pitch: height. The figure in these lines is taken from the sport of hawking, or falconry. Removing the scarfs from Cæsar's images is thus compared to plucking feathers from the wings of a falcon to prevent its flying too far and too high. (Compare our words *high-flyer* and *high-flown*.)

76. servile fearfulness: slavish terror.   **Exeunt:** they go out, — the plural of *exit*.

QUESTIONS AND TOPICS FOR DISCUSSION

1. What is the purpose, in your judgment, of the conflict between the tribunes and the mob at the opening of the play?

2. How does this opening foreshadow events that are to follow?

3. What is there humorous in this scene?

4. Are your sympathies with the tribunes or with the commoners? Why?

5. Why does the poet have the tribunes speak in verse, the commoners in prose?

6. What ideals of Roman citizenship are represented by the tribunes in their tirade against the mob?

7. Why do you think Shakespeare does not attempt to distinguish the characters of Marullus and Flavius?

8. What is there eloquent and poetic in the speech of Marullus beginning, "Wherefore rejoice"? Which lines of this speech do you like best?

189

9. If you were to stage this scene to-day how would you arrange the setting? What action and by-play would you have before Flavius first speaks? During the long speeches of the tribunes?

10. Why not omit this scene altogether? What would be lost? Do you think it is used in modern presentations of Julius Cæsar?

ACT I

Scene 2

With the second scene all the great characters are introduced. First is *Marcus Brutus*, the hero of the tragedy. Although the play bears the name of Julius Cæsar, Brutus is the veritable hero of it, for it is his fate that furnishes the motive for the entire piece, his is the only figure that moves to its tragic exit in unbroken dignity and majesty. With not a single touch does the poet derogate from the impression of moral greatness which he means we shall form of his Brutus. In his conception of Brutus' character he follows Plutarch, but goes further than his authority, as was dramatically right, and as he has done with the other chief persons of the drama, notably with Cæsar.

The main motive of the tragedy, — the essentially tragical point of it, — is the mistake of Brutus in undertaking a task for which his moral nature renders him unfit. The assassination of Cæsar is, in the play, incidental to the development of the career of Brutus. Brutus commands deference from all; and Cassius, who is Brutus's superior in practical sagacity, cheerfully yields to him in matters of crucial moment, being overawed by his commanding force of character. This force of personal character, joined with a reputation for absolute integrity of purpose, makes Brutus the natural leader of the men of his own rank with whom he is brought into contact. He stands well with the mob also, but does not make sufficient allowance for its fickleness, and foolishly imputes to it something of his own constancy and sense of honor.

As Shakespeare is not writing history or chronicle, but drama, — though indeed he is dramatizing a chapter of history, — he is no more bound to observe the exact proportions of character as these may be deduced from the records, than he is to respect the unities of time and place. For his present purpose he wished to enlarge and idealize Brutus, and to obscure and vulgarize Cæsar. For this procedure with regard to Cæsar he found a shadow of warrant in his historian. Plutarch is a gossip, by no means always careful to tell of his heroes only the grand achievements by which they won renown. Cæsar appears in his pages quite subject to the infirmities of human nature. The poet finds this aspect of the great dictator suitable to his purpose, exaggerates it in accordance with dramatic custom, — and so gives us his Julius Cæsar.

ANTONY, *for the course.* That is, ready to run the course: undressed.

SOOTHSAYER. One who claims to have supernatural foresight; a prophet or diviner. Literally, one who "says sooth," *i.e.* "tells the truth."

3. **in Antonius' way.** It was the custom at the Lupercalia for the priests to run through the streets of Rome, waving leather thongs and striking any whom they passed. Marcus Antonius at this time was at the head of one of the bands of *Luperci.*

8. **The barren.** Cæsar at this time had no children. His only daughter, Julia, who was the wife of Pompey, had died a few years before.

9. **sterile curse**: the curse of childlessness.

11. **Set on**: move on, start.

18. **ides of March**: March 15th.

24. **pass**: let us pass on. **Sennet.** A peculiar set of notes on the trumpet which Shakespeare frequently uses as a signal for a march, or to accompany a royal procession.

25. **the order of the course.** That is, the running of the priests in the streets.

28. gamesome : fond of games.

29. quickspirit : lively, gay spirit. (Compare "quick" here with *quick*silver, and with the word in the expression, " the *quick* and the dead.")

32. I do observe, etc. "I have been noticing you lately, Brutus, and," etc.

34. show : evidence. **as** : which, or "such as." **wont** : accustomed.

35. You bear too stubborn, etc. "You treat your friend too harshly and unfamiliarly." The picture is of a man driving a horse with too tight and too harsh a rein.

" This man, Caius Cassius Longinus, had married Junia, a sister of Brutus. Both had lately stood for the chief Prætorship of the city, and Brutus, through Cæsar's favor, had won it. . . . This is said to have produced a coldness between Brutus and Cassius, so that they did not speak to each other, till this extraordinary flight of patriotism brought them together." (Hudson.)

39. Merely : wholly, altogether.

40. passions of some difference : fluctuating, contradictory feelings ; a " discord of emotions."

41. only proper to myself : belonging exclusively to me ; peculiar to me alone.

42. give some soil . . . to : soil, tarnish, blemish. **behaviors** : manners, actions. Such plurals of abstract nouns are not uncommon in Shakespeare. Here it has the effect of repetition, or "behavior on several occasions." (Cf. line 133 below.)

45. cónstrue : explain, interpret. This word is always accented on the first syllable in Shakespeare's plays. Notice also " misconstrued " in " The Merchant of Venice " II, ii, 178 : " I be miscónstrued in the place I go to."

48. mistook your passion : misunderstood your feelings. Similarly Shakespeare has " spoke " for " spoken," " wrote " for " written," etc. (Cf. II, i, 125.)

49. By means whereof : because of which.

50. cogitations : thoughts.

53. But by reflection, etc. That is, the eye can see itself only by reflection in a mirror or some other polished surface.

54. 'Tis just: that is true; "that's so."

58. shadow: reflected image, reflection.

59. Where. Used loosely for "when" or "that," — much as we sometimes say, "I read in the paper *where* the governor," etc. **many of the best respect:** many of the most highly respected men in Rome.

66. Therefore. Ignoring Brutus's question, Cassius refers here to the wish which he has heard expressed, and which he is going to answer by what follows.

69. Will modestly discover: will disclose to you without exaggeration that side of yourself, etc.

71. jealous on me: doubtful, suspicious of me. In line 162 Brutus says: "That you do love me I am nothing *jealous*."

72. laugher: buffoon, jester. In the Folio editions of the play the word here is "laughter," which would mean "object of laughter or scorn." The change to "laugher," which was made by Pope in the 18th century, has generally been accepted. Do you feel, however, that perhaps the change was not necessary after all?

72, 73. did use to stale, etc. "were I accustomed to cheapen my love with too frequent oaths."

74. every new protester: every new claimant for my friendship.

75, 76. fawn on men, etc. "If you know that I am one who flatters men, holds them close to my heart, and afterwards defames them." Shakespeare often uses a noun as a verb in a strikingly forceful way, as "scandal" in this passage.

77. I profess myself, etc. "If I declare myself, when at banquets, a friend to all the company, then you should regard me as a dangerous flatterer." "Rout" of course is used contemptuously, as we might speak of "the mob," "the crowd," "the common herd." **Flourish.** This was probably a few notes on a trumpet. (See opening stage directions of this scene, and compare "Sennet" in line 24.)

80. How should this line be read to show Cassius' meaning?

85. the general good: the good of the community, the common weal.

86. Set honor, etc. "I will look upon honor and death together without emotion."

88. speed: prosper, bless.

91. your outward favor: your face, personal appearance. In this sense we still use "ill-favored," and in some parts of America we have now and then such an expression as "she *favors* her mother," meaning "she looks like her mother."

95. lief. To bring out clearly the play on "live," which Shakespeare undoubtedly intended, we should pronounce this word "lieve."

101. chafing with: rubbing against. (Any large dictionary will explain the interesting connection between this word and "chauffeur" and "chafing-dish.")

104. And swim to yonder point. This incident, apparently invented by Shakespeare, may have been suggested to him by Plutarch's statement that Cæsar was a great swimmer.

105. Accoutred: dressed, clothed.

108. With lusty sinews: with vigorous muscles.

109. stemming it: making headway against it. **hearts of controversy:** contending hearts, courage that contended against the torrent. Similar constructions are common in Shakespeare, as "passions of difference" in line 40 above, "thieves of mercy" for "merciful thieves," "mind of love" for "loving mind."

110. arrive the point. Point out other places where you have already noticed similar omissions of prepositions.

112. Æneas. According to the legend, the Trojan hero Æneas was the son of Anchises and Venus. The story of his wanderings, after the Greeks had sacked Troy, and his founding of Rome, is told in Vergil's great epic poem, the "Æneid."

119. He had a fever. This incident again was probably suggested by Plutarch's life of Cæsar: " . . . the falling sickness (the which took him the first time, as it is reported, in Cordoba, a city of Spain)."

122. His coward lips, etc. That is, "the color fled from his lips." The picture is evidently of cowardly soldiers fleeing from their colors, or their flag.

123. whose bend: whose inclination, frown.

124. his lustre: its brightness. (See note on "her shores," I, 1, 50.)

126. Mark: notice.

129. temper: nature, constitution, temperament. In "The Merchant" Portia says that "a hot *temper* leaps o'er a cold decree."

130, 131. So get the start, etc. The figure is from the running of a foot-race.

133. these applauses. Remember the plural "behaviors" in line 42 above.

136. Colossus. A gigantic bronze statue of Apollo erected in 280 B.C. on the shore of the harbor at Rhodes, and known as one of the "seven wonders of the world." Cassius here uses the word "bestride" because of the tradition that the statue stood astride the mouth of the harbor, so that ships sailed "under his huge legs." Why does he speak of the world as *narrow?*

140. our stars. That is, the planets that govern our lives. The plays of Shakespeare abound with references to the belief of his time that men's fortunes were controlled by the stars and planets. (Look up "astrology.")

141. underlings: inferiors, servile persons. Note the force of the ending *-ling* in these words: "hireling," "groundling," "changeling," "starling."

146. conjure with 'em, etc. That is, use them as means of summoning up, or "starting," spirits.

150. Age: the times, "the age in which we live."

152. the great flood. Not the flood of Noah and the Ark, but the great flood of Greek mythology from which Deucalion and Pyrrha were the sole survivors.

156. Rome indeed and room enough. We can understand Cassius' play upon words here when we remember that "Rome," in Shakespeare's time, was pronounced almost exactly like "room."

159. a Brutus. This was Lucius Junius Brutus who drove the tyrant Tarquin from Rome, and led in reëstablishing the republic. Our Marcus Brutus of the play, according to Plutarch, was descended from him. **would have brooked,** etc.: would have tolerated the Devil to rule in Rome as soon as a king. Shakespeare uses "eternal" several times for "infernal." "Perhaps," says Hudson, "our Yankee phrases, '*tarnal* shame,' '*tarnal* scamp,' etc., are relics of this usage. It seems that the Puritans thought *infernal* too profane for godly mouths, and so translated its sense to *eternal*."

162. am nothing jealous: do not doubt. Remember Cassius' "be not *jealous* on me" in line 71 above.

163. aim: guess, conjecture.

166. so: if, provided that, — as often in Shakespeare.

170. such high things: such important matters.

171. chew. This is a translation of the Latin "ruminate," which we still use in the sense of "reflect," "ponder."

172. a villager. To be a countryman, — a rustic, — from the point of view of a Roman citizen, was to be an outcast and a boor.

173. Than to repute: than consider myself. To-day we do not use "to" after the idiom "had rather."

174. as: which, such as. (A similar use of "as" occurred in line 34 of this scene.)

177. but: even. The figure here is from the starting of fire by the use of steel and flint. Later in the play Brutus describes his own cold nature thus:

> O Cassius, you are yoked with a lamb
> That carries anger as the *flint bears fire*,
> Who, much enforcéd, shows a hasty *spark*,
> And straight is cold again.

181. What hath proceeded, etc. "What has happened worthy of notice to-day." *Noteworthy* has become a common adjective to-day.

184. chidden: rebuked, censured, scolded.

186. ferret . . . eyes. The ferret has small reddish eyes.

187. seen him. That is, seen him look with.

188. crossed in conference: opposed in debate.

193. Sleek-headed men. According to Plutarch, Cæsar once said to friends who "complained unto him of Antonius and Dolabella, that they pretended some mischief towards him, 'As for those fat men and *smooth-combed heads*, I never reckon of them; but these pale-visaged and carrion lean people, I fear them most,' meaning Brutus and Cassius."

193. o' nights: at night.

194. Yond. An old form of "yon." (Cf. "yonder.")

197. well given: well disposed. This expression, like many others in the play, occurs in North's "Plutarch," from which Shakespeare drew the material for his tragedy.

199. if my name were liable to fear: that is, "If it were possible for me to be afraid." Cæsar uses "my name" for "myself."

204. he hears no music. Such a man Shakespeare evidently considered dangerous.

> The man that hath no music in himself,
> Nor is not moved with concord of sweet sounds,
> Is fit for treasons, stratagems and spoils;
> The motions of his spirit are dull as night
> And his affections dark as Erebus:
> Let no such man be trusted.
>
>   ("Merchant of Venice," V, 1, 83–88.)

205. sort: way, manner.

209. Whiles. An old form of "while," closely related to our "whilst."

217. sad. Probably here in the earlier sense of "grave," "serious."

228. marry. An exclamation about equivalent to our "indeed." Originally, as the word shows, it was an oath, being a shortened form for " by the Virgin *Mary*."

229. gentler than other: more gently than the other.

237. coronets. These were inferior to crowns, and in various forms denoted different degrees of noble rank less than sovereign. Here again the poet transfers to Rome an English custom.

239. fain: gladly, willingly.

243. rabblement: rabble, noisy crowd, mob.

244. chopt: chapped, rough and cracked. Macbeth speaks of the *choppy finger* of a witch.

247. swounded . . . 250. swound. Shakespeare uses these forms as well as the modern *swoon* and *swooned*.

250. soft: hold! stop! not so fast!

253. 'Tis very like: quite likely, it's very probable. **the falling-sickness.** That is, epilepsy, —a nervous disease accompanied, in its violent forms, with loss of consciousness, foaming at the mouth, and convulsions. Suetonius, in his life of Cæsar, says that the great Roman general was subject to fainting fits and that " he was twice seized with the falling-sickness while engaged in active service."

257. tag-rag: ragged and idle. (Cf. the expression " the rag, tag, and bobtail.")

260. no true man: no honest man.

264. plucked me ope his doublet: he opened his coat. The " me " in this construction is called the ethical dative (for me). It has no particular meaning here, though it may possibly add a little force to Casca's words.

The doublet (which did not come into use until the close of the 15th century) was a close-fitting outer garment with sleeves, and was belted at the waist. The expression " doublet and hose " occurs frequently in the plays.

265. An: if, — as often in Shakespeare. **a man of any occupation.** That is, " had I been a mechanic like those to whom he offered his throat."

266. at a word. We should say " at his word."

270. wenches: girls, — the sisters or daughters of the "commoners." As used here, and often in Shakespeare, the word corresponds almost exactly to the masculine "fellow."

274. sad. See note on "sad" in line 217 above.

277. he spoke Greek. How does Casca speak these words? What light do they throw on Cicero's character?

282. it was Greek to me: it was meaningless to me. The proverb here includes, of course, a play upon Casca's earlier remark, "Ay, he spoke Greek."

287. I am promised forth: I have promised already to dine out. In "The Merchant of Venice" Shylock says, "I am bid forth to supper," and "I have no mind of feasting forth."

293. blunt: dull, slow, — just the opposite of "quick mettle" in the next line, which means "of high or lively spirit."

297. this tardy form: this sluggish, slothful manner, — probably of talking, in reference to Casca's beating about the bush and hesitation in his story of Cæsar and the crown.

305. think of the world. That is, "think of the affairs of Rome." What is the significance of this remark as a farewell to Brutus?

307. metal: spirit, character. Point out two similar uses of the word earlier in the play.

307, 308. may be wrought From, etc.: may be moved, or changed, from that to which it is inclined.   **meet**: fitting, suitable.

311. bear me hard. That is, "Cæsar regards me with ill-will, or disfavor."

313. He should not humor me. "He (that is, Brutus) should not cajole me (play upon my humor) as I do him." (Warburton.) Cassius seems to think that he would not be as easy to work upon as he is finding Brutus.

314. hands: handwritings, — as often in Shakespeare.

316. tending to: setting forth, indicating.

318. glanced at: hinted at, suggested.

319, 320. let Cæsar seat him sure, etc. Let Cæsar establish himself firmly in power, for we will either overthrow him, or suffer the consequences of the attempt to unseat him.

Notice the rhyme (*sure . . . endure*) in these two last lines, similar to the ending of II, 3, V, 3, and the close of the play. Such a rhyming couplet often marked the close of a scene, or even the exit of an actor, in old plays before the days of curtains and elaborate changes of scenery. (See page 176.)

QUESTIONS AND TOPICS FOR DISCUSSION

1. Imagine and describe the setting of the scene. How does it make a splendid pageant on the stage to-day?

2. What is the first impression you get of Cæsar? Favorable or unfavorable? How?

3. Why do you think Shakespeare introduced the soothsayer at this point? What effect do his words have on the audience?

4. Does the soothsayer seem to have any effect upon Cæsar? Upon Cassius or Brutus?

5. How does Cassius skilfully lead up to his subject? What is his evident motive from the first?

6. How would you have Brutus appear and act during the long speeches of Cassius, 90–131 and 135–161?

7. Does Cassius seem to you to speak from personal enmity toward Cæsar, or solely from interest in the public welfare? Support your reasons by quoting various lines.

8. What is the effect of the distant shout and Brutus' comment? (131–133.)

9. What reasons does Cassius give for wanting Brutus to join the conspiracy?

10. Why do you think Cassius recalls to Brutus the deeds of his ancestors?

11. Compare the appearance of Cæsar's train as it returns with the spectacle at the opening of the scene.

12. How does Shakespeare give us an impression of what has taken place while Cassius has been talking to Brutus?

13. Why have Cæsar comment upon Antony, Brutus, and

especially upon Cassius, as he does? Do his words here have an important effect upon the audience?

14. Why does the poet have Casca speak entirely in prose?

15. What opinion do you form of Casca from his manner and his words?

16. Comment upon the words of Brutus in lines 293–294. How does Cassius turn these words to his own use?

17. What opinion do you form of Cassius from his last speech in this scene?

18. Can you explain why this last speech is often omitted on the stage to-day?

19. What contrast has Shakespeare already clearly made between Cassius and Brutus?

20. Quote any lines you particularly like and tell why you like them.

ACT I

Scene 3

In the preceding scene we saw Cassius sound Brutus' feelings concerning the growth of Cæsar's power in the state, and learned from his final soliloquy the result of his observations, —

> Well, Brutus, thou art noble, yet I see . . .

The third scene shows Cassius rapidly and with simple means winning Casca, and planning with Casca and Cinna the subtler devices which shall appeal to the moral sense of Brutus.

The previous scene took place on February 15th. A month has passed, and now it is the evening before the 15th of March.

1. brought you Cæsar home? Did you escort Cæsar home?

3. the sway of earth: the balanced swing, or regular movement of the earth; the established order of nature.

6. rived: split, cleaved. The form *riven* also is in use. In Cooper's "Deerslayer" there is an Indian chief named *Rivenoak*.

8. to be exalted, etc., so as to rise as high as the threatening clouds. In "The Merchant of Venice" the Prince of Morocco speaks of

> The watery kingdom, whose ambitious head
> Spits in the face of heaven.

11. civil strife in heaven : civil war among the gods.

12. too saucy with : too insolent towards the gods.

13. destruction. The metre requires four syllables, — *de-struc-ti-on*. At the end of a line it is not uncommon to find *ion* treated as two syllables, *i-on*.

14. more wonderful. That is, "more wonderful than this storm you have just been describing," or possibly Cicero may simply mean "more wonderful than usual." Which do you prefer?

15–27. These portents, or prodigies as Casca calls them, are all given in Plutarch's life of Cæsar. Compare the two versions. Which do you prefer, the prose or the poetry?

19. I ha' not since, etc. "You see, I still have my sword drawn." (Cf. stage directions at opening of scene.)

20. Against : opposite.

21. Who. Shakespeare frequently uses "who" to refer to inanimate objects and animals, just as he uses "which" sometimes when referring to persons. The relative pronouns had not become fixed in his time. (In the Bible of 1611 we find "Our Father, *which* art," etc.) **surly :** in a gruff or haughty manner. The word is an adjective and must not be confused with the adverbs *surely* or *sourly*. (There is an adverb *surlily*.)

23. Upon a heap : in a crowd or mob.

26. the bird of night. This, of course, is the owl, which, like the crow and the raven, has always been considered a bird of bad omen. Can you account for these strange superstitions by the habits, notes, and color of these birds?

Just before the murder of Duncan in "Macbeth" Lady Macbeth says :

> It was the *owl* that shrieked, the fatal bellman,
> Which gives the stern'st good-night.

29. conjointly meet : come together, happen at the same time.

30. These are, etc. That is, " Such and such are their causes."

31. portentous things : signs and omens.

32. the climate : the region, country, — as we use the " clime."

33. strange-disposéd : strangely ordered. Here again is an adjective where we should use an adverb. (Cf. " went surly by " in line 21 above.)

34. cónstrue. See note on line 45 of the previous scene.

35. Clean from : completely away from, — as we say, " I *clean* forgot it."

39. Is not to walk in. That is, is not fit or suitable to walk under. Some explain " sky " as meaning " weather," " atmosphere," though this is not necessary.

42. what night is this! We should say, " What a night this is ! "

47. Submitting me : exposing myself.

48. unbracéd : " with my doublet unfastened," — my coat unbuttoned. Shakespeare clothes his Romans in the English clothes of his own day. It is evident from this passage, and many others throughout the play, that actors in 1600 wore the costume of their own day, and did not attempt to dress according to the parts they played.

49. thunder-stone : the thunderbolt which many people still believe falls with lightning.

50. cross blue lightning : the zigzag flash, etc. How *blue ?*

58. you do want, etc. : you lack, or make no use of them.

60. put on fear, etc. : suffer fear and throw yourself into a state of wonder. Thus we say, " I was *thrown into* confusion."

63–66. Why. After each *why* we must supply some such expression as " we see."

64. from quality and kind. That is, why we see birds and beasts change their natures.

65. old men fool and children calculate : why old men act like fools and children think wisely, — that is, why everything is upside down.

66. their ordinance : what they were ordained or made to be.

67. preformed faculties : faculties created for special purposes.

68. To monstrous quality : to a strange, abnormal kind of thing. **why.** This is the turning-point of this long involved sentence, and is about equivalent to *now, well then.*

71. some monstrous state : some fearful state of affairs ; some terrible calamity in the government.

Cassius' long, complicated sentence (62–71) may be summed up briefly as follows : "These strange sights, these things contrary to nature, are a sign and warning from heaven."

77. prodigious : portentous, of the nature of a prodigy, — as generally in Shakespeare.

81. thews : muscles.

82. woe the while ! woe the time ! alas the day !

83. with our mothers' spirits. That is, by feminine rather than masculine impulses or feelings.

84. Our yoke and sufferance : our endurance of tyranny. A good illustration of hendiadys, a figure of speech, which you should look up in a large dictionary.

90. Cassius from bondage, etc. Cassius will free himself from slavery, as he says later, by killing himself.

95. Can be retentive, etc. Can repress, or confine, man's spiritual strength.

97. In the last act we shall see presented in actual deed "this Roman idea of taking one's own life when it became unbearable."

98. know all the world besides : let all the world know too.

101. bondman : slave, "bound-man."

108. begin it with weak straws. "Just as men start a huge fire with worthless straws or shavings, so Cæsar is using the degenerate Romans of his time to set the whole world ablaze with his own glory." (Hudson.)

109. offal : worthless, waste stuff.

114. My answer must be made. I must answer for my words.

117. fleering : deceitful, treacherously grinning. **Hold, my hand :** Here, take my hand.

118. Be factious: be active in forming a party, a faction, for redress of all these grievances.

123. undergo: undertake, — as often in Shakespeare.

124. honorable-dangerous. A similar compound adjective occurred in line 33 above, and later we find "high-sighted" and "honey-heavy."

125. by this: by this time.

126. Pompey's porch. The magnificent theatre of Pompey, where the statue of the great Roman general stood, was erected in 55 B.C. in the Campus Martius, or Field of Mars. The *porch* was an elaborate portico connected with the theatre.

128. the complexion of the element: the appearance of the heavens.

129. In favor's like: in aspect, or looks, is like the work, etc. (See note on "your outward *favor*," I, 2, 91.)

135. incorporate: closely united: heart and soul in sympathy with our efforts.

137. I am glad on't. Overlooking Cassius' last question Cinna expresses his pleasure at hearing that Casca has joined their conspiracy.   **on't**: of it. In I, 2, 71 Cassius said, "Be not jealous *on* me."

138. There's two or three. The grammar of our language was less rigidly fixed in Shakespeare's time than it is to-day. Thus we find in this play many instances of singular verbs with plural subjects, as just below in line 148, and again in line 155. Later we find "There *is* tears for his love." As a matter of fact, in conversation to-day even educated persons use such expressions as "There's several reasons" and "There's six or eight of us."

143. prætor's chair. The prætor was a city magistrate, annually elected, who watched over the administration of justice. He was distinguished by the presence of lictors, by the toga, and by the curule chair. Marcus Brutus had been made prætor by Cæsar in 44 B.C., or about two years before the conspiracy.

146. old Brutus' statue. This was Lucius Junius Brutus, to whom Cassius referred in I, 2, 159–161.

> There was a Brutus once that would have brooked
> The eternal devil to keep his state in Rome
> As easily as a king.

It is interesting to see how closely Shakespeare followed Plutarch's "Life of Brutus" here:

"For under the image of his ancestor Junius Brutus (that drave the kings out of Rome) they wrote: O, that it pleased the gods thou wert now alive, Brutus! and again, That thou wert here among us now! His tribunal, or chair, where he gave audience during the time he was Prætor, was full of such bills "Brutus, thou art asleep, and art not Brutus indeed."

148. Is. See note on "There's two or three," line 138 above.

150. hie: hasten, hurry, — often with a pronoun as in "The Merchant," "Hie thee, gentle Jew."

152. Pompey's theatre. See note on "Pompey's porch" in line 126 above.

154, 155. three parts of him is. See note on "There's two or three" in line 138 above. Such expressions as this were really not bad grammar in Shakespeare's English.

159. his countenance: his approval, his countenancing support. **alchemy.** This was the art by which men for centuries tried to turn the base metals, such as lead and iron, into gold. From the Greek Midas, who was able to turn everything he touched into gold, down to modern times, literature is full of references to alchemy and the alchemist.

162. You have right well conceited: you have formed an excellent idea of Brutus and our great need of him.

QUESTIONS AND TOPICS FOR DISCUSSION

1. Compare the Cassius of this scene with the Cassius of Scene 2, especially the manner of his winning Casca and Brutus.

2. What would probably be the effect upon the audience of the thunder and lightning during this scene? Of the "portentous things" described by Casca?

3. What are some of the superstitions associated with the owl? (Line 26.)

4. What does the last speech of Casca (157–160) add to our knowledge of Brutus?

5. From what you now have seen of Cassius, describe his appearance in some detail.

6. How far has the plot been developed by this first act?

7. In what ways has Shakespeare aroused your interest and curiosity?

8. Judging by this first act, what part would you assign to the leading actor in your company of players? What to the next?

ACT II

Scene 1

We must imagine that an hour or more has passed since the end of Act I, for it now is nearly daylight of the 15th of March. A little later Cassius hears a clock strike three.

Brutus' orchard. We should say "Brutus' garden." Shakespeare uses these two words as synonyms.

1. What, Lucius! "What" and "when" (line 5 below) were common words of exclamation or calling, like our colloquial "Hi, there," or "Oh." When Shylock is leaving his house he calls to his daughter inside to come out and speak to him: "What, Jessica! . . . Why, Jessica, I say!"

3. how near to day. We must supply "it is "

7. taper. A sort of wick or small candle, probably made of wax.

11. to spurn at him: to reject him, or almost "to strike at him." Later Cæsar says, "I spurn thee like a cur out of my way," which is the more common use of the word.

12. the general: the public, the community.

14. It is the bright day, etc. Just as snakes come out to bask in the warm sun, so the "sunshine of royalty,—the dazzle of being king,—will kindle the serpent in Cæsar."

15. that craves wary walking: that demands careful, watchful walking. Notice that here, and again at the end of his soliloquy (32–34), Brutus has not forgotten his comparison of Cæsar and a serpent. — **that**. be that so; suppose him crowned.

17. do danger with: do what is dangerous, — like our expressions "do mischief," "do harm," "do wrong," etc.

18. when it disjoins remorse: when it separates mercy, or pity, from power.

20. his affections swayed: his emotions, or feelings, governed him more than his reason.

21. a common proof: a common experience, a thing commonly proved.

26. the base degrees: the lower steps, the lower rounds of the ladder. A *degree* is literally a "step down."

28. prevent: anticipate, get ahead of him.

28, 29. since the quarrel will bear no color, etc. That is, "Since our case against him cannot be justified by what he is now, let us state our argument thus," etc. Professor Hudson thus sums up Brutus' reasoning: "Since we have no apparent ground of complaint against Cæsar in what he is, or in anything he has yet done, let us assume that the further addition of a crown will quite transform his nature, and make him a serpent."

33. as his kind: like the rest of its kind, or species.

34. kill him. That is, — let us, therefore, kill him in the shell.

35. closet. This word was formerly used for any small room devoted to retirement, privacy, or study, and was not confined to a room for storing clothes or dishes. Here Lucius refers to Brutus' private study. (See line 7 above.)

36. a flint. A piece of stone used with tinder for striking a fire.

44. exhalations: meteors. The ancients believed that the sun drew vapor up from the earth and then *exhaled* it, or breathed it forth, in the form of meteors.

47. redress: set right that which is wrong.

48. Brutus, thou sleep'st. See note on I, 3, 146.

50. I have took. Compare this with "mistook your passion" in I, 2, 48, and see note.

53. My ancestors. This is a reference to Lucius Junius Brutus. See note to I, 3, 146.

61. whet: excite, arouse, — literally, "sharpen," as in the expression "to whet one's appetite." (Cf. *whet*stone.)

64. motion: impulse, motive.

64, 65. the interim is like a phantasma: the time between is like a nightmare.

66. The genius, etc.: the soul and the bodily powers; the spiritual and physical powers; the guardian angel of man and his passions, — but just exactly what Shakespeare meant by "genius" and "mortal instruments" in this famous line will always remain a mystery. The editors have written pages upon these words.

67. the state of man: the government of man. Man is compared to a kingdom, or state, in which civil war arises between the various elements, — the "genius and the mortal instruments."

69. The nature of: something like.

70. your brother. Really brother-in-law, for Cassius had married Brutus' sister, Junia.

72. moe: more, — frequent in Shakespeare.

> Friends, I owe moe tears
> To this dead man than you shall see me pay.
>
> (V, 3, 101.)

73. their hats, etc. Here is another good illustration of Shakespeare's disregard of the costumes actually worn in Rome. "The Roman *pileus* was a close fitting cap of felt without any brim, and the *petasus* was worn only to keep off the sun. Shakespeare dressed his Romans in the slouched hats of his own time." (Wright.) But does this make the least particle of difference in our enjoyment of the play, or injure its dramatic quality?

76. By any mark of favor: by a special distinction of

features. Do you remember when Cassius said to Brutus, "I do know your outward favor"?

77. faction. A body of persons combined for a certain purpose, — here the conspirators.

79. When evils are most free. That is, when crimes are most free from the law, — most unrestrained.

82. affability : courteous words, gentle manners.

83. path. Here the word is a verb and means to *walk, walk forth*; but it may be a printer's error. *Put* has been suggested by many of the critics. *Path* as a verb, however, occurs in writers of Shakespeare's time. **thy native semblance on** : in thy true form.

84. Erebus. This was a place of darkness, according to Greek mythology, part way between the earth and Hades; but here, as often in literature, the term is applied vaguely to the lower world.

85. prevention : discovery, — which would lead to prevention or inference.

86. we are too bold. etc. : we are too bold thus to break in upon your rest.

100. Shall I entreat a word : May I have a word with you?

104. fret : adorn, ornament with lines or pencillings. Hamlet speaks of "this majestical roof (the heavens) *fretted* with golden fire."

107, 108. a great way growing, etc. The sun rises far to the south, considering the early time of year. Casca is rather inaccurate, for on March 15th the sun would rise almost exactly in the east.

110. the high east : exact, or perfect, east, — as we say "*high* noon."

112. your hands all over : all your hands once more. Brutus shook hands with the conspirators when they arrived; now after talking with Cassius he shakes hands with them all again.

114. the face of men. Probably, the look of disapproval of Cæsar in the faces of men.

115. sufferance: suffering.

116. break off betimes: let's throw up the whole business at once.

117. hence to his idle bed: go to bed and remain there idle. So we often say "a *sick bed*," and Shakespeare in "Troilus and Cressida" has "upon a *lazy bed*."

114–118. The broken grammatical structure of these lines makes them a little difficult. Summed up, the meaning is: If the unspoken words in men's looks, together with our own suffering and the abuses of the time, are not sufficient motives for our conspiracy, let us give up our scheme, go home, and allow proud tyranny to flourish.

119. drop by lottery. That is, "die at the mere whim of the tyrant, just as by the mere chance of a lottery." (Thorndike.) **if these.** That is, these three motives just enumerated.

123. What: Why. The figure, of course, is from horseback riding, the source of many comparisons and figures in Shakespeare. How do you account for this?

125. Than secret Romans: that of secret Romans. **have spoke.** Compare this with "have took" in line 50 above, and see note on I, 2, 48.

126. palter: quibble, act trickily.

129. cautelous: crafty, sly, — a rare word even in Shakespeare.

130. carrions. Literally "carcasses." Here "men as good as dead."

133. The even virtue: The calm, firm virtue.

134. the insuppressive mettle: the nature of our spirits which cannot be suppressed.

135. or our cause or. This construction, instead of *either . . . or*, occurs in English poetry as late as Tennyson.

136. Did need: ever could need.

138. a several bastardy: a special treason against his noble birth.

144. his silver hairs. At this time Cicero was sixty years old. Of course Metellus remembers that he has just used "silver" when in the next line he speaks of *purchasing* good opinion," — that is, a good reputation, — and *buying* men's voices.

148. Our youths, etc. That is, our light, uncontrolled youth shall not be in evidence at all.

150. break with him: tell him, — as we say "break the news."

157. of him: in him. In the previous line "of" = by. Notice other variations in the use of prepositions as you read the play.

158. A shrewd contriver: an evil plotter or schemer. According to Plutarch, all of the conspirators, except Brutus, wished to slay Antony as well as Cæsar.

164. envy: hatred, malice, — as usually in Shakespeare. So "envious" in line 178 below means "malicious," "evil."

169. come by: get hold of.

175–178. Let our hearts rouse our hands to act, and then after the deed is done they may reprove them, just as clever masters arouse their servants to an outrageous act, and then find fault with them for doing it. What do you think of this advice?

178. Our purpose necessary. That is, seem necessary and not malicious.

180. purgers: cleansers, healers. They will *heal* Rome of its disease of tyranny.

184. ingrafted love: love so deeply implanted that it has become a part of him.

187. take thought and die. This was an old expression for "grieve one's self to death." In Elizabethan English "thought" often meant "worry," as in the New Testament, — "Take no *thought* for the morrow," which means, of course, "be not anxious or solicitous about the morrow."

188. And that were much, etc. That would be a great deal for him to do, — as Brutus explains in the next line.

190. no fear in him: nothing to be feared in him. **Clock strikes.** Clocks such as Shakespeare had in mind were unknown to the Romans; thus we have here another anachronism. Can you explain it?

192. stricken. Shakespeare also uses the forms "struck" and "strucken." We still use the word in such expressions as "he was *stricken* with the disease," and "the words were *stricken* from the record."

196. Quite from the main opinion: wholly contrary to the strong opinion.

197. fantasy: imagination. **ceremonies:** superstitious rites.

198. apparent prodigies: manifest, clearly seen signs and omens.

200. augurers, or **augurs,** were interpreters of omens, especially of those seen in the entrails of animals which were sacrificed to the gods. No Roman would set about an important undertaking without consulting the augurs for favorable omens.

203. o'ersway: win him over, change his mind.

204. According to early stories, the unicorn in its fury would drive its horn into a tree behind which the hunter had dodged for safety, and before it broke free again was captured or killed. Bears were supposed to be easily shot while they remained motionless, gazing into a mirror that had been set up to attract them. Elephants were captured by means of pitfalls, covered with straw or leaves, and lions were snared with nets or *toils.*

208. flattered. Pronounced *flat-ter-ed.* Do you see why?

210. humor: state of mind, temper. The word "humor" is used by Shakespeare in many different senses, some of which are not familiar to us to-day.

213. the uttermost: the very latest. We probably would say "latest" or "utmost."

215. doth bear Cæsar hard: bears ill-will toward Cæsar, hates Cæsar. Do you remember where Cassius said, "Cæsar doth bear me hard"?

216. rated: reproved, berated.

218. go along by him: go home by way of his house.

219. given him reasons. That is, for caring for Brutus.

220. fashion him: mould him, win him to our cause.

225. our looks put on, etc. Let not our looks put on an expression that will betray or reveal our plans.

227. formal constancy: unbroken, unchanged dignity of outward appearance; "dignified self-possession."

230. honey-heavy dew, etc. "Slumber as refreshing as dew, and whose heaviness is sweet." (Wright.) Notice the compactness and suggested pictures in Shakespeare's one phrase.

231. no figures nor no fantasies. That is, "Thou hast no pictures or fancies created by the imagination." Double negative constructions (*nor . . . no*) were common in the English of Shakespeare's time.

238. Stole. Compare this form with "broke" for "broken," "wrote" for "written," which occur frequently in the plays.

246. wafture: wave. A rare word, used only here by Shakespeare.

248. impatience. Four syllables, *im-pa-ti-ence*, like *de-struc-ti-on* in I, 3, 13, *q.v.*

250. humor. Here, "caprice" or some "whim." In line 262 below we find still another meaning of this word.

251. his: its, — as often in Elizabethan English.

253. shape: physical appearance in contrast to "condition" in the next line.

254. prevailed on your condition: influenced or changed your state of mind.

255. Dear my lord. Shakespeare has this peculiar order in other terms of address, such as "Sweet my mother," and "Good my lord."

261. physical: good for the health, wholesome.

262. unbracéd: with clothes unfastened. Do you remember where Cassius walked "unbraced," and "bared his bosom to the thunder-storm"? **humors:** mists, moisture.

263. dank: damp. Which of these words is the more poetic?

266. rheumy: damp, causing catarrh or *rheum*atism. **un-purgéd air:** foul air; air that has not yet been purified by the sun's rays.

268. some sick offence. That is, some grief that makes you sick.

271. charm: conjure, entreat. Do you think Pope's alteration of this word to "charge" a necessary or wise change?

273. incorporate. The next four words almost translate this expression.

275. heavy: sad, — as we say "a heavy heart," "a light heart."

281. Is it excepted, etc. "Is there an exception made that I should not know your secrets?"

283. in sort or limitation: only after a fashion, and in a limited way. Notice here, and often in this play, the compactness of Shakespeare's language, — the extensive meaning pressed into a word or two.

285. the suburbs. That is, in the outskirts, not in the center of your heart.

287. harlot: mistress.

289, 290. the ruddy drops that visit, etc. Harvey's discovery of the laws governing the circulation of the blood were not published until twelve years after Shakespeare's death, though much earlier, as these words clearly show, men had begun to have notions that such a circulation prevailed.

295. well-reputed: of good name; honorable. **Cato's daughter.** Portia was the daughter of Marcus Cato, sometimes called "the last of the Romans," because of his struggle to bring back to Rome a republican form of government. His hatred of Cæsar led him to commit suicide after that great imperial leader had defeated the followers of Pompey.

299. constancy: firmness.

300. a voluntary wound. Portia wounded herself with a knife to test, by her power to endure physical pain, her ability to keep her husband's secrets. This incident — indeed, the whole interview between Brutus and Portia — follows Plutarch very closely. See page 112 for a comparison of the historian and the dramatist.

307. construe: explain, interpret.

308. All the charactery of my sad brows, etc.: all the marks of sadness on my countenance.

312. how? Brutus utters this as an exclamation rather than as a question. He is surprised to see Ligarius wearing a "ker-chief."

313. Vouchsafe good morrow: deign, or condescend, to accept good morning.

315. kerchief. Used here in its literal meaning, — a covering for the head. It was evidently the custom in Shakespeare's time for sick men to wear such head-coverings.

323. an exorcist: one who raises spirits, a conjurer.

324. My mortified spirit. That is, my spirit that was dead.

331. To whom: To him to whom. **Set on your foot**: go ahead. In I, 2, 11, Cæsar used a similar expression: "Set on; and leave no ceremony out."

QUESTIONS AND TOPICS FOR DISCUSSION

1. What does Lucius add to this scene? Would you omit his part as unnecessary to the main action?

2. In what ways has Brutus changed since we saw him in Act I?

3. What opinion do you form of Brutus from his soliloquies in this scene? Do they increase your respect for him or not? Why?

4. Why do you think the poet has Brutus ask Lucius about "the ides of March"?

5. What is the purpose and effect of having Brutus and Cassius whisper aside? (101–111.) What do you think they talk about?

6. Point out and comment upon Shakespeare's skill in man-aging the other actors on the stage during the whispered con-ference between Brutus and Cassius.

7. Have you any definite knowledge, before Brutus speaks in line 112, of his decision as to the conspiracy?

8. What are the objections to including Cicero in the con-spiracy?

9. What do you think of Brutus' arguments to spare Mark Antony? Do you agree with him or with Cassius?

10. How do you explain the words, "The clock hath stricken three," when clocks, as we know them, did not exist in Cæsar's time?

11. What is there effective in lines 229–233? Do these words increase your admiration for Brutus or not?

12. What impression does the scene between Portia and Brutus leave with you? Would you omit it in a modern presentation of the play on the stage?

13. What is there heroic in Portia's character? Bassanio in "The Merchant of Venice" says of the heroine,

> Her name is Portia, nothing undervalued
> To Cato's daughter, Brutus' Portia.

14. In what ways does Portia fulfil your idea of the noble Roman matron?

15. Describe the setting of the conspiracy in Brutus' orchard, and point out the elements that make this one of the finest scenes in English drama.

ACT II

Scene 2

The story of Calpurnia's crying out in her sleep, of the ill omens announced by the augurs, and of Cæsar's irresolution, is all in Plutarch, and is not exaggerated by the poet. This scene between Calpurnia and Cæsar and the similar one between Portia and Brutus should be compared with reference to differences of character in the actors which the dialogue brings to light.

It is now nearly eight o'clock, and the ides of March has come.

night-gown: Not in its modern sense, but "dressing-gown," as usually in Shakespeare.

1. Nor heaven nor earth: neither heaven, etc., — like "*or* our cause *or* our performance" in the previous scene (II, 1, 135 and note).

217

5. **do present sacrifice**: perform the sacrifices at once.

6. **their opinions of success**: That is, their opinions as to the outcome,— as to what will *succeed* or happen,— if Cæsar goes forth.

10. **Cæsar shall forth**: Shakespeare often omits the verb "go" in this and similar expressions. Later we find "We'll along ourselves"; "We must out and talk"; "I will myself into the pulpit"; etc.

13. **stood on ceremonies**: regarded omens or prophecies.

16. **the watch**: the watchman,— a familiar figure in Shakespeare's London, though not in Cæsar's Rome.

20. **right form of war**: regular battle array.

22. **hurtled**: crashed, clashed.

24. **ghosts did shriek**, etc. Ghosts were believed to have the power of speech, as we see later in this play. In connection with these lines, it is interesting to read the words of Horatio in "Hamlet," a tragedy written about the same time as "Julius Cæsar."

> In the most high and palmy state of Rome,
> A little ere the mightiest Julius fell,
> The graves stood tenantless and the sheeted dead
> Did squeak and gibber in the Roman streets.

25. **all use**: all custom, all we are used to.

27. **Whose end is purposed**: the completion of which is planned by the gods.

29. **Are to the world**, etc. That is, these prophecies apply just as much to the world in general as they do to Cæsar.

37. **augurers**: augurs, priests who read the omens, especially the entrails of animals. See line 200 of the last scene, and note.

42. **should**. In modern usage this would be "would," but it was the regular form for the simple future in Elizabethan English.

46. **We**. That is, Danger (personified) and I.

56. **humor**: caprice, whim,— as in II, 1, 150.

73. **satisfaction**. Pronounced *sat-is-fac-ti-on*. Do you see why?

76. to-night: last night, as in III, 3, 1. "I dreamt to-night that I did feast with Cæsar"; and Shylock in "The Merchant of Venice" says,

> For I did dream of money-bags to-night.

More often the poet uses the word in its present meaning.

76. statuë. Pronounced here, and again in act III, as a three syllable word, — *sta-tu-a.* How should it be treated in line 85 below?

78. lusty: vigorous, robust. Where did Cassius speak of "*lusty* sinews"?

80, 81. portents, and evils imminent: signs and approaching dangers.

83. all amiss interpreted. That is, the meaning of your dream has been explained entirely incorrectly.

89. tinctures: stains. This is an allusion to the old custom of dipping handkerchiefs in the blood of great men, especially of saints and martyrs, and then preserving them as relics. **cognizance**: memorial, badge.

96, 97. a mock apt to be rendered: a sneering reply likely to be made.

103. To your proceeding. That is, my love for, or interest in, your advancement, — your career.

104. reason to my love, etc. Reason (which would have kept me from speaking so frankly) is subject to, subordinate to, my love. Or, as Rolfe puts it, "My love leads me to indulge in a freedom of speech that my reason would restrain." (Notice here again how much the poet puts into a phrase of six words.)

113. ague (ā'gue): fever.

114. 'tis strucken eight. Five hours earlier, Cassius said, "The clock hath *stricken* three." (See II, 1, 192 and note.) Notice throughout this part of the play the exact time of each important event that develops the plot is stated exactly. See II, 4, 22.

116. long o' nights. Where did Cæsar speak of men who "sleep o' nights"?

118. So to, etc. Much as we familiarly say, "The same to you!"

120. what, Trebonius! Like the exclamatory, impatient "what" at the opening of Act II,

> What, Lucius, ho!

128. That every like, etc. That is, to be *like* a friend is not to be a friend. Brutus, of course, is referring to the words Cæsar has just spoken.

129. yearns: grieves, pains, — as always in Shakespeare. Brutus here, just for a moment, seems to have a pang of remorse.

QUESTIONS AND TOPICS FOR DISCUSSION

1. Compare Cæsar's superstitions here with those of I, 2. Why do you think Shakespeare makes so much of them in the play?

2. Is it Calpurnia or the report from the augurers that determines Cæsar to remain at home? Give reasons for your decision.

3. What opinion do you form of Calpurnia? Do you like her as well as Portia? Contrast the two.

4. What are the arguments of Decius Brutus to induce Cæsar to "come forth"?

5. What do you think of Cæsar's sudden change of mind as to the augurers' warning? Is it flattery alone that wins him?

6. How do you account for Calpurnia's silence while Decius is persuading Cæsar to come to the Senate?

7. How would you have Calpurnia look and act when Cæsar decides to go forth?

8. Does Decius Brutus impress you as a heroic, noble-spirited man in this scene? Can you defend him for his deception?

9. Do Cæsar's words and actions in this scene raise him or lower him in your estimation?

10. Are your sympathies at this point with Cæsar or the conspirators? Give your reasons in detail.

11. What new glimpse do we get here of Antony's character? (116, 117.)

12. Why are the last two lines of the scene usually omitted on the stage to-day?

ACT II

Scene 3

7. security gives way to. Over-confidence makes a way for conspiracy. Have we seen anything to show that Cæsar was wholly confident of his own security?

8. lover: friend, — as frequently in Shakespeare. So later Brutus calls the citizens " Romans, countrymen, and lovers!" and in " The Merchant" Lorenzo speaks of Antonio as " a lover" of Bassanio.

12. Out of the teeth of emulation: safe from the teeth of jealousy; "free from the attacks of envy."

14. contrive: conspire, plot.

QUESTIONS AND TOPICS FOR DISCUSSION

1. Of what incidents earlier in the play does this scene remind you?

2. Why do you think this short scene is often omitted when presenting the play to-day?

3. Do you see any good reason for having the warning written in prose, but the words of Artemidorus that follow in verse?

4. Describe Artemidorus as you imagine his appearance and dress.

ACT II

Scene 4

Nearly an hour has passed since the conspirators entered Cæsar's house to " taste some wine " with him ; and the time draws on when they are to escort him to the senate-house.

221

1. prithee. A contraction of "pray thee."

6. constancy: resolution, firmness. Do you remember where Portia said,

> I have made strong proof of my *constancy?*

9. to keep counsel: to keep a secret.

14. went sickly forth: went out looking sick.

18. rumor: murmur, noise. I hear a noise of some excitement, like a struggle.

20. sooth: truly, indeed. Remember the opening line of "The Merchant of Venice":

> In *sooth* I know not why I am so sad.

Enter the Soothsayer. This is the same man that interrupted Cæsar's procession at the beginning of the play with the cry "Beware the ides of March!" There is no reason for believing him to be Artemidorus, as some of the editors wish to make him. Why is it better to have *two* distinct persons try to warn Cæsar?

34. prætors: city magistrates.

36. I'll get me to a place more void. That is, I'll move along to a more open place, — in contrast to the "narrower street" where he now stands talking with Portia.

38. Ay me: alas.

41. Brutus hath a suit, etc. These words are evidently spoken to Lucius to allay any suspicion that may arise from her exclamation: "The heavens speed thee in thy enterprise!" For a moment she had forgotten the boy's presence.

QUESTIONS AND TOPICS FOR DISCUSSION

1. Comment upon the great change that has come over Portia since we last saw her. How do you account for it?

2. What contrast is there between her feelings and those of Lucius? How does the dramatist make this contrast striking?

3. From her conversation with the soothsayer, what do you think is in Portia's mind? Has Brutus told her the plans of the conspirators, or is she merely suspicious?

4. How do you explain Portia's words, —

> Brutus hath a suit
> That Cæsar will not grant ?

Is this said aside or to Lucius?

5. Why do you suppose Shakespeare wrote this scene? Does it add anything to the plot of the tragedy? Would you omit it on the stage to-day?

ACT III

Scene 1

It is a little after nine o'clock in the morning of the ides of March. The outcome of the conspiracy is approaching, and with it the first great climax of the tragedy.

Flourish. Notice that here, as in Act I, a *flourish*, or notes on a trumpet, precedes the entrance of Cæsar and a formal procession of nobles. This, again, was an English rather than a Roman custom.

2. Ay: yes, — pronounced like "I." In line 38 of the previous scene the word is used in a different sense.

8. us ourself. The poet here has Cæsar assume the language of royalty. Do you see why? **served:** presented, — as in the expression "to *serve* a summons."

18. he makes to: he advances or presses toward.

19. Be sudden, for, etc.: Be quick, for we fear interference.

21. Cassius or Cæsar, etc. That is, one of us two shall not return alive, for I will slay myself if we do not succeed in killing him.

22. constant: firm, as already twice in the play.

28. presently: immediately.

29. addressed: ready.

33. puissant: powerful, — pronounced here in two syllables instead of three as to-day.

36. couchings. Same as *crouchings*.

38. pre-ordinance and first decree : that which has been ordained and decreed from the beginning. Notice the grandiloquence, — the "big talk," — of Cæsar in this passage.

39. the law of children. That is, into childish laws, — unstable, liable to change. **Be not fond :** be not so foolish as to think, etc. ; **fond :** foolish, simple, silly, as frequently in Shakespeare.

> Grant I may never prove so *fond*
> To trust man on his oath or bond.
>
> (" Timon of Athens.")

41, 42. That will be thawed, etc. As will be softened or changed from its true nature by that sort of pleading which melts fools.

43. Low-crookéd court'sies. Curtsies in which the knee is crouched or bent low.

46. I spurn thee, etc. Shylock in " The Merchant " says to Antonio, " You . . . foot me as you *spurn* a stranger cur Over your threshold." Where did Brutus say, " I know no personal cause to spurn at him " ?

47, 48. Know, Cæsar doth not wrong, etc. To the student of Shakespeare these are two of the most interesting lines in the play, for they seem to be an alteration of the words as they stood in the tragedy when it was acted in 1601, and the change may be traced to a criticism by the poet's friend, Ben Jonson. In his " Discoveries " Jonson says of Shakespeare, " Many times he fell into those things [that] could not escape laughter, as when he said . . . , ' Cæsar, thou dost me wrong,' Cæsar replied, ' Cæsar did never wrong but with just cause.' " If Jonson is quoting the lines as he actually heard them at the theatre, it may be that his ridicule of them in " Discoveries " resulted in their being altered to the form we find in the Folio, that is, as they stand here in our text. Some of the editors have even gone so far as to print Jonson's quotation as being the words that Shakespeare really wrote.

51. repealing : recalling, — and so " repeal " four lines further on.

57. enfranchisement: the rights of citizenship.

60. constant: fixed, firm, — as in line 22 above.

61. resting: steadfast.

62. fellow: equal, — as often in Shakespeare.

67. apprehensive: endowed with apprehension, — hence, intelligent, quick of mind.

69, 70. holds on his rank, unshaked, etc.: "continues to 'hold his place' (like the star), resisting every attempt to move him." (Rolfe.)

74. wilt thou lift up Olympus? That is, "Wilt thou attempt what is impossible?" It is significant, and in keeping with his style of speech here, that Cæsar should compare himself with Olympus, the great mountain in Greece which was the abode of the gods.

75. bootless kneel: kneel in vain.

76. Speak, hands, for me! Brutus, Cassius, Cinna, and Decius have spoken in behalf of Metellus' brother with words. So far Casca has said nothing, but now he calls upon his hands to speak instead of his tongue. Remember it was agreed (line 30) that Casca should be the first to strike.

77. Et tu, Brute! "And thou, too, Brutus!" There seems to be no ancient authority for these famous words. They do not occur in Plutarch; but, as has been pointed out many times, this very exclamation is found in two different works which were printed shortly before Shakespeare wrote "Julius Cæsar." Thus in "The True Tragedie of Richard Duke of Yorke," printed six or seven years before our play was acted, Edward cries to Clarence, "Et tu, Brute, wilt thou stab Cæsar too?"

80. the common pulpits. The pulpits, or rostra, from which speakers addressed the people of Rome.

90. good cheer. Much as we say, "Cheer up!"

92. Nor to no Roman else. Another double negative construction like "Yet 'twas *not* a crown *neither*" (I, 2, 236), and "*No* figures *nor no* fantasies" (II, 1, 231).

95. abide: be held responsible for, suffer for.

99. As it were doomsday: as though it were the Day of Judgment.

100. 'tis but the time, etc. "How long we can draw out our life, is the only question we concern ourselves about." (Hudson.)

107. let us bathe our hands in Cæsar's blood. Remember Calpurnia's dream in which she saw "many lusty Romans" bathing their hands in Cæsar's blood.

113. this our lofty scene: this scene of our great deed.

116. on Pompey's basis lies along: lying prostrate at the base of Pompey's statue.

118. the knot of us: our band.

120. shall we forth? The verb "go" is omitted, as in "Cæsar shall forth" (II, 2, 10).

122. most boldest. Another double superlative like this occurs later: "This was the most unkindest cut of all," and a similar double comparative often quoted is Shylock's "How much more elder art thou than thy looks!" ("The Merchant of Venice," IV, 1, 240.)

123. Soft!: But wait! Stop! — an exclamation common in Elizabethan plays.

131. vouchsafed: grant, permit.

132. resolved: informed, satisfied.

137. Thorough. Shakespeare uses this spelling (pronounced in two syllables) and also *through*. In "The Merchant" he has "throughfares" where we should use "thoroughfares." **the hazards of this untrod state**: the risks of this unexplored state of affairs.

141. so please him come. Expanded to its full form this would be, "If it so be that it please him to come."

143. presently: at once, immediately, — as in line 28 above, and generally in Shakespeare.

144. to friend: as a friend, — an idiom we still use in the expression "to take, or have, to wife."

146, 147. my misgiving still, etc.: my suspicions always hit

226

the mark; things always happen just about as I expect they will. *Still* usually means *always* in Shakespeare's English.

153. be let blood. That is, be bled, referring to the ancient custom of bleeding people for all kinds of ailments, whence the word "leech" for a doctor. Here, of course, Antony really means "bled to death" or killed.   **rank**: too full of blood or life, and therefore needing to be "let blood." Johnson explains *rank* as "grown too high for public safety," as we speak of *rank* grass or *rank* weeds.

158. bear me hard: bear me any ill-will.   Where did Cassius say that Cæsar bore him hard?

159. reek: smoke, steam, — with Cæsar's hot blood.

160. Live: If I live, — just as Portia says to Bassanio, "Live thou, I live," when he is about to make his choice of the caskets. ("The Merchant," III, 2, 61.)

161. so apt: so ready, so fit.

162. mean: means.   Shakespeare uses both singular and plural forms.

163. by Cæsar. That is, here near Cæsar, referring to the place where he would wish to die.   Antony then plays upon this meaning of "by" in his next few words.

168. we do.   That is, "we do appear bloody and cruel."

170. pitiful.   Not *pathetic*, but literally "full of pity or compassion."

172. As fire drives out fire.   This was a familiar saying.   It is an allusion to the old custom of taking the pain out of a burn by holding it up to the fire.   Thus in "Romeo and Juliet" Benvolio says to Romeo:

> Tut, man, one fire burns out another's burning,
> One pain is lessened by another's anguish.

174. leaden points in contrast to sharp iron points.   That is, "our swords to you are harmless."

175. Our arms in strength of malice, etc.   "Our arms, even in the intensity of their hatred for Cæsar's tyranny, and our hearts in their brotherly love for all Romans, do receive you in."

(White.) Or, as explained by Professor Neilson, " Our arms, though their strength has just been manifested in what seems malice, and our hearts in genuine brotherly affection, do receive you."   The passage has been freely altered by the critics to get rid of " malice," which seems to them to be a blunder.   " Welcome " and " amity " are two of the words suggested in place of " malice."

182. deliver: declare, relate, tell.

193. conceit: conceive of, think of, judge.   So earlier in the play Cassius said to Casca, " You have right well conceited Brutus."

197. dearer: more intensely.   Shakespeare often uses " dear " in the older sense of " keen," " heartfelt," " coming home to one closely."

203. close: agree, make a compact, — as in our expression " to close an agreement."

205. bayed: brought to bay, cornered.   The picture is that of a deer, or hart, hemmed in by the hounds.   Notice how Antony carries on this figure in the next five lines.

207. Signed in thy spoil: bearing the marks of thy destruction, *i.e.* covered with blood.   Hunters sometimes dipped their hands in the blood of the slaughtered game.   **thy lethe**: thy slaughter.   In Greek mythology Lethe was the river of Oblivion, or Forgetfulness, in the lower world.   From it all souls drank before passing to Elysium, that they might forget the sorrows of this world.   Thus the expression " crimsoned in thy lethe " may be rendered " crimsoned in the stream that bears thee to oblivion, — to Heaven."   This interpretation, however, seems far fetched, and the word remains a puzzle to the critics.

209. the heart of thee.   Notice the play on the words " heart " and " hart."   The same pun occurs in " As You Like It " :

> *Celia :* He was furnished like a hunter.
> *Rosalind :* O, ominous ! He comes to kill my heart.

210. strucken.   We have already had the expressions " 'Tis strucken eight," and " The clock hath stricken three."   Can you find them?

214. cold modesty: moderation.

217. pricked: marked, — as in IV, 1: "Their names are pricked." A pin, or some other sharp point, was formerly used instead of a pencil or pen to mark off names on a list.

220. Swayed from the point: turned from the subject in hand.

225. full of good regard: entitled to favorable consideration.

229. Produce: carry, bear forth, — the literal meaning of the Latin *produco*. **the market-place**. By this Shakespeare of course means the Forum, in which there were several *rostra*, or pulpits, as the poet calls them, for addressing the people.

231. in the order of: in the course of the funeral ceremonies.

236. By your pardon: Excuse me, let me explain.

243. advantage more than do us wrong. That is, letting Antony speak will help us more than harm us.

244. fall: happen, be*fall*.

258. in the tide of times. That is, in the ebb and flow, — in the ever changing course, — of the times.

259. costly: precious, rare.

263. the limbs of men. We should be more likely to say "the heads of men." Many substitutes for "limbs" have been suggested by doubting editors, such as, "sons," "lives," "times," "tombs," "minds," etc. Do you think any change is necessary?

265. cumber: burden, oppress, — more common to-day in the form *encumber*.

266. so in use: so usual, so common.

269. quartered with: torn to pieces by the hands of war.

270. All pity choked, etc.: All sense of pity being choked by the frequency of cruel deeds.

271. ranging: wandering over the earth.

272. Ate. In Greek mythology the goddess of discord and vengeance.

273. these confines: these regions; within the confines of this empire.

274. "Havoc." It is said that in battles of ancient times this

cry was the signal that no quarter was to be given to prisoners.
let slip the dogs of war.   Here Antony comes back once more to
the language of hunting.   (See lines 205–211 above.)   To "let
slip" a dog was to release it from the leash when it was time to
begin the pursuit.   It has been suggested that "the dogs of
war" are *fire, sword,* and *famine,* for in "Henry V" the poet
says of the warlike king,

> and, at his heels,
> Leashed in like hounds, should Famine, Sword, and Fire
> Crouch for employment.

275.   That: so that, — as often in Shakespeare.

276.   With carrion men: with the decaying bodies of men.

284.   Passion, I see, is catching: Emotion, sorrow, I see, is
contagious.

290.   No Rome of safety.   Possibly we have here again the
pun that Cassius made in I, 2, 156: "Now is it *Rome* indeed
and *room* enough."

295.   issue: deed, or "result of the action" of these bloody
men.

296.   According to the which: according to which way they
take my oration.

298.   Lend me your hand.   As there was no curtain at the
front of the stage in Shakespeare's theatre, the body of Cæsar
must be removed by some of the actors before the scene closes.

QUESTIONS AND TOPICS FOR DISCUSSION

1. What is the effect of the reference again (line 1) to the
"ides of March"?

2. Explain the crisis when Artemidorus tries to present his
schedule.   How would you manage the scene between Decius
and Artemidorus?

3. Why do you think Shakespeare has Popilius say, "I wish
your enterprise to-day may thrive"?   What do these words
suggest?

4. How would an audience naturally be influenced by the uncertainty of the conspiracy during the first lines of the scene?

5. Are your sympathies at this point with Cæsar or with the conspirators? How does the dramatist wish the audience to feel?

6. Point out how skilfully the poet gathers the conspirators about Cæsar for the fatal blow. Do you feel that this scene is natural and convincing?

7. What effect upon our feelings for Cæsar does his last speech have? (Lines 58-73.) Is it in keeping with his words in II, 2?

8. What is the signal to strike? Are the words significant? Can you suggest any reason for having Casca rather than Brutus or Cassius speak them?

9. What do you believe are Brutus' thoughts as he uses his dagger? How would you have him look at this moment and directly after?

10. Why is it that none of the senators rush to Cæsar's aid? Explain the situation in detail as you imagine it.

11. What was Antony's purpose, in your judgment, when he sent the messenger to the conspirators? Why did he not go to them himself?

12. What do you think of Antony's action in pretending to join the conspirators? Was it justifiable?

13. Does Shakespeare mean to have Antony win the sympathy of the audience? Does he succeed?

14. What is your opinion of Antony's speech when left alone with Cæsar's body? (Lines 255-277.)

ACT III

Scene 2

The scene of the famous speeches to the citizens of Rome,— two of the most widely known passages in all Shakespeare. Notice that Brutus speaks with studied plainness of manner, disdaining oratorical tricks and presenting his case with fewest possible words. He believes that his cause is plainly right and needs no defence. He tries to seem to have brought no passion to his deed as assassin. Antony, on the contrary, uses all the tricks of a mob leader. He is overwhelmed with grief and apologizes for his emotion, which, however, he displays before the people with clever effect. He evidently understands his audience better than does Brutus.

It is still the ides of March, a few hours perhaps after Cæsar's death. Up to this point the conspirators have carried everything before them, but in this scene the tide turns and the spirit of Cæsar begins to work out its revenge.

4. part the numbers: divide the crowd.

7. And public reasons, etc.: And reasons for Cæsar's death shall be publicly set forth.

11. is ascended. We should say "has ascended." The poet frequently uses forms of "be" with verbs that to-day take "have," as later (V, 3, 25) "my life *is* run his compass."

13. lovers: friends, — as often in Shakespeare. So in 44 below, "I slew my best *lover*," and "Thy *lover* Artemidorus" (II, 3, 8).

15. have respect to: consider, look to.

16. censure: judge, — not "find fault with."

26. There is tears. This construction, common enough in Shakespeare's time, has already occurred in the play. Do you remember "Three parts of him *is* ours"? "There's two or three of us"? "*Is* Decius and Trebonius there"?

29. bondman: slave. Where did Casca say,

> So every *bondman* in his own hand bears
> The power to cancel his captivity?

36, 37. The question of his death, etc. That is, a statement of the reasons why Cæsar was put to death is placed in the official records of the Capitol.

38. extenuated: lessened, diminished. **enforced.** Here just the opposite of extenuated, — that is, enlarged, exaggerated.

42. the commonwealth. According to Cassius, while Cæsar

lived, all Romans were "bondmen"; now that he is dead, Brutus believes that the commonwealth will be restored.

52. clamors: cheers.

57. Do grace to: honor, pay respect to.

58. Tending to: indicating, touching upon.

61. Save I alone. Shakespeare often uses the nominative case of pronouns after prepositions where modern grammatical usage demands the objective. See "save only he" in V, 5, 69.

65. I am beholding: I am beholden, or under obligations to you. Notice the marked contrast between Antony's style and that of Brutus.

74. to bury Cæsar. The Romans burned their dead. Shakespeare is speaking to an English audience and thinks of English manners and customs, as when he speaks of the *coffin* in 106 below.

76. oft interréd: often buried.

89. the general coffers: the public treasury. In "The Merchant" Portia speaks of the treasury of Venice as "the privy coffer of the state."

103. withholds you then to mourn: keeps you from mourning.

114. dear abide it: dearly pay for it. Where did Brutus say, "Let no man abide (suffer for) this deed But we the doers"?

120. so poor to do: so poor as to do, etc. Antony says there are now none so poor or humble but that Cæsar is too low for their regard.

129. closet: room, private study, — as in II, 1, 35, where Lucius said to Brutus, "The taper burneth in your *closet*, sir."

130. the commons: the common people.

133. napkins: handkerchiefs.

137. issue: children, descendants.

141. meet: fitting, proper.

150. I have o'ershot myself. That is, I have gone too far I have spoken more than I should. To overshoot is to shoot beyond, or over, the mark.

165. hearse: bier, coffin.

167. **far**: further,—as often in Shakespeare.

168. **Bear back**: fall back, move further away.

173. **That day he overcame the Nervii.** Cæsar tells of his great victory over the Nervii, "the stoutest warriors of all the Belgæ," in the second book of his "Gallic War." Perhaps none of his conquests had contributed more to his fame and popularity with the common people of Rome, who looked upon him as their great military hero.

175. **envious**: malicious, spiteful. (Cf. II, 1, 178.)

179. **resolved**: informed, assured. Where did Antony send to Brutus to "be resolved How Cæsar hath deserved to lie in death"?

181. **angel.** That is, Brutus was one whom Cæsar could trust as he would his guardian angel. Possibly *angel* is equivalent here merely to "best-loved friend," "favorite."

183. **most unkindest cut.** Cassius used a similar double superlative when he spoke of "the most boldest and best hearts of Rome." (See III, 1, 122 and note.)

194. **dint**: impression, influence.

197. **marred . . . with**: mangled by.

213. **private griefs**: personal grievances.

221. **wit**: understanding.

222. **utterance**: gift of speech. Antony's repeated assertion that he is not eloquent is summed up by his "I only speak right on."

243. **every several**: each separate. **seventy-five drachmas.** This is the sum given by Plutarch. The drachma was a Greek coin, worth approximately twenty cents; but of course the purchasing value of the fifteen dollars left by Cæsar to each citizen was far greater then than it would be to-day.

249. **orchards**: gardens,—as in the stage direction of II, 1.

250. **On this side Tiber.** Cæsar's gardens were in reality on the right bank of the river, or *beyond* the Tiber. Shakespeare copied the error from North's incorrect translation of Plutarch. **left them you.** The "you" is placed out of its natural order, and

at the end of the line, for emphasis. Contrast this arrangement of the words with "he hath left you them."

252. To walk abroad, etc.: For walking out and refreshing yourselves.

260. forms: seats, benches.

267. He comes upon a wish. That is, he comes just at the time I most wished or desired.   **Fortune is merry.** As we say, "Fortune smiles upon us."

270. Are rid: have ridden. (We still use both *chid* and *chidden* as past participles of "chide.")

271. Belike they had, etc.: Probably they had some information of how I had moved, or stirred up, the people.

272. Bring: escort, accompany.

QUESTIONS AND TOPICS FOR DISCUSSION

1. Why do you think Shakespeare allows us to hear the speech of Brutus rather than that given by Cassius?

2. Do you believe that Cassius was more or less successful than Brutus in addressing the mob?

3. Do you see any reasons for having Brutus speak in prose? (Notice the form of Antony's oration beginning with line 73.)

4. What are the most striking qualities of Brutus' speech? How would it have affected you had you been in the crowd?

5. Contrast the opening words of the speeches made by Brutus and Antony to the citizens. Which is the more appealing?

6. Point out several ways in which Antony shows greater knowledge of human nature than does Brutus, — also greater skill as an orator.

7. What is the effect of Antony's pause at line 107? Is this merely an oratorical trick?

8. What do you feel is the most successful point made by Antony?

9. What is the effect of Antony's repeated reference to the "honorable Brutus"? How would you read these words throughout the speech?

10. Can you explain why Brutus had no lasting effect with the citizens? Would he have been more successful had he followed Antony?

11. Did Antony, in your judgment, foresee his influence upon the mob? Can you follow his plan?

12. Describe the Roman mob as you imagine it.

13. What is it that has made the speeches in this scene so famous? Quote the lines from each that you like best.

14. Read the account of these speeches in Plutarch (pages 112–114), and then comment upon the changes and improvements made by Shakespeare in his play.

ACT III

Scene 3

This scene, which shows us the rage of the mob in its lawless violence, evidently follows directly after Antony has left the citizens to run their riot of burning and killing.

1. to-night: last night, — as in II, 2, 76, where Cæsar said that Calpurnia "dreamt *to-night* she saw my statuë."

2. things unlucky charge my fantasy: things of bad omen weigh on my imagination.

3. forth of doors: out of doors.

9. directly: clearly, explicitly. Do you remember where Marullus said to one of this same group of Roman citizens, "Answer me directly"?

18. you'll bear me a bang for that. That is, you'll get a whack from me for saying that.

27. Cinna. The conspirator was Cornelius Cinna; this is Helvius Cinna.

34. turn him going: let him go.

QUESTIONS AND TOPICS FOR DISCUSSION

1. Is this scene necessary to the development of the plot? Would you omit it on the stage to-day?

2. Explain how this scene might be made the conclusion of Scene 2.

3. What is there rather grim and even a bit humorous in this short scene?

4. Can you see how this scene may serve as a means of "comic relief" in the unbroken course of tragedy? (Compare this with the famous Porter's Scene in "Macbeth.")

ACT IV

After the first scene the entire act is devoted to the unfolding of the character of Brutus, whom we see placed in the most interesting and moving situations, — the quarrel and reconciliation with Cassius, the reception of the news of Portia's death, the night scene with the boy Lucius, the interview with the ghost. Every detail is meant to exalt our estimate of the nobility of Brutus. Historically this is not an accurate picture of the man as he was. In making him his hero Shakespeare naturally exaggerates his virtues and overlooks many of his faults.

Scene 1

Some time has evidently elapsed since Cæsar's death. In reality this meeting of the three men, who formed the Second Triumvirate, occurred in November, 43 B.C., nineteen months after the events of Act III.

A house in Rome. History tells us that the actual meeting place was on an island in the river Rhenus near Bononia (now Bologna). Do you see any particular reason for Shakespeare's transferring it to Rome?

1. **their names are pricked**: marked.

> Will you be *pricked* in number of our friends,
> Or shall we on, and not depend on you?
>
> (III, 1, 217, and note.)

6. **with a spot I damn him**: with a mark (a prick) I condemn him to death.

9. **charge**: expense. Antony proposes to use some of Cæsar's legacies, of which he spoke in his oration to the people, for war expenses against Brutus and Cassius.

11. **Or here, or.** Notice other uses of this expression for *either . . . or* in these last two acts.

12. **slight**: insignificant. Cf. Brutus' "Away, *slight* man!" (IV, 3, 37.) **unmeritable**: without merit.

14. **The three-fold world**: Europe, Asia, and Africa.

16. **took his voice who**: took his vote as to who, etc.

20. **divers slanderous loads**: various disagreeable charges.

22. **business**: Here pronounced in three syllables, *bus-i-ness*. So *sol-di-er* in line 28 below.

27. **commons**: The commons of an English village in Shakespeare's time were the pasture lands held in common by the townspeople for their cattle. Boston "Common" was originally such a public grazing field.

30. **appoint him store of provender.** That is, provide him with an abundance of corn and hay.

32. **wind**: turn, wheel.

33. **His corporal motion**: the movements of his body, his *physical* motion.

34. **in some taste**: in a sense, in some ways.

36. **barren-spirited**: lacking spirit, or character.

37. **abjects**: things thrown away, leavings. **orts**: scraps, broken fragments, — about the same as "abjects."

37–39. "Lepidus is a man," says Antony, "who is always interested in things that everybody else has grown tired of and thrown aside." [The Folio reading of "abjects, orts" is "objects, arts," changed by Staunton, and generally adopted by later editions.]

38. staled: made stale or common.

39. Begin his fashion: "Are the newest fashion with him." (Clarendon.)

40. a property: a piece of property, a tool, — which we can use as we wish.

41. Listen great things. Later in the play we have "list a word," and in "Much Ado about Nothing," "To listen our purpose." The omission of prepositions was common in Elizabethan English.

42. powers: forces.   **straight make head.** That is, we must raise an army at once.

44. our means stretched. We must exert ourselves to the utmost. The line is defective; it will not scan. Many alterations have been suggested, one of which will do for a sample: "Our best friends made secure, our means stretched out."

45. presently: at once, — as often in Shakespeare.

46. How covert matters, etc. As to how secret, hidden matters, etc.

47. answeréd: faced, met.

48, 49. at the stake, and bayed about, etc. The figure is from the old sport of bear-baiting, in which a bear was tied to a stake to be "bayed" at, bitten, and tormented by a pack of dogs. When besieged in his castle and attacked on every side by his enemies, Macbeth exclaims,

> They have tied me to a stake; I cannot fly,
> But, bear-like, I must fight the course.

QUESTIONS AND TOPICS FOR DISCUSSION

1. Discuss Antony's reasons for sending Lepidus to Cæsar's house.

2. What opinion do you form of Lepidus from this scene?

3. In what ways does Antony seem to have changed since we last saw him in Act III?

4. Does Octavius give any indications of being the man who is later to oppose and conquer Antony?

5. What is the purpose of this scene? Can you explain why it is generally omitted on the stage to-day?

ACT IV

Scene 2

Historically this scene takes place nearly a year after the meeting between Antony, Octavius, and Lepidus. The remaining events of the play occur in the autumn of 42 B.C., about two years and a half after the feast of the Lupercalia in 44, when the action of the drama began.

Sardis. An ancient city of Asia Minor, the capital of Lydia. The account of the action about Sardis, and the quarrel between Brutus and Cassius, is taken with but slight change from Plutarch.

5. To do you salutation: to salute you. So in " Richard III," " The early village cock hath twice *done salutation* to the morn," and similarly we have had already in this play " none too poor to *do* him reverence," and " *Do grace* to Cæsar's corse."

6. He greets me well. That is, his greeting finds me well, or possibly " his greeting is friendly."

7. In his own change, etc. By a change of his feelings toward me, or through the misconduct of his officers.

12. full of regard: full of qualities worthy of esteem, as in III, 1, 225, " Our reasons are so full of good *regard*."

14. How: as to how, — as often in Shakespeare. **resolved**: informed.

16. familiar instances: instances or examples of familiarity; " assurances of friendship."

21. enforcéd ceremony: artificial courtesy.

23. hot at hand: restless, spirited when held in check. Notice that the figure from horsemanship continues through the four lines following.

26. fall their crests: let fall, lower their crests — that is lose their courage, are *crestfallen*.   **jades**: old, worn-out, worthless horses; nags.

40. sober: serious.

41. be content: contain, restrain yourself; be calm.

46. enlarge your griefs: set forth your grievances at large or fully.

48. charges: troops under their *charge*, or command.

QUESTIONS AND TOPICS FOR DISCUSSION

1. What do you imagine has been taking place since Brutus and Cassius were driven from Rome?

2. In what way does Brutus here remind you of Brutus the conspirator?

3. Does it seem more natural for Brutus than for Cassius to suggest that they conceal their quarrel from the soldiers? Why?

4. Is this scene necessary to the development of the plot? What would be lost were it omitted on the stage?

5. Has your interest in the play begun to flag now that Cæsar is dead?

ACT IV

Scene 3

2. noted: set a mark or stigma upon him; disgraced him. Shakespeare took the expression "condemned and noted" directly from Plutarch.

4. praying on his side: pleading in his behalf.

5. slighted off. We should say simply "slighted."

8. every nice offence, etc.   That is, every petty, trivial offence should bear *its* comment, or be criticized.

10. condemned to have: accused of having.   **an itching palm.** The expression is explained by the next line. An interesting comparison is our slang word "palm-grease," — money given as a bribe or tip.

11. mart: sell, barter, — a contraction of *market*, used more frequently as a noun.

16. chastisement: punishment. "Your name and position, Cassius, protects you in this practice of selling your offices for gold."

20. What villain, etc. That is, who of those that killed Cæsar was such a villain as to stab him with any other motive except justice?

27. bay the moon. Compare this with line 121 of Goldsmith's "Deserted Village":

"The watchdog's voice that *bayed* the whispering wind."

28. bait: provoke, anger. Several editors have substituted "bay," thus making Cassius repeat the word and thought of Brutus. Is this change necessary? Is it an improvement?

30. hedge me in: hamper, restrict me, — by interfering with my affairs.

32. To make conditions. That is, to arrange the terms on which offices should be distributed and the campaign conducted. **Go to.** An expression of exhortation, and sometimes of scorn, common in Shakespeare, and about equivalent to our *well, come now*, or *bosh*.

> Well then, it now appears you need my help;
> *Go to*, then; you come to me, and you say,
> 'Shylock, we would have moneys.'
> ("Merchant of Venice," I, 3, 104-106.)

36. Have mind upon your health: Consider your safety.

37. slight: insignificant, petty. Of whom did Antony say earlier in this act, "This is a *slight* unmeritable man"?

38. Is't possible? Cassius' questions in lines 41 and 50 below also refer, of course, to Brutus' language and attitude toward him.

39. rash choler: quick and irritable temper.

45. observe you: treat you with reverence.

46. testy: fretful, irritable.

47. the venom of your spleen: the poison of your ill temper. The spleen, an organ near the stomach, was formerly considered the seat of various emotions; hence its figurative use to-day for *ill temper*, *spitefulness*, *melancholy*, etc.

48. Though it do split you. That is, though the digesting of the poison cause you agony. So we speak of a *splitting* headache or pain.

50. waspish: snappy, irritable, quick to sting like a wasp. Compare this word with *wolfish*, *bearish*, *currish*, *mulish*, *foxy*, *elephantine*, etc.

52. vaunting: boasting, bragging.

54. noble. Some of the editors have substituted "abler" for *noble*, referring to what Cassius said above, "Older in practice, *abler* than yourself." Why does this change seem unnecessary and unwise?

69. respect: regard, heed,— the usual meaning in Shakespeare.

73. drachmas. The drachma was a Greek coin equal to about twenty cents. Where have we had the word before?

75. indirection. Literally, an action not direct or straight and so *dishonest means*, or "crookedness." Cf. "the *straight* and narrow path."

79. covetous: stingy, miserly, avaricious.

80. To lock such rascal counters, etc.: As to lock up such contemptible coins from his friends. *Counters* were round pieces of metal used in casting accounts and making calculations. Here the word is used in contempt for money.

81. thunderbolts. What is the effect of omitting the "and" at the end of the line? The thunderbolt was regarded by the Romans as the peculiar weapon of Jupiter, who hurled it upon those mortals with whom he was angry or displeased.

84. rived: broken,—literally, split or cleaved. Do you remember Casca spoke of having

> seen tempests, when the scolding winds
> Have *rived* the knotty oaks?

91. Olympus. A great mountain of northern Greece, 9750 feet high, and the fabled residence of the gods.

94. Cassius is aweary of the world. So in "The Merchant of Venice" Portia says to Nerissa: "By my troth, Nerissa, my little body is aweary of this great world." (I, 2, 1–2.)

96. Checked: rebuked, censured.

97. conned by rote: studied until learned by heart, — like a lesson.

101. Plutus. The Greek god of riches, son of Iasion and Demeter, who had under his charge all the gold in the earth. The Folio reading here is "Pluto's," plainly a misprint.

107. it shall have scope. That is, your anger shall have indulgence, — shall be allowed to have its run, — shall have free play.

108. dishonor shall be humor. I shall consider any dishonorable action the result of mere caprice, — the result of your testy humor.

109. yokéd with a lamb: you are united with one who has the nature or disposition of a lamb. Pope changed this to "with a man," and several critics say that "lamb" can hardly be right.

110. as the flint bears fire. Where did Cassius say,

I am glad that my weak words
Have struck but this much show of fire from Brutus ?

111. much enforcéd: greatly irritated.

114. blood ill-tempered: disordered condition.

118. to bear with: to be patient with.

119. that rash humor: that hasty, reckless temper.

Enter Poet. Here again the dramatist follows the story as told by Plutarch : "This Favonius at that time, in despite of the door-keepers, came into the chamber, and with a certain scoffing and mocking gesture, which he counterfeited of purpose, he rehearsed the verses which old Nestor said in Homer :

'My lords, I pray you hearken both to me,
For I have seen mo years than suchie three.'

Cassius fell a-laughing at him; but Brutus thrust him out of the chamber, and called him dog, and counterfeit Cynic. Howbeit his coming in brake their strife at that time, and so they left each other."

131. cynic. The Cynics were a sect of Greek philosophers founded by Antisthenes, a pupil of the great Socrates. Later the name became a symbol of ignorant and insolent self-satisfaction. Diogenes was the most noted of the Cynics.

132. sirrah: sir, fellow, — generally used in anger or contempt, or to an inferior.

135. jigging: rhyming, ballad-making.

136. Companion. Used here contemptuously, like our "fellow."

144. If you give place, etc.: If you give in to misfortunes that are beyond your control.

148. scaped: escaped, — a common form in old English. We have to-day "scapegallows," a man who has escaped hanging, though deserving it. In "The Merchant of Venice" Launcelot says, "Then to *scape* drowning thrice."

150. Upon. What preposition would we use to-day? **Impatient of my absence,** etc. Notice the confused construction in these lines, which are perfectly clear in spite of the loose grammatical structure. How does this confusion of language correspond, in a way, to Brutus' emotions?

153. fell distract: became distracted, crazed.

154. swallowed fire. "For Portia . . . determining to kill herself (her friends carefully looking to her to keep her from it) took hot burning coals, and cast them into her mouth, and kept her mouth so close that she choked herself." (Plutarch.)

163. call in question: discuss, talk over.

168. Bending their expedition: directing their march. **Philippi.** A city of Macedonia in Northern Greece named for Philip II who conquered it from Thrace. It fell under the Roman power in B.C. 168. It was here that the Apostle Paul founded a Christian church, to which he addressed the Epistle to the Philippians.

169. the selfsame tenor: the same general drift or purport.

171. by proscription and bills of outlawry. That is, by outlawing and proclaiming that they were to be killed and their

245

property confiscated. . Plutarch, in the "Life of Brutus," says, "These three . . . did set up Bills of Proscription and Out-lawry, condemning two hundred of the noblest men of Rome to suffer death; and amongst that number, Cicero was one."

181. Nor nothing. Notice the intensive force which the double negative has here. Compare this with "Yet 'twas *not* a crown *neither*" in I, 2, 236.

182. methinks: it seems to me. This word, now rarely used except in poetry, is not our "think," but is derived from the Anglo-Saxon *thincan: to seem*.

189. once: sometime or other, sooner or later.

192. in art: in theory, in my stoic philosophy.

192, 193. Cassius means that he would not have the ability to bear calmly so sad a loss, though in theory he believes, with Brutus and other Stoics, that to give way to grief or strong emotion is unmanly and weak.

194. to our work alive: to the work that we the living have to do, — without further thinking upon the dead, that is, Portia.

195. presently: at once, — as usually in Shakespeare.

199. offence: injury, harm.

201. of force: of necessity, perforce.

207. new-added: reënforced, "newly-added to."

210. These people at our back. That is, "the people 'twixt Philippi and this ground" behind us, and not facing us in the army of Antony and Octavius.

211. Under your pardon: Pardon me. Why does Brutus ask Cassius to pardon him?

218. Omitted: neglected.

220. a full sea. That is, the tide "taken at the flood."

222. ventures: goods, merchandise, whatever was ventured or risked on shipboard in hope of profit. The word is frequently used in this sense in "The Merchant of Venice," as,

> I thank my fortune for it
> My *ventures* are not in one bottom trusted,
> Nor to one place.   (I, 1, 41–43.)

246

222. **with your will**: as you wish.

226. **niggard**: supply stingily, sparingly.   Craik says "this is probably the only instance in the language in which *niggard* is used as a verb."

239. **knave**: boy, — here used affectionately, though in Shakespeare's time the word had begun to take on the modern meaning of *rogue, rascal*, and sometimes it is so used by the poet. **o'erwatched**: worn out with watching.

240. **other**: others, — as often in Shakespeare.

249. **I shall otherwise bethink me**: I shall possibly think, or decide, otherwise.

253. **Bear with me**: Be patient with me.

256. **an't**: if it.

266. **mace.**   The club, or staff, borne by an officer of justice. Here Slumber, which the poet calls "murderous" because sleep is regarded as the image of death, is spoken of as an officer arresting Lucius by touching him with his mace.   "Leaden" suggests the heaviness of sleep.

271.   What is the effect of the repeated "Let me see"?   **the leaf turned down.**   The Romans, of course, had no books with leaves that "turned down," any more than they had clocks that struck the hour.   This is only one more illustration of the way in which Shakespeare gives to the Romans of the first century B.C. the customs and conditions of England in his own time.

273.   **How ill this taper burns!**   According to an old superstition, the approach of a ghost would cause lights to burn dimly. In "Richard the Third," when the ghosts first appear, Richard exclaims, "The lights burn blue!"

278.   **to stare**: to stand stiff, to bristle, — much as we say "to stand on end."

285.   **Now I have taken heart.**   Similarly in "Macbeth" when the ghost of Banquo vanishes, Macbeth says, "Why so; being gone, I am a man again."   ("Macbeth," III, 4, 108.)

289.   **false**: out of tune.

305.   **set on his powers betimes before**: have his forces advance early. Where did Cæsar say, "*Set on;* and leave no ceremony out "?

QUESTIONS AND TOPICS FOR DISCUSSION

1. With whom do you sympathize in the famous quarrel between the two generals?   Give your reasons.

2. How does each of the generals show his true character in the quarrel?

3. Explain just why Brutus was vexed with Cassius.

4. What is there dramatic about the quarrel? Can you see why it makes an effective scene on the stage even to-day?

5. What do you think of Cassius in lines 92–106? Do you think he is sincere or speaking simply for effect?

6. How do you explain the reconciliation in lines 115–121? What leads naturally to it?

7. How does the interruption of the poet bring the generals closer together again?   Does this interruption serve any other purpose?

8. Does it seem natural for Brutus not to have spoken of Portia sooner?

9. Do you admire or dislike Brutus for his apparent lack of emotion?   Do you think he is really indifferent to Portia?

10. Point out two other places where Brutus and Cassius disagreed as to the conduct of affairs.   Who so far has offered the wiser counsel?

11. Do you agree with Brutus or Cassius in their plans for the approaching battle?

12. Why do you think Shakespeare has Brutus again informed of Portia's death?

13. What does the news concerning Cicero show us of conditions in Rome?

14. Compare the first scene in which we saw Lucius with this one in Brutus' tent before Sardis.   How are they somewhat alike?

15. What effect upon the audience has the music and song of Lucius? Also his sleepiness, and the words of Brutus just before the ghost enters?

16. What is there in this ghost scene that makes it on the stage even to-day one of the most dramatic and stirring moments of the play?

17. Can you name other plays by Shakespeare in which ghosts appear?

18. What is there similar in the warning words of the ghost and the soothsayer at the opening of the play?

19. How would you stage this scene, especially the make-up and actions of the ghost?

20. Can you explain why such a supernatural scene as this had a more profound effect upon an audience in Shakespeare's time than it does to-day?

ACT V

Historically, there were two battles at Philippi, separated by an interval of two weeks. It is the earlier of these battles that the poet adopts as the ground-work of his representation, though the death of Brutus took place immediately after the second. Such changes of time are common in Shakespeare, as in all historical drama and historical romance.

Scene 1

The brief but sharp disagreement between Octavius and Antony (17–20) is not in Plutarch, who, however, does speak of a disagreement between Brutus and Cassius on the same question as to which one should take command of the right wing, or the position of honor. Cassius, the older man, yields to Brutus in this matter, as we have seen him do whenever difference of opinion arose between them. This grudging acquiescence of Antony in the leadership of young Octavius the poet invents as a foil to set

off the ready and willing deference paid by Cassius to Brutus.
We are not told in the play that Brutus went into the battle in
command of the right of his army; but as we learn from V, 3,
51–53, that Brutus' wing confronted that of Octavius, and have
seen that Octavius has insisted on having the command of his
own right, we must infer that the poet, if he thought the matter
out, gave to Brutus the subordinate position on the left, choosing
herein to differ from his authority. Plutarch tells us: "Brutus
prayed Cassius he might have the leading of the right wing, the
which men thought was farre meeter for Cassius: both because
he was the elder man, and also for that he had the better experience. But yet Cassius gave it to him," etc. In his life of Antony,
Plutarch says: "When they had passed over the seas, and that
they began to make warre, they being both camped by their
enemies, to wit, Antonius against Cassius, and Caesar against
Brutus: Caesar did no great matter, but Antonius had alway the
upper hand, and did all." It is interesting to consider why
Shakespeare, who in so many things follows Plutarch exactly,
prefers not to follow him in this.

Several days have elapsed since the previous scene in Brutus'
tent near Sardis. It is the autumn of B.C. 42, and the day has
come that "must end that work the ides of March begun." For
Philippi, see note on IV, 3, 168.

1. **our hopes are answeréd**: our wishes are granted.

3. **regions.** Pronounced in three syllables, *re-gi-ons*, like
"sol-di-er" in IV, 1, 28.

4. **battles**: battle array, battalions.

5. **warn**: summon, challenge to fight.

7. **I am in their bosoms**: I know their real motives; I see into
their hearts. We speak of a *bosom* friend, and a *bosom* sin, with
much the same significance.

8. **they could be content**: they would be glad, or would prefer.

10. **With fearful bravery**: with bravado, or a show of bravery,
that is full of fear, and in reality, cowardly. "With timorous,
faint-hearted show of bravery." **this face**: this appearance,

this show, this outward effect, — as we speak of "putting on a bold *face*," and "*facing* it out."

14. Their bloody sign of battle. According to Plutarch, "the Signall of Battell . . . was an arming Scarlet Coat."

15. something to be done: something should be done.

16. lead your battle softly on: lead your forces slowly on.

19. exigent: exigency, critical moment.

20. I will do so. That is, I will do as I have said, — lead the right wing. This gives us a glimpse of the true character of Octavius, who, as history tells us, always stood firm against Antony. Even here, when but a youth of twenty-one, he shows the stuff that later made him the great Emperor Augustus.

24. answer on their charge: await their attack ; let them begin the battle.

25. Make forth: "step forward" (Craik).

33. The posture of your blows: The place where your blows are to fall ; or possibly, "The nature of your blows."

34. the Hybla bees. Classical writers often speak of Hybla in Sicily as a town famous for its honey. Cassius, of course, is speaking tauntingly. Our expression "*honeyed* words" suggests beguiling, flattering language, — "smooth talk," — and is not exactly complimentary.

41-44. Compare these lines with the scene in the Capitol when Cæsar was slain. Is it a faithful or an exaggerated description of the assassination ?

46. This tongue: that is, Antony's tongue. To what does Cassius refer ?

48. the cause: the real issue ; "let's get down to business!"

49. The proof of it. That is, the proof of the matter about which they are arguing, namely, the real fighting.

52. goes up again: is again put into its sheath.

53. three and thirty wounds. Plutarch gives the number of wounds as *twenty*-three ; but to change Shakespeare's statement is to make arithmetic out of poetry. What is the difference, anyway ?

54, 55. till another Cæsar have added slaughter, etc. That is, until my own death has added another Cæsar to the list of those murdered by the swords of traitors. "Either you or I shall die," says Octavius.

59. thy strain: thy race, thy family.

60. honorable. We should say "honorably," but Shakespeare frequently uses an adjective for an adverb.

61. peevish: foolish, silly. Remember that Octavius at this time was only twenty-one, hence Cassius' taunting "schoolboy."

62. a masker and a reveller. Where did Brutus say of Antony, "he is given to sports, to wildness and much company"?

66. stomachs: spirit, courage. "He which hath no stomach to this fight, let him depart." ("Henry V," IV, 3, 35.)

68. all is on the hazard: all depends on the fortune of war.

71. as this very day. In this phrase "as" is redundant, or unnecessary for the sense. So Shakespeare often has "when as" where we should use merely "as."

74. As Pompey was. This is an allusion to the battle of Pharsalia, B.C. 48, into which Pompey was forced, against his own wishes, by younger and inexperienced officers. He was easily defeated by Julius Caesar.

74, 75. to set upon one battle, etc.: to risk our independence upon *one* battle; to stake everything on one fight.

76. I held Epicurus strong: I strongly believed in the teachings of Epicurus. The followers of this Greek philosopher believed that the gods were concerned but little with human affairs, and that pleasure was the chief end of life. As an Epicurean, Cassius would therefore not pay much attention to signs or omens.

78. presage: portend, foretell things to come.

79. our former ensign: our foremost banner.

82. consorted: accompanied.

84. kites. The kite is a small bird of prey of the falcon family. Ravens and crows were generally regarded as birds of evil omen.

86. As we were sickly prey: as if we were weak and feeble prey (for them to devour).

91. constantly: firmly. So in III, 1, 22, Brutus said, "Cassius, be constant."

92. Even so: just so, quite true. This refers, of course, to something Lucilius has just said, which we have not heard.

93. The gods to-day stand friendly: May the gods be friendly to us to-day!

94. Lovers: friends,—as in Brutus' address to the people, "Romans, countrymen, and lovers!" and so often in Shakespeare.

96. Let's reason with the worst, etc. Let's confer together in view of the possible ruin of our cause in the impending battle.

100. Even by the rule, etc. That is, I am determined to act in accordance with that rule, or principle, by which I condemned Cato for killing himself. Brutus then goes on to explain further his feelings against suicide.

104, 105. so to prevent the time of life: to anticipate the end of life by suicide.

106. stay: await.

110, 111. In these lines Brutus seems strangely inconsistent. First he declares that he will not take his own life,—that "he finds it cowardly and vile" to commit suicide,—and that he will await patiently the action of Providence. Then in the next breath, when Cassius asks him whether he will be "contented to be led in triumph Thorough the streets of Rome," he very decidedly implies that rather than be so degraded he will kill himself. It has been suggested that the humiliation mentioned by Cassius alters his purpose; but such a sudden and complete change of mind, just after his strong words against suicide, seems most improbable. The explanation probably lies in the bad punctuation and confusing translation of North's "Plutarch," which Shakespeare followed so closely, and here, we must admit, so blindly, that he wrote a passage that not only seems weak and inconsistent, but one that does not give the facts as the old Greek historian stated them. Plutarch in reality tells us that Brutus *in his youth* blamed Cato for killing himself, but that now before the battle, he was of a different opinion.

We must remember, however, that Shakespeare wrote his plays to be acted on the stage, not studied intensively; and not one person in a hundred at the theatre, then or to-day, would notice this inconsistency. It is therefore a matter of little importance, except as it shows us to-day the methods of composition which the dramatist used.

QUESTIONS AND TOPICS FOR DISCUSSION

1. Comment upon the words of Octavius in line 20, in relation to his later control over Antony and the Roman Empire.

2. What is there in the wrangling parley of the four generals that pleased the audience in Shakespeare's time?

3. Contrast this verbal battle with the methods of modern warfare.

4. Can you explain why this wrangling scene is nearly always omitted on the stage to-day?

5. What do you think of the omens of which Cassius speaks? Compare these with other superstitions in the play.

6. How does Shakespeare suggest to us that Brutus and Cassius will be defeated in the approaching battle?

7. Which of the two generals seems to you the wiser military leader? Why?

8. What is there noble and moving in the parting scene between Brutus and Cassius? Quote any lines you particularly admire.

ACT V

Scene 2

Alarum: notes on a bugle or horn; a call to arms. This older form of "alarm" is common in Shakespeare. See opening of Scene 3 just below.

1. bills: notes, dispatches. This is the word used by Plutarch in the "Life of Brutus."

2. **on the other side.** That is, on the left wing which was commanded by Cassius.

4. **cold demeanor:** a lifeless, indifferent manner.

ACT V

Scene 3

2. **to my own.** That is, to one of my own army, — the standard-bearer referred to in the next lines.

4. **it:** the standard. The word "ensign" was used then, as it is to-day, both for the flag and the man who carried it. Here Cassius uses the word with both meanings in the same sentence.

7. **Took it too eagerly:** followed up too eagerly the advantage which he gained over Octavius.   **fell to spoil:** went to work plundering. According to Plutarch, whom Shakespeare follows closely here, Cassius was "marvellous angry to see how Brutus men ran to give charge upon their Enemies, and tarried not for the word of the Battell, nor commandment to give charge: and it grieved him beside, that after he had overcome them, his men fell straight to spoil, and were not careful to compass in the rest of the Enemies behind." It was against Cassius' best judgment that Brutus was given command of the right wing, a concession which this time leads to fatal consequences.

18. **yond:** yonder. Where did Cæsar say,

Yond Cassius has a lean and hungry look ?

19. **with a thought:** as quick as thought; "in the twinkling of an eye."

21. **My sight was ever thick.** Plutarch's words are, "Howbeit, Cassius himself saw nothing, for *his sight was very bad,* saving that he saw (and yet with much ado) how the Enemies spoiled his Camp before his eyes."

Pindarus ascends the hill. Here probably Pindarus went up to the balcony over the inner stage. See page 173.

25. My life is run his compass. In the words of Macbeth,

> I have lived long enough; my way of life
> Is fallen into the sear, the yellow leaf.

31. light: alight, dismount.

38. I swore thee, saving of thy life: I made thee swear when I saved thy life, — or spared thee.

42. search: pierce, probe.

43. hilts. A common use in Shakespeare, where we should say "hilt" for the handle of a sword.

51. It is but change. The battle is an *interchange* of victory and defeat.

66. Mistrust of good success: doubt as to the issue. In Shakespeare's time the word "success" often meant simply "outcome," "issue," and thus needed a qualifying adjective such as "good" here. So Cæsar said,

> Go bid the priests do present sacrifice,
> And bring me their opinions of success.
>
> (II, 2, 6.)

68. the apt thoughts: the impressionable, receptive thoughts.

70. happy: fortunate.

84. misconstrued. Pronounced here miscónstrued, as in "The Merchant of Venice," II, 2, 171, "I be miscónstrued in the place I go to."

86. bid. Shakespeare often uses this form, as well as *bade*, for the past tense of "bid." Cf. "that tongue that *bade* the Romans mark him." (I, 2, 125-126.)

88. regarded: esteemed, reverenced.

94. O Julius Cæsar, thou art mighty yet, etc. Hudson remarks on this passage, "Brutus here strikes the proper keynote of the play." He then quotes Froude: "The murderers of Cæsar, . . . such of them as were in Italy were immediately killed. Those in the provinces, as if with the curse of Cain upon their heads, came one by one to miserable ends. In three years the tyrannicides of the Ides of March, with their aides and abettors, were all dead; some killed in battle, some in prison, some dying by their own hand."

Remember, too, Antony's prophecy over Cæsar's body in Act III :

> A curse will light upon the limbs of men ;
> And Cæsar's spirit, ranging for revenge,
> Shall in these confines with a monarch's voice
> Cry " Havoc," and let slip the dogs of war.

96. In our own proper entrails : into our own entrails. " Proper " simply emphasizes "own."

97. whether. Here a word of one syllable, probably pronounced " whe'r," as in I, 1, 62 :

> See, *whether* their basest metal be not moved.

101. fellow : equal, counterpart.   **moe** : more, — an old comparative of " many." Do you remember where Lucius says, " No, sir, there are *moe* with him " ?

104. Thasos. An island in the Ægean sea off the coast of Thrace where, according to Plutarch, Cassius was buried.

105. funerals. Although we use this word to-day in the singular form, we still speak of *nuptials*.

108. set our battles on : move forward our army ; advance our line.

109. ere night. This second battle in reality did not take place for twenty days. Why does Shakespeare transfer it to the day of the first conflict? Does this change seem justifiable to you?

QUESTIONS AND TOPICS FOR DISCUSSION

1. Explain, after reading page 173, how probably in Shakespeare's time this scene of Pindarus on the hill was acted.

2. Why did Cassius kill himself? What has he said about suicide earlier in the play?

3. Explain the actions of Titinius, as you understand them. What caused Cassius to "misconstrue everything"?

4. What does Titinius mean by exclaiming, just before he stabs himself, "This is a Roman's part"?

5. Explain and comment upon Brutus' words upon finding the body of Cassius, "O Julius Cæsar, thou art mighty yet!"

6. Compare Brutus' words and constrained feelings here with his manner upon hearing of Portia's death.

7. Do you admire Cassius in this scene? Has he risen or fallen in your estimation since the beginning of the play? Discuss in detail.

ACT V

Scene 4

2. What bastard doth not? "Who is such a base-born coward as not to do so?"

7, 8. And I am Brutus, etc. In the Folio no name is given to the speaker of these two lines, so that we may give them to Lucilius instead of Brutus. This is possibly the better arrangement, in view of what takes place immediately following.

12. Only I yield to die. I yield only in order to die.

13. There is so much, etc. "Here, I give thee so much money on condition that thou wilt kill me at once." Considering the fact that the stage-direction, *offering money*, is not in the Folios, Lucilius may mean that so much can be laid to his charge that the soldier is certain to kill him at once. Remember that Lucilius is pretending to be Brutus in order to lead the soldiers of Antony and Octavius away from his general.

16. Brutus is ta'en, etc. This incident of Lucilius' pretending to be Brutus is taken from Plutarch.

24. or alive or dead. This use of *or . . . or* for *either . . . or* is still common in poetry.

32. is chanced: has befallen, has turned out.

ACT V

Scene 5

2. Statilius show'd the torch-light. Plutarch's account of this incident runs as follows: "There was one called Statilius, that promised to go through his enemies, for otherwise it was impossible to see their camp: and from thence, if all were well, that he would lift up a torch-light in the air, and then return again with speed to him. The torch-light was lifted up as he had promised, for Statilius went thither. Now Brutus seeing Statilius tarry long after that, and that he came not again, he said, 'If Statilius be alive, he will come again.' But his evil fortune was such that, as he came back, he lighted in his enemies' hands and was slain."

3. He came not back. We should say, "he has not come back." **or ta'en or slain**: either taken or slain. Where before have you noticed this *or . . . or* construction?

5. Whispering. This stage direction is not found in the Folio edition of the plays, but was added by the early editors.

13. that noble vessel. The figurative use of the word *vessel* for a person, suggesting the fitness or capacity to contain something or other, was common in Shakespeare's time. Thus we find in the Bible: "he is a chosen *vessel* unto me"; "the *vessel* of wrath"; "giving honor to the wife as to the weaker *vessel*."

14. That it runs: so that it runs over. What is Brutus doing?

19. Philippi fields. "The Romans called the Valley between both Camps, the Philippian Fields." (Plutarch, "Life of Brutus.")

23. have beat us to the pit: have beaten and driven us, as hunters drive animals, to the edge of the pitfall.

27. Even for that our love of old: for the sake of our old friendship. **prithee.** An old and abbreviated form of the expression *pray thee*. Who was it that earlier in the play said, "I prithee, boy, run to the senate-house"?

28. sword-hilts. For a similar use of the plural *hilts*, see V, 3, 43, and note.

45. of a good respect: of good esteem; held in high regard. Similarly in I, 2, 59, Cassius said, " many of the best respect in Rome."

46. smatch: smack, taste.

50. Cæsar, now be still. Brutus refers to Cæsar's ghost, which, as we know, had been restless and walked the earth. Now that the murder has been avenged the spirit will " be still."

55. can but make a fire of him. This refers to the custom among the Romans of burning their dead on the funeral pyre.

60. I will entertain them: I will take them into my service.

61. bestow thy time with me: give up thy time to me; enter my service.

62. prefer: recommend. In the " Merchant of Venice " Bassanio says to Launcelot,

> I know thee well; thou hast obtained thy suit:
> Shylock thy master spoke with me this day,
> And hath *preferred* thee.

69. save only he: except only him. The nominative case after prepositions was common in all writers of Shakespeare's time.

71, 72. in a general honest thought, etc. Brutus, declares Antony, acted, as he honestly thought, for the good of all. This is one of those involved Shakespearean sentences the meaning of which, however, is perfectly clear.

73, 74. the elements so mixed in him, etc. According to a commonly accepted belief of Shakespeare's time, man was composed of the four elements, earth, air, fire, and water. Human perfection depended upon a well-balanced mixture of these four elements or " humours."

76. virtue: worth, character.

79. ordered honorably: treated with honor.

80. call the field to rest: sound the signal for the army in the field to cease fighting.

81. part: divide, share.

QUESTIONS AND TOPICS FOR DISCUSSION

1. What is the effect of the whispering and rapid conversation at the opening of this scene?

2. Why does Shakespeare have Brutus ask three of his companions to hold his sword before Strato consents to do the deed?

3. Comment upon Brutus' words:

> My heart doth joy that yet in all my life
> I found no man but he was true to me.

4. What effect have the one-syllable words of these two noble lines?

5. Contrast the deaths of Cassius and Brutus. Which seems to you to make the more pathetic scene?

6. Describe the setting of the stage as you would have it at the close of the play.

7. Discuss Antony's last speech in view of what you know of Brutus and the other conspirators.

8. Are you pleased with the conclusion of the tragedy? Would it have been better, in your judgment, to have Brutus and Cassius live?

9. What decided the fate of the battle?

10. Do you think the play would be more appropriately entitled "Brutus"? Discuss fully.

SUBJECTS FOR ORAL AND WRITTEN COMPOSITIONS

[Other subjects for discussion and written exercises will be found at the end of the notes on each scene. Subjects starred (*) are taken from various college entrance examination papers.]

INCIDENTS IN THE PLAY

1. The Clash between Tribunes and Commoners.

[Describe the scene and explain the actions and feelings of Flavius, Marullus, and the mob. Bring out the effect of this scene upon the audience.]

2. Marullus Rebukes the Mob.*

[Put into your own words the fine speech of Marullus, I, 1, 33-56. Discuss the spirit in which it is spoken, and the way the people take it.]

3. The Procession.

[Describe the entrance of Cæsar in I, 2. What opportunities are there for making a gorgeous spectacle of this scene? How would you stage it in a performance of the play to-day?]

4. Hatching the Conspiracy.*

[How did Cassius set about to win Brutus? Explain his motive and his methods.]

5. The Influence of Cassius over Casca.

[Explain how Cassius wins Casca to the conspiracy. Contrast his methods in I, 3 with those used when talking with Brutus in the previous scene.]

263

Subjects for Compositions.

6. The Plot against Cæsar is Formed.*

[Tell the story of the meeting in Brutus' orchard. Try to make your account spirited and dramatic.]

7. The Advice of Brutus concerning Mark Antony.

[Give the reasons for Brutus' wishing to spare Antony. Why was his advice accepted? How did he blunder?]

8. Brutus and Portia.

[The story of their interview after the departure of the conspirators. What is the effect of this scene upon your interest in the plot?]

9. Cæsar Changes His Mind.

[Show how Calpurnia induced Cæsar to remain at home, and then how Decius Brutus prevailed upon him to go to the senate.]

10. The Death of Cæsar.*

[Describe the scene as you see it and tell the story of the murder. This may be told in the form of a dialogue between one of the conspirators and a Roman who was not present when Cæsar was slain.]

11. Brutus Blunders Again.

[The story of the interview between Antony and the conspirators. Make clear Brutus' reasons for allowing Antony to speak at Cæsar's funeral.]

12. Brutus' Speech to the Roman Citizens.*

[Give his arguments for killing Cæsar, and show their effect upon the people.]

13. The Funeral Oration of Mark Antony.*

[Point out the various ways in which Antony holds and finally wins the mob.]

14. The Speeches of Brutus and Antony.

[Contrast the style and construction of the two speeches. Which of the two men is the greater orator? Why?]

15. The Roman Mob.

[Explain how the commoners are worked upon by Antony and what they do. Compare their feelings and actions with those of the mob that stormed the Bastille, as described by Dickens in "A Tale of Two Cities."]

16. Getting Rid of Lepidus.*

[How Antony prevails upon Octavius to set aside their partner.]

17. The Quarrel.*

[The scene and causes of the famous quarrel between Brutus and Cassius. Make clear which of the two you sympathize with, and why.]

18. Brutus and Cæsar Meet Again.*

[Describe the scene in which Cæsar's ghost appears before Brutus and the effect it has upon him.]

19. Wrangling Words before Battle.

[Read again V, 1, 19–66 and contrast this scene with methods of modern warfare.]

20. The Deaths of Cassius and Brutus.

[Tell how each of the generals meets his end; contrast the feelings of Antony and Octavius for their enemies, Cassius and Brutus.]

GENERAL SUBJECTS

[The following subjects are less specific than the first twenty. Many of them require a consideration of the play as a whole.]

21. Brutus and Cassius.*

[Contrast the characters of these men, especially their motives for doing away with Cæsar. Give your own personal opinion of each.]

22. The Superstitious Element in Cæsar's Character.

[Point out the various superstitions which Cæsar shows, and explain the effect that these have upon your opinion of the great Roman.]

Subjects for Compositions.

23. A Character Sketch of Cæsar.

[Draw a picture of the Cæsar Shakespeare has portrayed in the play. If you have read the Gallic War, compare the impression of Cæsar gained there with Shakespeare's portrayal.]

24. Cæsar's Will.*

[Discuss the reading of the will by Antony, its effect upon the mob, and the light it throws upon Cæsar.]

25. Cæsar's Ambitions.

[An account of what you have learned from the play of Cæsar's ambitions, especially from Act I and from the speeches of Brutus and Antony in Act III.]

26. The Part of Portia in the Play.

[The story of Portia's part in the drama, with your reasons for Shakespeare's introducing her at all.]

27. Friends of Cæsar.

[An account of the different ways in which Cæsar was warned of impending danger, from the soothsayer's words in I, 2, to Calpurnia's dream.]

28. The Part Played by Cicero.

[Who was Cicero? What does he do in the tragedy and what important references are made to him? See I, 2, 276, II, 1, 141-152, etc.]

29. Brutus Justifies Himself.*

[Tell in your own words how Brutus justifies his part in the conspiracy. This may be made interesting by being written as a dialogue between Brutus and Portia. See II, 1, 305-308.]

30. Details of the Conspiracy.

[A full account of the plot against Cæsar, — reasons for it, by whom suggested, names of leaders, meeting place, watchword, plans, etc.]

266

Subjects for Compositions.

31. Brutus, the Central Figure of the Play.

[Point out in detail how it is Brutus rather than Cæsar that holds our interest as the central figure of the tragedy.]

32. Brutus the Roman Patriot.*

[Show how Brutus was the typical Roman to whom the state, and not the individual, was of chief importance.]

33. The Climax of the Play.

[Compare the death of Brutus with that of Cæsar as the real climax of the drama.]

34. After the Fall of Cæsar.

[Point out in what ways Shakespeare keeps up our interest in the play even after Cæsar has been killed.]

35. The Title of the Play.

[Why do you think Shakespeare called the tragedy "Julius Cæsar," rather than "Marcus Brutus" or "The Conspiracy"? Discuss other possible titles.]

36. Shakespeare's Use of Plutarch.*

[After reading pages 108–115, explain how the dramatist made use of Plutarch's "Lives." What scenes and speeches are his own?]

37. The Failure of the Conspiracy.*

[Explain why Brutus and the other conspirators failed in their great object after they had been successful in killing Cæsar.]

38. The Three Great Scenes of the Play.

[Point out the elements that make the conspiracy in Brutus' orchard, the murder of Cæsar before the Capitol, and the quarrel of the generals stand out as the three most stirring scenes of the tragedy.]

39. The Minor Scenes of the Play.

[Imagine yourself a stage manager, and decide what scenes you would omit in a presentation of the drama to-day. Give your reasons.]

267

Subjects for Compositions.

40. My Favorite Lines in " Julius Cæsar."

[Quote several passages and give reasons for your choice.]

IMAGINATIVE SUBJECTS

[The following subjects call for imagination and originality as well as knowledge of the play. Some of them may be told in the first person in the form of a letter or journal. Others may be written in dialogue, or as one-act short plays, which then may be presented by members of the class. In all of them, start with the facts and suggestions given you by Shakespeare. Then use your imagination freely, though what you imagine should always be possible and the more probable the better.]

41. The Commoners Talk It Over.

["They vanish tongue-tied in their guiltiness" said Flavius, after he and Marullus had berated the citizens. What did they do and say after the tribunes left them?]

42. Disrobing the Images.

[Follow Flavius and Marullus about the city and describe some of their adventures.]

43. " The Ides of March."

[Describe the soothsayer as you imagine him. How do you think he obtained his knowledge of future events?]

44. Cassius Saves Cæsar's Life.

[Tell with further details the story of Cassius and Cæsar swimming in the Tiber. See I, 2, 100–115.]

45. " He had a Fever when he was in Spain."

[Enlarge upon the incident related by Cassius in I, 2, 119–127. This may well be told in dialogue.]

Subjects for Compositions.

46. Cæsar Is Offered a Crown.

[Have one of the citizens tell the story which Casca relates to Brutus and Cassius, remembering Casca's words, "There was more *foolery* yet, if I could remember it."]

47. Cicero's Speech on the Feast of Lupercal.

[Casca reports that Cicero "spoke Greek." Write his speech in your own English, fitting his words and style to your knowledge of the great Roman orator.]

48. Marullus and Flavius Rebuked.

["Marullus and Flavius, for pulling scarfs off Cæsar's images, are put to silence." Tell the story of their experiences.]

49. Brutus Decides That Cæsar Must Die.

[Give in detail Brutus' reasons for joining Cassius and the other conspirators. This may be told in the form of a letter or monologue.]

50. The Whispered Conference between Brutus and Cassius.

[Report the whispered conversation while Cinna and Casca are discussing which way "lies the east." (II, 1, 101 ff.) This may well be written as a dialogue.]

51. Portia Overhears the Conspirators.

[Imagine what might have taken place had Portia been told by Lucius, or heard herself, the conversation in the orchard.]

52. Cæsar Reads the Letter of Artemidorus.

[Read again III, 1, 1–10, and write an account of the events that might have followed had Cæsar looked at the "schedule" presented to him by Artemidorus.]

53. Antony Remains with the Conspirators.

[Trebonius knows his time; . . .
        He draws Mark Antony out of the way.
What might have happened had Trebonius failed?]

Subjects for Compositions.

54. Antony after the Murder.

[What did Antony do when he "fled to his house amazed"? Imagine his thoughts, plans, and actions. See III, 1, 124-149.]

55. Octavius Learns of Cæsar's Death.

[Remember that Antony said to the servant, "Post back with speed, and tell him what hath chanc'd." Report the scene when the servant tells Octavius what he saw in Rome. Put this into a lively dialogue.]

56. Cassius Addresses the Mob.

[We have the speeches of Brutus and Antony. Write the speech made by Cassius, trying to adapt it to the character of the man as you know him.]

57. Brutus and Cassius Driven Out of Rome.

["Brutus and Cassius are rid like madmen through the gates of Rome." Describe the scene, making it as full of action as possible.]

58. Cassius Loses Control of His Temper.

["Urge me no more, I shall forget myself." Imagine the scene and consequences had Cassius struck Brutus at the height of the quarrel.]

59. The Death of Portia.

[Have a servant report to Brutus, or to Cassius, the circumstances of Portia's death in Rome.]

60. Cæsar's Ghost Again Appears.

["Thou shalt see me at Philippi." Write a graphic account of the second appearance of the ghost in "Philippi fields." This may be told by Brutus to Volumnius, or described as a scene by itself.]